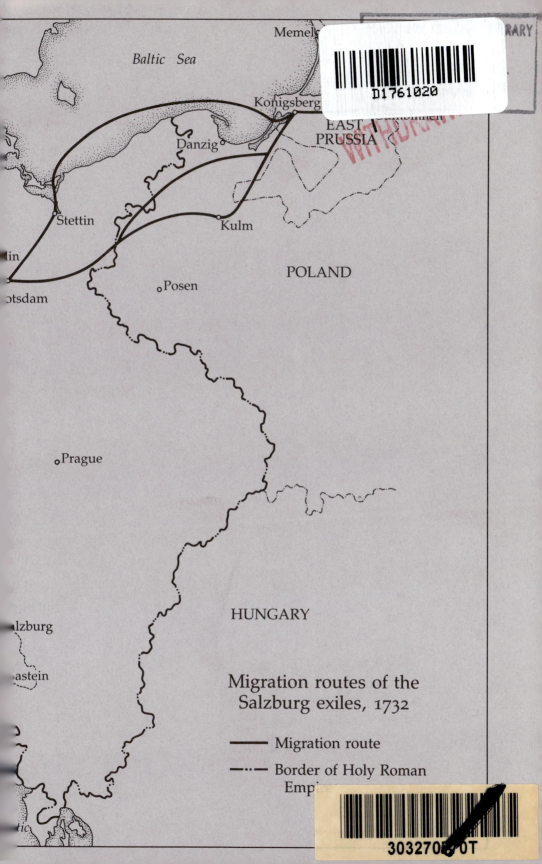

Baltic Sea

Memel

Konigsberg

EAST
PRUSSIA

Danzig

Stettin

Kulm

in

otsdam

POLAND

Posen

Prague

HUNGARY

lzburg

astein

Migration routes of the
Salzburg exiles, 1732

———— Migration route

—·—·— Border of Holy Roman
Empi

The Salzburg Transaction

The Salzburg Transaction

EXPULSION AND REDEMPTION IN
EIGHTEENTH-CENTURY GERMANY

Mack Walker

Cornell University Press

Ithaca and London

First published 1992 by Cornell University Press.

International Standard Book Number 0-8014-2777-0
Library of Congress Catalog Card Number 92-52774
Printed in the United States of America
*Librarians: Library of Congress cataloging information
appears on the last page of the book.*

♾ The paper in this book meets the minimum requirements
of the American National Standard for Information Sciences—
Permanence of Paper for Printed Library Materials, ANSI Z39.48-1984.

To Eleanor and Franklin Ford

CONTENTS

ILLUSTRATIONS
AND MAPS

Illustrations

Maps

PREFACE

The expulsion of the Salzburg Protestants in 1731–32 was the most dramatic religious confrontation in Germany after the Thirty Years' War. Unlike earlier post-Westphalian confessional encounters, critical though these were for the political constitution of Germany, the expulsion was played out largely on a public stage. By its dramatic effects the episode gave sharp definition to religious differences in Germany, challenged the leadership of the House of Habsburg in the Holy Roman Empire of the German Nation and thus threatened the imperial constitution itself; it made an indelible mark on the political depiction and traditions of the Prussian state, and generated a legendry that has left appreciable traces on modern German religious and political consciousness.

In most academic histories the episode appears as an instance of anachronistic religious obscurantism and intolerance. In those histories but especially in informal confessional traditions and anecdotage, the story has been a source of Protestant pride and righteous outrage, and of Catholic embarrassment and defensiveness where it is mentioned at all. So it has been since the eighteenth century.

In composing the rendition that follows, I have neither pursued the partisan issues nor, least of all, set about striking some judicious balance among them. I began, rather, having in mind the naive historian's problem: that there may be many legitimate ways to tell a story, all of them different and yet all of them true. This complication is not simply a matter of point of view, or of angle of vision, with their intimations of interest and distortion, but more nearly, of the different ways in which a story or text may emerge when told in different contexts. To acknowledge this condition does not authorize any suspension of customary scholarly standards of evidence, verification, skepticism, and accountability. To allow the possibility of many historical truths is not to allow that there is no truth at all; nor does it yield indifferent legitimacy to stories that are false.

I set out to tell the story of the Salzburg expulsion as a way of pursuing that problem, as successive narrations of one event: the story as it appears as an episode in the history of the Salzburg archepiscopate, as one in the history of the Prussian state and monarchy, as another in the political and constitutional life of the Holy Roman Empire, and yet another in the experience of the emigrants themselves, and inevitably, in the legendry of German Protestantism. Inasmuch, however, as the main action and focus of the story moves over time among these several contexts, it has been possible and technically convenient to lay these renditions chronologically end to end, with a minimum of repetitions, flashbacks, and cross-references. Moreover, when most of the methodological verbiage and scaffolding has been stripped away, something like a traditional general narrative exposition emerges. This development was not wholly voluntary but prompts little dismay, for I believe that each of these renditions retains its autonomy in the context of its own protagonists and may be told on its own. They intersect at the point of the participation and interest each protagonist has in the expulsion itself, and so I have entitled the whole text *The Salzburg Transaction*.

Initially I chose to examine this particular episode because it combined three aspects of German history to which, despite their importance, I had never before given serious attention: the history of religion, of rural society, and of the Prussian state. This motive grounds a second confession: at the end I discovered that I had written a study in the history of migration, of social relations and processes, and of the law and politics of the Holy Roman Empire—all topics I had indeed studied in the past or at least written about. But once again, this combination of predispositions may have provided as fruitful a position from which to examine the Salzburg expulsion as those that have preceded it.

A third discovery bearing on the nature of this book has been the realization of an obligation even greater than I had supposed. Very often in the composition of the piece I have found myself uncertain, even anomic when it came to audience: how to judge the intelligibility of an expression, the legitimacy of an observation, the persuasiveness of an argument. When this happened I found myself, quite reflexively, testing the language against the response I might expect from my first teacher in the writing of history, and ever since it seems: from Franklin Ford, at Harvard nearly forty years ago. I am not sorry about that either, and commit this story to grateful recognition of that obligation and that influence.

Some real though lesser and particular obligations I have incurred during the preparation of the present book. The whole story and argument have been substantially influenced and modified by comments on earlier briefer renditions, especially by Hartmut Lehmann, Heide Wunder, and Axel von dem Bussche, and on constructive language found by Hans Medick for a presentation in German. I was able to begin the research during 1982–83 as a fellow at the Wissenschaftskolleg zu Berlin, owing to the support of its officers and of the senate of the city of Berlin; and I essentially finished it at the Max-Planck-Institut für Geschichte during 1989–90, through the hospitality of Rudolf Vierhaus and his colleagues at Göttingen and the financial support of the Alexander von Humboldt-Stiftung. My colleagues at the Johns Hopkins Department of History have borne extra burdens on my account patiently, or at least silently. Administrators and staff at the Konsistorialarchiv and the Landesarchiv at Salzburg and the Geheimes Staats-Archiv at Berlin-Dahlem have been generous with counsel and assistance. Three recent scholarly works, listed in the Bibliography, need special mention here because without them this book would have been quite impossible: Artur Ehmer's *Das Schrifttum zur Salzburger Emigration* (Hamburg, 1975), Horst Kenkel's *Amtsbauern und Kölmer im nördlichen Ostpreussen* (Hamburg, 1972), and Angelika Marsch's splendid *Die Salzburger Emigranten in Bildern*, 2d ed. (Weissenhorn/Bayern, 1979). Unless otherwise indicated, all translations are mine.

My wife, Irma, has done her best to suppress complacency of opinion or interpretation on my part and caught very many embarrassing technical errors as well. Barbara Walker and Bill Bowman located weaknesses in the text, some of which I have been able to remedy. The publisher's readers have made seriously important suggestions and have brought about real improvements in my text—or where not, not for want of trying—and this is no common mark of generous attention. For essential help with the proofs, I am indebted to Jean Johnson, Tanya Kevorkian, and, again, Irma Walker. Finally let me thank the editors, designers, and staff of the Cornell University Press for their patience, care, and flexibility in completing a task for which these qualities have been indispensable.

MACK WALKER

Baltimore, Maryland

ABBREVIATIONS

AÖG	*Archiv für österreichische Geschichte*
BBK	*Beiträge zur bayrischen Kirchengeschichte*
CC	*Continuity and Change: A Journal of Social Structure, Law and Demography in Past Societies*
FHK	*Festschrift für Herbert Klein*. Published by the Gesellschaft für Salzburger Landeskunde. Salzburg, 1965.
GStA PK	Geheimes Staats-Archiv, Preussischer Kulturbesitz
GT	*Geographisches Taschenbuch*
HG	*Hannoversche Geschichtsblätter*
HTR	*Harvard Theological Review*
HZ	*Historische Zeitschrift*
JGPÖ	*Jahrbuch der Gesellschaft für die Geschichte des Protestantismus in Österreich*
JWG	*Jahrbuch für Wirtschaftsgeschichte*
KAS	Konsistorialarchiv Salzburg
MAGW	*Mitteilungen der Anthropologischen Gesellschaft in Wien*
MGSL	*Mitteilungen der Gesellschaft für salzburger Landeskunde*
MIÖG	*Mitteilungen des Instituts für österreichische Geschichtsforschung*
NABB	*Neuer Anzeiger für Bibliographie und Bibliothekswissenschaft*
ÖAK	*Österreichisches Archiv für Kirchenrecht*

OGS	*Oxford German Studies*
REP	Friederike Zaisberger, ed. *Reformation/Emigration: Protestanten in Salzburg.* Salzburg, 1981.
SDF	*Sudetendeutsche Forschungen*
SLA	Salzburger Landesarchiv
SMB	*Salzburger Museumsblätter*
ZAA	*Zeitschrift für Agrargeschichte und Agrarsoziologie*
ZBK	*Zeitschrift für bayerische Kirchengeschichte*
ZKG	*Zeitschrift für Kirchengeschichte*
ZPG	*Zeitschrift für preussische Geschichte*
ZRG Kan	*Zeitschrift der Savigny-Stiftung für Rechtsgeschichte, Kanonische Abteilung*

The Salzburg Transaction

PRELATES AND PEASANTS

The archbishops of Salzburg and the cattle farmers of the alpine districts of the principality were alien to each other, by circumstance and by preference. They were seldom obliged to think about each other, and when they did it was with reluctance and aversion. For neither furnished the other with something the other valued, whether wealth, dignity, loyalty, or affection; encounters between them made for irritation, repugnance, or enmity, depending on the intimacy of the contact. So they maintained their natural distance as best they could, expending little trust on each other, and little truthfulness.

It is easy to suppose here at the outset that it was the broken alpine landscape that separated them from each other; and in a primitive and protean sense, it was. But the political, economic, and cultural features of their respective worlds as they had separately evolved, especially from the sixteenth century to the eighteenth, were more telling than the geological and topographical ones. Meanwhile, neither archbishop nor peasantry was isolated from the German Empire or from Europe, or from imperial and European Christian associations. In some operative ways, the external connections of each with the out-

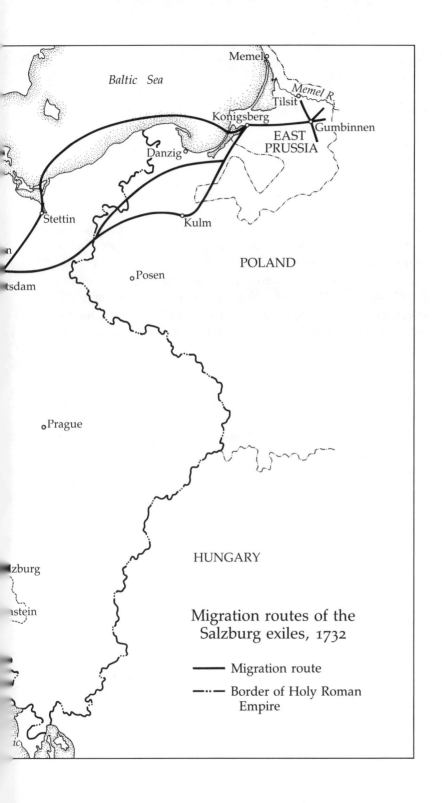

Memel

Baltic Sea

Memel R.

Tilsit

Königsberg

Gumbinnen

EAST
PRUSSIA

Danzig

Stettin

Kulm

n

tsdam

Posen

POLAND

Prague

HUNGARY

lzburg

stein

ic

Migration routes of the
Salzburg exiles, 1732

——— Migration route

—··— Border of Holy Roman
Empire

side were stronger than their association with each other. The expulsion and emigration of 1732, the central event that unites the accounts that follow, was guided by their respective associations with the outer world—or worlds, including those of the German emperor, of the king in Prussia, and of the political champions of the German Evangelical or Protestant faith, the three other main participants in the event.

Indeed, these wider associations, economic, political, and confessional, deepened the local disassociation of archbishopric and mountain peasantry, despite geographical conventions that would locate them in the same space on a political or ecclesiastical map. The scattered lone priests and officials of the river valleys and market towns, who stood functionally between prince and people and upon whose effectiveness the reality of such a map depends, may have been the most thoroughly isolated of all, for they held the confidence and respect neither of their overlords at the central capital and court, nor of their subjects of the outer slopes and upland valleys.

It is important to attend at the beginning to this separation of the inner and outer worlds of the archepiscopal capital from the inner and outer worlds of the mountain settlements, because the archbishop's expulsion of the farmers in 1731–32 has been the most notorious episode in Salzburg's history at least before the time of Mozart, so that historians have inevitably thought about archbishopric and peasantry in conjunction. The emigration was brought about by an outright encounter between the two, a shock and a surprise because of their normal condition of mutual aversion, ignorance, and evasion. There were to be sure some earlier and lesser encounters, which I shall sketch later in this Prologue, for they form the common context for the five chapters that follow.

In the stylized and retrospective language of history, the convention of posing archbishop and peasants in engagement seems fair enough, but the convention began in 1731–32, and hardly any chronicler or observer would have thought of writing about Salzburg that way before that. The peripatetic court-ier Karl Ludwig von Pöllnitz, for example, visited Salzburg in 1730 and announced in his travel memoirs: "The surroundings of Salzburg are not disagreeable; and although the valley in which it is situated is closed in by mountains, still, it provides a variety of pleasant prospects." By "pleasant prospects" he meant some parks and palaces, and not the alpine scenery, let alone whoever might live out there.[1]

The Salzburg archepiscopal court and state that Pöllnitz saw and described were not unlike other middle-sized German ecclesiastical principalities of the time. Salzburg might be compared with other places of its rank with respect to the splendor of its court, its patronage of the representational arts, and its university. Its government was surely acquainted with the old-regime afflictions of nepotism, favoritism, and unchaste prelates, but not to an unusual degree. In its treatment of its subjects it was probably no worse than most others, and maybe a bit better. On the whole Salzburg was a relatively enlightened ecclesiastical polity, geographically somewhat remote, to be sure, and not wealthy enough to sustain the imperial and family politics that were everyday life for the great Rhenish archbishoprics like Cologne, Mainz, and Trier, or the key Franconian bishoprics of Bamberg or Würzburg. If compared with these rich imperial dignitaries, a proud Salzburger prelate might point to the ecclesiastical history of the archdiocese. It had been founded in the eighth century and had maintained its independence against the secular houses of Austria and Bavaria through the centuries of medieval violence. An archbishop of Salzburg had occupied the chair at the Imperial Diet at Worms in 1521, where Martin Luther had made his dramatic open break with a church that could neither burn nor buy him, and where the young Emperor Charles had taken his definitive

---

[1] Charles-Louis [=Karl Ludwig v.] Pöllnitz, *Mémoires, contenant les observations qu'il a faites dans ses voyages*, vol. 2 (Liège, 1734), p. 99. But for the publication in 1734 he inserted new material about the Evangelical peasantry, the archbishop, and the king of Prussia: see below, Chapter 3, pp. 142–43.

stand with Mediterranean Catholicism; and in 1529 the archbishop of Salzburg was made primate of Germany, replacing
the archbishop of Magdeburg when that northern metropolis
fell away from the church. Salzburg alternated with Austria
and Burgundy as president of the Bench of Ecclesiastical
Princes at the Imperial Diet in Regensburg, and with Austria as
director of the entire College of Princes. In the early eighteenth
century the archbishop of Salzburg was metropolitan over
seven suffragan bishops: three of them imperial (Passau, Freis-
ing, and Brixen [or Bressanone] in the Tyrol), three in Carinthia
and Styria under Austrian secular jurisdiction (Seckau, Lavant,
and Gurk), and Chiemsee in Bavaria. He held immediate pastoral authority over not only the territory of Salzburg itself but
also parts of Bavaria, Upper and Lower Austria, and the Tyrol.[2]

These offices, endowments, and patronages provided important revenues; but more important by far to church and state
were the mineral resources, most of which were owned by the
archbishop as territorial prince and which by the eighteenth
century consisted almost entirely of the salt works near Hallein, close to the city and alongside the route leading south
toward the mountain districts. These works were valuable less
for direct revenue than as producers for export; even more important, they provided a base for credit, always vital to court
societies of the time. The mines were directly managed by the
treasury, the *Hofkammer*; and indeed, the fiscal administration
of the archdiocese was largely built around the development
and administration of this resource. Since these mines required
quantities of timber and water, forest and riparian rights were
also strictly controlled.[3]

---

[2] The standard modern general history is Hans Widmann, *Geschichte
Salzburgs*, 3 vols. (Gotha, 1907–14). The basic and still indispensable ecclesiasti-
cal histories are Judas T. Zauner, *Chronik von Salzburg*, 11 parts in 10 vols.
(Salzburg, 1796–1826); and Marcus Hansiz [=Hansitz], *Germania Sacra*, vol. 2,
Archiepiscopatus Salisburgensis (Augsburg, 1729).

[3] There is a convenient summary in Widmann, *Geschichte Salzburgs*, 3:346–59;
monographic detail is in Gerhard Ammerer: "Funktionen, Finanzen und Fort-

During the later seventeenth and early eighteenth centuries there was an elaboration and a sharpening of uniform rules governing the Salzburg economy and the everyday behavior of Salzburg subjects. This activity may be conveniently dated with the reign of the energetic archbishop Max Gandolf (1668–87); but it matches similar developments in other states of the Empire, programs associated with the historians' word "absolutism" and with the *Polizei* of German contemporaries. In Salzburg as elsewhere in Europe this development was resisted by the estates of the principality, here meaning in effect the capitulars of the cathedral chapter, a body that habitually, in keeping with the usual political patterns of the time, contested the archbishops' assertions of sovereignty. Traditionally this quasi-hereditary cathedral chapter had extracted concessions from the archbishops and had imposed limitations upon them, at a time and as a price and condition of their election, in the electoral contracts called *Wahlkapitulationen*, until these were invalidated and forbidden by the papacy in 1695; the last Salzburg Wahlkapitulation was inscribed in 1688. The archbishops seem to have paid little attention to these promises, once elected and in office; nevertheless to reach office they did have to be elected, and, by hook or crook, to be elected by the chapter—which eventually would select their successors. The capitulars continued to assert their influence, as opportunity allowed, in the realm of religious exercise and authority, but also for direction of policy and patronage both inside and outside the archbishopric. They particularly insisted that no new clerical orders should be introduced into the archdiocese without the chapter's consent: by this prohibition they usually meant the Society of Jesus, Benedictines being the generally dominant order in the archdiocese.[4]

---

schritt: Zur Regionalverwaltung im Spätabsolutismus am Beispiel des geistlichen Fürstentums Salzburg," *MGSL* 126 (1986), 341–518, and *MGSL* 127 (1987), 151–418.

[4] Reinhard R. Heinisch, *Die bischöflichen Wahlkapitulationen im Erzstift Salzburg*

The pattern of political contention between prince and estates thus did not differ markedly from the pattern of the time in other German principalities of comparable size and resources, except that in this instance the prince was a priest as well: a prelate. Political sovereignty generally included ecclesiastical authority in secular principalities too, but for a priest-prince it could become a particularly sensitive element of his authority, touching the special dignity of his spiritual estate. Within the immediate circle of the Salzburg court and capital, however, the Salzburg Pöllnitz saw in 1730, it was not. Formerly disaffected townspeople, nobility, and clergy had been effectively purged or returned to Catholic discipline in the course of the sixteenth century, so that within the inner sphere there was little sign of or inclination to religious enthusiasm or doctrinal passion. Religious conformity, or laxity, or a reasonable compound of both, were a necessary part of the climate within which the modern state, secular or ecclesiastic, could be proclaimed, represented, and made real. *Religions-Eyfer*—enthusiasm—was an opprobrious term in the Salzburg that Pöllnitz saw.

We may turn now to the other Salzburg of this story. The main emigration area of 1731–32 was the alpine region of the Pinzgau but especially the Pongau, centering about seventy-five present-day kilometers south of the city of Salzburg and upstream, on both sides of the Salzach and its tributaries. A handful of small market towns and villages were strung along the valley bottoms: such places might have some shops, a church and priest, perhaps a district official or two, and townspeople's gardens on its outskirts. These market and administrative settlements were firmly Catholic and saw next to no emigration in 1731–32.

1514–1688 (Vienna, 1977); Corbinus Gärtner [=Maurus Schenkel], *Geschichte der Bauernauswanderung aus Salzburg, unter dem Erzbischoff Firmian* (part 10 of Zauner, *Chronik*, above note 2: [Salzburg, 1821], hereafter cited as Gärtner, *Chronik*), pp. 400–407.

The bulk of the population lived widely scattered on family-sized holdings on the mountainsides and the high valleys, only rarely grouped even in villages. The families had no special need and less regard for the political and religious agencies of the provincial towns. In their everyday lives and domestic culture they were further from the valley towns nearby than the towns were from the capital; economically too they lived rather independently from the towns and visited them rarely. Reciprocally, pastoral and administrative work with the mountain people was difficult and unrewarding, unlikely to attract the energies of ambitious, able, or confident officers; and the provincial priests and prefects showed little perceptible enthusiasm for their work.

The fundamental social and economic unit of the mountain rural culture was the family farmstead, the *Gut*. I will have more to say about this in the chapter called "The Migrants," which treats the transition of the country people from the rural circumstances of alpine Salzburg to those of lowland East Prussia. Note for now that about four out of five inhabitants of these farmsteads were fully participating family members, and the remaining fifth of the population were Gut residents but with insecure and inferior status: wage or contract laborers, or relatives a stage removed from the domestic unit. Serfdom did not exist in this region. There were several thousand of these farmsteads in the area affected by the emigration. Legal tenure on such properties, though technically varied, usually was secure, heritable, and alienable, and properties changed hands often, commonly within the space of a generation or two or even less, in what appears to have been a lively land market among a locally mobile population.[5]

---

[5] Johannes W. Pichler, *Die ältere ländliche Salzburger Eigentumsordnung* (Salzburg, 1979), esp. pp. 81–101; Kurt Conrad, "Der Bauer und sein Hof," in *REP*, pp. 151–66; for frequent turnover of *Güter*, assessed values based on most recent sales are recorded in KAS 11/69e: Reformation. Emigrationspatent 1731. Verkauf der Emigrantengüter im Beisein des preuss. Gesandten. Verzeichnis der Güter 1734–38, etc.; and GStA PK Rep. 5 Tit. 21 Nr. 15, vols. 1–3: Acta,

At the time of the emigration this population was growing, too, in density and gross numbers, though not necessarily in number of households. There are substantial indications that the German Alps had become relatively overpopulated during and since the Thirty Years' War.[6] General figures are scarce and they cannot be projected usefully on local situations; but a close look at one characteristic mountain valley in the Pongau emigration region, which cannot be proved typical but which certainly is not eccentric, yields striking results, offering numbers that are specific enough to withstand any caviling.[7] During the period 1620–1920, the population of Wagrain-Kleinarl was at its most dense in the 1720s, the decade just preceding the emigration or expulsion. It reached peak density, of all these three centuries, precisely in the emigration year 1732. Then after the emigration, the population of the valley stabilized at a lower level, an ecologically "natural" level, perhaps, at which it remained without significant change for the next two hundred years.

Other statistical indicators for Wagrain-Kleinarl elaborate the pattern. The marriage rate there reached its highest level, of the entire three centuries, during the same 1720s; but the birthrate, in statistical contrast, was then at its *lowest* level in the

---

wegen Liquidation der von den Salzburgern in ihrem Vaterlande zurückgelassenen Forderungen . . . 1735–38. Pichler, pp. 47–56, identifies an obligation of personal loyalty to the *Landesherr* as a condition of possession, with dispossession a consequence of emigration, but I find no trace of this notion in the contemporary materials, where if effective it surely would have been mentioned. For some general observations on the ecology of *Streusiedlung* (scattered settlement), Johann H. G. v. Justi, *Grundfeste zu der Macht und Glückseligkeit der Staaten*, vol. 1 (Königsberg, 1760; reprint Aalen, 1965), pp. 355–58; and Heide Wunder, *Die bäuerliche Gemeinde in Deutschland* (Göttingen, 1986), pp. 62–63 and the sources cited there.

[6] Hermann Wopfner, "Güterteilung und Übervölkerung Tirolischer Landteile im 16., 17. und 18. Jahrhundert," *SDF* 3 (1938), 202–32; Ernst Nowotny, *Die Transmigration ober- und innerösterreichischen Protestanten nach Siebenbürgen im 18. Jahrhundert* (Jena, 1931), pp. 35–37.

[7] Matthias Schönberger, "Bevölkerungsstatistik eines Salzburger Gebirgstales, 1621–1920," *MAGW* 66 (1926), 271–78.

past fifty years. The population was dense and growing; there were many marriages but few births, implying domestic strictures, personal stress and anxiety. And moral statistics follow this pattern over time, showing a steady rise in the proportion of illegitimate births during those preceding fifty years, but after the migration a sharp decline to about a third the levels of the pre-emigration years. Mortality rates, following slight declines during the preceding couple of decades, fell steeply in the 1740s.[8]

What are we to make of this remarkable regularity? Social historians of recent times might find in these statistical correlations all the explanation the story needs, and end it here. Self-consciously Catholic historians also invoke social-economic (not to say deterministic) arguments, albeit uneasily, to explain the emigration. Indignant Protestants by ironic contrast reject such sober calculations, thereby keeping moral responsibility for the expulsion fixed on Archbishop Firmian, his church, his will, and his intentions.[9] One might even combine the two and credit, or condemn, Archbishop Firmian and his government

---

[8] But I find nothing in serial price or wage figures to distinguish the times or places of emigration (see, for example, Alfred L. Pribram et al., *Materialien zur Geschichte der Preise und Löhne in Österreich*, vol. 1 [Vienna, 1938]), though this does not exclude the possibility of local or momentary fluctuations that escape the tabulations. Neither does any contemporary comment on the emigration that I have seen mention such matters.

[9] Representative of scholarly Protestant accounts are Carl F. Arnold, *Die Ausrottung des Protestantismus in Salzburg unter Erzbischof Firmian und seinen Nachfolgern*, 2 vols. (Halle, 1900–1901), and the milder and more recent Gerhard Florey, *Geschichte der Salzburger Protestanten und ihrer Emigration 1731/32* (Vienna, 1977); on the Catholic side, Ludwig Clarus [=Ludwig Völkel], *Die Auswanderung der protestantisch gesinnten Salzburger* (Innsbruck, 1864), and the judicious but firmly Catholic account by Franz Ortner, *Reformation, Katholische Reform und Gegenreformation in Salzburg* (Salzburg, 1981). But the authorized contemporary account by Johannes Baptist Gaspari [=Giovanni Battista Caspari di Nuovomonte], *Aktenmässige Geschichte der berühmten salzburgischen Emigration*, trans. Franz X. Huber (Salzburg, 1790), is a valuable, intimate, and generally reliable view from inside the archepiscopal court. Gaspari was *Hofbibliothekar* and *Hofmeister* to the Salzburg *Edelknaben* at the time of the emigration.

with a neat bit of demographic sanitation. Remarkably, a memorandum of 1735, at the Austrian Court Chancellery in Vienna, advocated a "transmigration" of Austrian Protestant subjects "especially since there is so excessive a population in the Salzkammergut anyhow, that hardly a tenth of them can be provided with sufficient work there."[10] But this reflection was offered after the Salzburg emigration had been successfully accomplished. It has no counterpart at all in the Salzburg materials before or during the expulsion of 1731–32 that I am aware of. The decisions and actions that brought the emigration about had quite other reasons and causes. And of course a great many demographically and economically similar places, in the Salzburg archbishopric and elsewhere, saw no emigration in 1731–32.

How to identify partial causes and how to maintain separate but equal narrative truths will be matters for coming chapters. As for the place of gross population and its relation to the emigration: like the alpine geology it is a primitive and a protean cause, with many potential consequences. But one secondary and conditioned cultural phenomenon turns out to provide an important link: I mean the regular practice of wandering northward in search of seasonal work, which was traditional and commonplace among the alpine population of the Pongau and a persistent element of its particular culture.

This practice in turn involves a principal social and domestic distinction within the alpine population, already touched upon, which will become more important when I turn to emigration itself: the distinction between that predominant part of the population which lived regularly and by entitlement as members of established households, and the 20 percent or

---

[10] "Wo zumahlen ohnedem so viel überflüssigen Volkes auf dem Salzkammerguth sey, dass kaum der zehende Theil mit genugsamer Arbeit versehen werden könne, auch *leichter* seyn würde *in puncto religionis* allda eine bessere Einrichtung zu machen, wann selbes von den Verstockten und Unverbesserlichen vorhero würde gesäubert seyn." Quoted in Nowotny, *Transmigration*, p. 35.

thereabouts who did not. The former were considered *ansässig*, settled; the others were called the *Nichtangesessenen*, the unsettled or undomiciled. The latter was partly a category of family connection and economic expectation, or rather their absence, inasmuch as it included those who had no home farm family membership and thus no hope of inheritance. But in this farmstead population it was not a social category mainly but a generational one, encompassing grown, unmarried sons and daughters of propertied families, who worked away from home for day wages or on contract. Many and perhaps most of these subsequently attained or recovered ansässig status by inheritance or marriage into a Gut.

The domestic organization of rural economy and society into family farms, subject to a growing natural population, obliged or encouraged many of these Nichtangesessenen to travel northward, out of the mountains to the flatlands around Regensburg, Augsburg, Nürnberg, and beyond: across the confessional borders, therefore, out of Catholic into Protestant territory. There was no appreciable demand for rural labor in the Salzburg market towns and capital itself. Indeed it seems quite likely that of all Salzburg subjects, the mountain peasantry had the most regular contact with foreigners, and especially with Protestant foreigners, on account of these annual treks northward: migration *laboris causa* in the language of the Salzburg police, a practice already noted in the sixteenth century.[11] Some of the seasonal workers brought books home with them, to sell or to keep, another and equally important link with Germany to the north, bypassing the capital. Books were almost a tribal

[11] Aurelia Henökl, *Studien zur Reformation und Gegenreformation im Pongau unter besonderer Berücksichtigung der Vorfälle im Pfleggericht Werfen* (Vienna, 1979), pp. 206–14; Ortner, *Reformation*, pp. 50–52 and passim. There are hundreds of examinations of returning migrant workers about their contacts abroad in the Konsistorialarchiv in Salzburg: KAS 11/53b: Reformation. Religions Kommissikons-Akten 1672–1728. Verschiedene Orte. Verhöre; and in other bundles nearby (see Bibliography), many of them quite entertaining duels between dumb-playing rustics and undeceived ecclesiastical officials.

totem of the mountain peasant culture, related to the family and Gut household as organic principles of the society: devotional books, designed for religious exercise where there was no priest, and thus mainly Protestant books. Books were central objects of domestic worship, the *Hausandacht*.[12] I call them totems to mark them as objects that endowed this otherwise scattered and dispersed alpine population with a distinct and conscious cultural identity. (Totemism as an aspect of bookishness might reward wider application and speculation.) This cultural identity of the mountain peasantry linked them therefore with the German north, even as it estranged them from their own prince, a Catholic bishop, and from his court and culture. The baroque splendors of the Counter-Reformation, like its disciplinary strictures, did not penetrate the alpine parishes of the Pongau.

These linkages and totems were well known to state and church authorities throughout the Salzkammergut and Upper Austria generally; and efforts to suppress the importation of books had led to a lively smuggling trade, far exceeding such portable contraband as peasant boys' summer wages might buy. A commercial traveler passing through the mountains might collect orders and payments for books that he bought in Regensburg or Nürnberg; cattle drivers, peddlers, and carters joined in the trade.[13] Discharged soldiers converted some of

---

[12] I shall not pursue the perplexed legal question of the constitutional right to domestic devotions, for however important such devotions were to religious exercise and religious discipline, the legal position was ambiguous and rarely observed, and had little bearing on this episode, even in the view of the Protestant constitutional expert Johann J. Moser: *Von der Landes-Hoheit im Geistlichen* (Frankfurt/M., 1773), pp. 54–55; and *Von der Teutschen Religions-Verfassung* (Frankfurt/M., 1774), pp. 130–35.

[13] The main authority on this subject is Paul Dedic; see his "Besitz und Beschaffung evangelischen Schrifttums in Steiermark und Kärnten in der Zeit des Kryptoprotestantismus," *ZKG* 58 (1939), 476–95; "Die Einschmuggelung lutherischer Bücher nach Kärnten in den ersten Dezennien des 18. Jahrhunderts," *JGPÖ* 60 (1939), 126–77; "Verbreitung und Vernichtung evangelischen Schrifttums in Innerösterreich," *ZKG* 57 (1938), 433–58. Salzburg counterparts

their savings into books and brought them home in their packs. The market was there, "because," according to a 1722 report from Austrian Carinthia next door, "just about every inhabitant here can read and many can write, but they never learned or allow [their children] to learn reading and writing in the towns and markets, for fear of the religious instruction and catechizing that would go with it there, but rather from a local schoolmaster or very often from a peasant, where in wintertime especially even the farmhands and maidservants come together for this, and take such instruction with no other purpose, than to read and to understand the old or newly arrived Lutheran books."[14] Into this culture children were initiated as they were read to, or as they learned to read. Literacy was widespread among women; a striking number—at a guess, perhaps a third—of the (male) peasants who were examined on account of book possession or literacy, these conditions being prima facie evidence of Protestant heresy, testified that they had learned to read from a female relative or housemistress.[15] They hoarded books that might have been found in the library of a burgher family in the German north: Arndt's *Wahres Christentum* and *Paradiesgärtlein*, Habermann's *Gebetbuch*—the "Habermändl"—and Lutheran catechisms and hymnals.[16] One family was found to own eighty-six devotional

---

to these Upper-Austrian studies could easily be constructed from the comparable sources in the Salzburg state and consistorial archives, which are filled with testimony on contraband books and literacy.

[14] Dedic, "Einschmuggelung lutherischer Bücher," p. 157.

[15] I record this impression unsystematically from my reading of the interrogations reported in the consistorial records identified under KAS in the Bibliography, especially the records of the Religions Kommission for 1672–1728 in 11/53b, and for 1706–26 in 11/54b. There are some signs, though, that persons asked who had taught them to read preferred to incriminate women.

[16] Compare Rolf Engelsing, *Der Bürger als Leser: Lesergeschichte in Deutschland 1500–1800* (Stuttgart, 1974), pp. 56–78. As in Engelsing's findings, I find no examples of "Hausväterliteratur" or other economic topics in the Salzburg inventories and interrogations; to be sure it was religious books these investigators were looking for.

books in the spring of 1731, eighty of them Protestant and six Catholic (an exceptionally large collection, to be sure), about a quarter of them published before 1555, close to half before 1648, the rest since the Thirty Years' War.[17] In Vienna itself around that time, of thirteen bookdealers, ten were Protestant. These were readily tolerated in the culture of the Habsburg capital and court; but Protestantism among the alpine peasantry, Austrian as well as Salzburger, was quite another matter.[18]

In the Salzburg archbishopric the capital and the mountain cultures lived apart, except when an aggravated religious issue brought them face to face. Yet religious issues are never far from the history of their alienation either, since Reformation times.[19] Ecclesiastical abuses of the kind that troubled the German church in the fifteenth and early sixteenth century were common enough in Salzburg, scandalizing the populace and the imperial court, and stimulating a revival of the territorial estates of prelates, nobility, and towns, with irregular attendance from the mountain districts.[20] Reformist preachers of Saxon and Franconian stamp appeared in Salzburg in the 1510s, as did Thuringian miners. In 1520 Martin Luther's old teacher and confessor, Johann von Staupitz left the Saxon order of Reform Augustinians and retired to Salzburg. He ended his days (in 1524) as abbot of the dominant Benedictines but

[17] Friederike Zaisberger, "Der Salzburger Bauer und die Reformation," *MGSL* 124 (1984), 392–94. There are very many interrogations of book owners and inventories of seized books in the Konsistorialarchiv documents listed in the Bibliography.

[18] Heinrich Benedikt, *Monarchie der Gegensätze*, vol. 2 (Vienna, 1947), p. 78.

[19] There is a useful summary in Johann Sallaberger, "Das Eindringen der Reformation in Salzburg und die Abwehrmassnahmen der Erzbischöfe bis zum Augsburger Religionsfrieden 1555," in *REP*, pp. 26–33.

[20] On the period of estates activity, see Sallaberger, "Eindringen der Reformation"; Ortner, *Reformation*, pp. 25–26; Herbert Klein, "Die Bauernschaft auf den Salzburger Landtagen," *MGSL* 88–89 (1948–49), 51–78; Klein, "Salzburg und seine Landstände von den Anfängen bis 1861," in *FHK*, pp. 115–36; and Peter Blickle, *Landschaften im Alten Reich: Die staatliche Funktion des gemeinen Mannes in Oberdeutschland* (Munich, 1973), pp. 60–67, which hopefully reads official representation from the mountain *Gerichte* as peasant participation.

left behind a Protestant fragment in the history of the archdiocese.

The Peasants' War of 1525–26 ended the tentative representation of the mountain districts in the Salzburg estates. In its
aftermath the estates themselves became firmly subordinated
to the archbishop as territorial prince, and then disappeared
altogether, leaving only the cathedral chapter with an organized political voice of its own, which it exercised mainly at election times. Its interests, placemanship apart, were parochial
and made no assertion of territorial responsibility except insofar as the chapter occasionally harassed archbishops for their
unseemly religious laxity. Visitation reports of 1528 and again
of 1555 found little Lutheran doctrine at work in the mountains, though considerable resentment among the populace
against an undisciplined local clergy, and associated with this
resentment a strong sentiment in favor of taking the sacrament
in both kinds, especially among the miners at Gastein, at the
far southern end of the Pongau. Within the city of Salzburg
itself, Lutheranism was well known at that time and was prac-
ticed, though privately and discreetly, by leading citizen families and possibly native nobility. But in 1554, the Wittelsbach
archbishop, Duke Ernst von Bayern, was forced into early retirement because he refused (after fourteen years as archbishop) to accept consecration as a priest, and his successor
was obliged to swear before the chapter his perpetual allegiance to the church, on behalf of himself and his subjects.[21]

The imperial Religious Peace reached at Augsburg in the following year forbade the interference by any German prince in
the religious affairs of any other. Two consequences of that settlement will be important here: the constitutionally legitimized
survival of powerful Protestant princes in the German Empire;
and the exclusive authority and freedom of any German
prince, secular or ecclesiastic, to regulate religious organization
and practice within his territory. These doctrines combined to

[21] Ortner, *Reformation*, pp. 52–74.

found the *ius reformandi*, meaning the authority of a prince of the Empire to impose religious conformity in either of the two recognized Christian confessions on his subjects or citizens. Persons unwilling for conscience' sake to accept such regulation were guaranteed the right to emigrate to another place, a right restated and elaborated in the Peace of Westphalia in 1648. This may seem small consolation, but it was looked upon as a considerable concession to liberty of conscience at the time, when productive population meant wealth and power and confession was the touchstone of politics; and on reflection, this was a greater freedom than has prevailed for political or racial or even religious inconformity in most of the world of the present century. But note that the right freely to emigrate was a *confessional* right in imperial law and could be claimed by that law only on grounds of confessional difference.

Emigration was the solution to religious difference Martin Luther himself had favored, and with direct reference to Salzburg at that: in 1532 Luther had written to a troubled gold-miner and councilman at Gastein that he could in good conscience avoid trouble with the authorities over communion merely by taking the sacraments not "bodily" at all, but only "spiritually." If, however, he was unsatisfied without bodily communion, and still his prince forbade communion in both kinds, "then you must leave the land, and seek another place, as Christ said: Fly to another town, if they persecute you in one, for here there is no other way."[22] One wonders what advice this experienced ecclesiastical politician might have given exactly two centuries later—an eerie coincidence of dates, of a kind that recurs often enough in this story, or more nearly, that links these several stories. Coincidence need not mean accident.

[22] Martin Luther, *Werke, Kritische Gesamtausgabe*, Abt. IV, *Briefwechsel*, 6. Bd. (Weimar, 1935), pp. 352–53. The biblical reference is to Matthew 10:23. Luther had adopted that position at the time of the Peasants' War, in a commentary on the Twelve Articles: see *Werke* Abt. I, 18. Bd. (Weimar, 1908), pp. 323–24.

Not much was done in the Salzburg archbishopric to enforce Tridentine doctrine and practice until a papal visitation of the 1580s, followed by the election of the ambitious Wolf Dietrich of Raitenau (1587–1612), who in 1588, Armada year, made an unprecedented personal journey to Rome to express his allegiance (it was Habsburg or Wittelsbach papal loyalty, apparently, that inspired him) and upon his return launched a campaign to extirpate Protestant dissent.[23] The campaign was effective in city and court circles; many wealthy and influential families were forced to attend church and otherwise to conform, or to emigrate, leaving in place a wholly Catholic society and culture. City councilmen were directed to take oaths of Catholic loyalty and orthodoxy; and they did so. But when a comparable order went out to the mountain districts, no rebels or heretics could be found to enforce the order upon; or so it was reported. The peasantry knew all about new brooms, perhaps, and archepiscopal authorities beyond the mountain passes were quite unlikely shock troops for the Counter-Reformation. Confessional deceit now became accepted practice among the alpine peasantry, and lying to public officials about religion, a regular element of the culture. Unlike the city of Salzburg, there was little resistance or emigration from the mountain districts. A partial exception appeared among the miners, but not among the farmers, of the Gastein district; and there, special official dispensation had to be made in favor of Protestant miners lest their possible emigration leave the mines, which were already in precarious financial condition, wholly inoperative.[24]

After this calculated opening flurry, religious confrontation lapsed for the remainder of Wolf Dietrich's reign, until 1612. An archbishop who had fifteen children by a mistress named

---

[23] There is a good account of the reign of Wolf Dietrich in Ortner, *Reformation*, pp. 102–9.

[24] Heinrich v. Zimburg, *Die Geschichte Gasteins und des Gasteiner Tals* (Vienna, 1948), pp. 123–31.

Salome Alt was himself an unlikely champion of the Tridentine Reforms, especially when Archduke Ferdinand of Austria was in full cry next door about such clerical abuses and debilitations of ecclesiastical authority; and Wolf Dietrich near the end of his life refused to join the Catholic League of counter-reforming political militants.[25] He was deposed then, in 1612, by an alliance between Maximilian of Bavaria, head of the league, and reformists in the Salzburg cathedral chapter; and he was imprisoned in the Hohensalzburg castle, where he died five years later. His successor, Markus Sittikus (1612–18), selected by the victorious reform party in the chapter, launched a serious visitation and Catholic reform program that lasted until it was broken off by the archbishop's early death and the outbreak of what became the Thirty Years' War.

The visitation begun by Markus Sittikus and his reform party initially reported shocking conditions in the church, especially in the alpine districts of Pongau and Pinzgau.[26] There were only thirty-odd priests in that whole area, and of these only five were native Salzburger. Priestly concubinage was common—*vide* Wolf Dietrich and his Salome—and this was a particularly touchy point in the alpine districts because the Tridentine rules on marriage conflicted directly with a common marriage practice there, a custom whereby the bride moved in with the bridegroom immediately after the marriage contract between their families, but priestly consecration came only later, when the bridegroom took over the farmstead. A concubinary priest who called this fornication, however, was in an implausible position. The peasantry also claimed, on scriptural grounds, a right to the sacrament in both kinds, a Lutheran position but also an expression of their disrespect for the clergy. This archbishop meant business, however, and Markus Sitticus dispatched Capuchin missionaries to the mountain dis-

[25] Heinisch, *Wahlkapitulationen*, pp. 65–66; Ortner, *Reformation*, pp. 109–11.
[26] The reform program of Markus Sittikus is closely and sympathetically examined by Ortner, *Reformation*, pp. 110–24.

tricts, with soldiers to support them, to bring about religious order. The reformers moved from parish to parish, house to house, giving particular attention to backsliding priests and the "unsettled" part of the lay population. Among the latter, confraternities or *Bruderschaften* were organized, as favored Counter-Reformation instruments for religious instruction, discipline, and example; rosaries and catechisms were distributed; and efforts made to enforce orthodox marriage rules.[27] Of some ten thousand suspected dissidents, nine thousand now took oaths to the Catholic faith; perhaps another thousand, who would not, were declared banished.

The Markus Sittikus reforms (he was also the builder of the Lustschloss Hellbrunn with its antic waterworks, consecrater of the present cathedral, and founder of the gymnasium and lyceum that later became the university) were the most serious and most thoroughgoing effort fully to Catholicize the mountain population since the Peasants' War. Probably they would have succeeded if the archbishop had not died at age forty-five, or if the great war had not broken out in the year of his death. He was replaced by his still younger political adviser, Paris Graf Lodron (1618–54). Paris Lodron devoted his considerable talents to keeping the archbishopric out of war and internally at peace, which seems accomplishment enough. Reports from the mountain districts were now encouraging: the reforms seemed to have taken effect. The peasantry, with no taste for wandering northward either by choice or compulsion in those war years, was remarkably quiet; there was no sign of the violent disturbances that took place among their counterpart populations of Habsburg Austria in 1626, and a half-hearted tax revolt in the remote Zillertal in 1645 found no recognition or support elsewhere.[28]

---

[27] Henökl, *Pongau*, pp. 214–19; more generally on confraternities Markus Klammer, *Das religiöse Bruderschaftswesen in der Diözese Brixen vom Konzil von Trent bis zur Aufhebung, 1787* (Innsbruck, 1984). Compare Timothy Tackett, *Religion, Revolution, and Regional Culture in Eighteenth-Century France* (Princeton, 1986), pp. 232–33, and the citations there.

[28] Reinhard R. Heinisch, *Salzburg im dreissigjährigen Krieg* (Vienna, 1968), pp.

Confessional peace became the rule within the archbishopric
from the start of the Thirty Years' War until the eve of the
emigration of 1731–32, with the exception of a flurry of events
in the early 1680s. This was the time of the Turkish Danube
campaign that brought the armies of Islam from the east to the
gates of Vienna; to the west the French monarchy had
mounted its domestic religious campaign that ended with the
expulsion of French Protestants, and confessional politics were
at a fever pitch in the maritime countries. Witch hunts were
active in Europe and in America. The concurrent scare in
Salzburg took the strange form of the Zauberer-Jackl affair.
This occurred during the reign of Max Gandolf von Kuenberg
in Salzburg (1668–87), a vigorous Jesuit-trained nobleman
whose visitations to the mountains were directed more toward
policing the moral and social practices of the population (including marriage practices and the high illegitimacy rate to be
sure) than to ensuring their confessional purity. What his
agents found was not so much heresy as witchcraft and super-
stition.[29]

Just who Jake the Magician was—he was never found, but
probably there was some such person—and what his powers
and purposes were, nobody was clear about, which was an
essential part of the scare. But over a hundred members of his
blood brotherhood were identified and executed. The peak of
this affair coincided with a campaign to expel vagabonds and
beggars from the archbishopric, and of those executed most by
far were officially identified as beggars—not, it may be argued,
because the wizard hunt was an excuse for a social purge but
because it was presumed that Jackl was most likely to find re-
cruits and disciples among such folk, a point upon which the

184–89; Josef K. Mayr, "Bauernunruhen in Salzburg am Ende des Dreissigjährigen Krieges," *MGSL* 81 (1951), 1–106; Ortner, *Reformation*, pp. 124–35.

[29] Widmann, *Geschichte Salzburgs*, 3:332–33, 353–59; Ortner, *Reformation*, pp.
139–53; Heinz Nagl, "Der Zauberer-Jackl–Prozess: Hexenprozesse im Erzstift
Salzburg 1675–1690," *MGSL* 112–13 (1972–73), 385–539, and 114 (1974), 79–241.

authorities and the population at large were likely to agree. No doubt an implicit connection existed between a widespread popular distrust of strange folk and fear of strange events— attitudes endemic to those times—and the official campaign for social and moral order.

The Zauberer-Jackl affair seems not, however, to have been related to the older problem of heresy in the mountains, except perhaps indirectly, by arousing the moral police. Protestantism itself was neither examined nor denounced as sorcery or witch-craft in any of the Zauberer-Jackl trials.[30] Nor were the regions and populations subsequently affected by the emigration of 1731–32 particularly contaminated with sorcery in the 1680s, and these districts remained passive throughout the episode. Pongau and Pinzgau were also untouched by another event of the 1680s which bears on this story: the expulsion of Protes-tants from the Defereggental.

Sorcery was not Protestantism, nor was the Defereggental the Pongau. Nevertheless, the Zauberer-Jackl affair did draw the capital's attention to states of mind out in the mountain valleys, and one of the remotest, highest, and poorest valleys was in the Defereggen chain, in the East Tyrol, across the Hohe Tauern and beyond the Great Glockner. Economic condi-tions and arrangements were quite different there from those of the Pongau, let alone the distant ecclesiastical capital at Salzburg: the political and legal status of the region was com-plex and in dispute, land tenure was precarious, agriculture and husbandry were hopeless. Once there had been work un-certainly available in the mines, but these had been worked out and were deserted now. As the Deferegger traveled about seeking odd jobs or peddling cheap goods, they became known as troublesome and unstable folk.[31]

---

[30] But persons judicially condemned to death who were adjudged *unbussfertig* were executed by burning alive, rather than by the garrote or the ax allowed to the *Bekehrten*.

[31] The main treatments are Paul Passler, "Die lutherische Bewegung im Def-

In 1683 a merchandiser of religious articles complained to Salzburg officials of the Defereggers' abuse and contempt for holy pictures. A Capuchin mission, sent out in 1684 to investigate the matter, reported the inhabitants' scornful disbelief in hellfire, rosaries, and other such aids to orderly life and devotions. Intensive religious examinations and oath takings began in that year, and the refusal of clergy to administer sacraments to people who failed the tests crystalized hostility and unleashed public outbursts directed aganst the Capuchin missionaries. As the tension escalated, soldiers and more clergy were dispatched. On October 20, 1684, an order of expulsion was issued at Salzburg (anticipating that of Louis XIV against the Huguenots by just a year less two days), requiring all those who refused to acknowledge the discipline of the church to leave the archbishopric; children under age fifteen were to be left behind, and half the property of emigrant parents—those who had property—was forfeit to the archdiocese to help pay for the maintenance and proper education of the children. By midsummer 1685, over five hundred had emigrated; many managed to smuggle their children out with them, but most of these were captured in Innsbruck and returned by courtesy of the government of the Austrian Tyrol. Other dissidents were preparing to leave when the government at Salzburg, from failure of nerve or in the belief that the problem had been squelched, or both, found acceptable ways for them to recant, and subsequently even tried to bring back some who had already emigrated, though with little success. The episode seemed ended, to everybody's relief, with the succession of Archbishop Ernst von Thun in 1687.

The Deferegger expulsion is a nasty story even when baldly

ereggental," *JGPÖ* 49 (1928), 1–107; and Alois Dissertori, *Die Auswanderung der Deferegger Protestanten 1666–1725* (Innsbruck, 1964). See also Ortner, *Reformation*, pp. 154–65; Widmann, *Geschichte Salzburgs*, 3:325–30; Grete Mecenseffy, *Geschichte des Protestantismus in Österreich* (Gratz, 1956), pp. 190–92; and Zaisberger, "Salzburger Bauer," pp. 390–91.

told three hundred years later. It has a long legendary history, and remains sensitive and controversial. Catholic partisans at the time and historians since have been pained by it, especially the part about the children, which inevitably is a major part of the story. I have not examined the event itself in detail here because its relation to the far larger emigration of 1731–32 is not that of an early parallel or forerunner, but more that of an indirect but still possibly essential cause of it. The Deferegger expulsion was a stimulus to confessional partisanship of a particular kind, particular to the political and constitutional state of Germany and Europe. To be sure this event was partly a result of widespread confessional tension as well. On the European scene the year 1685 was a conjunctural year of confessional politics, one of converging tensions among the major religious and dynastic networks. The Deferegger expulsion represented Salzburg's phase and Salzburg's participation in that conjuncture. At another and less portentous time the incident would have attracted little notice, even assuming that it would have happened at all. But in 1685 French Protestant refugees streamed eastward into Germany; Britain and the Low Countries were braced for a showdown between a Catholic Stuart succession and a Protestant parliament; the Habsburg emperor had turned his back on a confessionally divided empire in favor of a campaign down the Danube after the retreating Ottomans. In Germany the expulsion of the Deferegger became a rhetorical focus of the religious politics of the Empire and its princes, and confessional rivalry on that stage belongs intimately to the history of the emigration of 1731–32.

Before we turn to that stage, however, one more Salzburg incident needs attention because of its contribution to the story following: the banishment of a number of dissident salt miners of Dürrnberg and of their spokesman, Joseph Schaitberger.[32]

---

[32] Wilfried Keplinger, "Die Emigration der Dürrnberger Bergknappen 1732," *MGSL* 100 (1960), 171–208; Ortner, *Reformation*, pp. 165–72; Zaisberger, "Salzburger Bauer," pp. 390–92.

Dürrnberg is the center of the salt-mining district that lay between the Salzburg town of Hallein and the upper Bavarian
town of Berchtesgaden. Lutheran religious inclinations had
long been known there, but the governments of Salzburg, Bavaria, and of Cologne (whose Wittelsbach archbishop was at
this time, on account of that office, provost over the Berchtesgaden part of the mining enterprise) had long turned a blind
eye to the religious peculiarities of their miners to avoid dis-
turbing the orderly exploitation of the mines. This prudent laxity broke down amid the excitement of the Turk Year 1683,
when leaders among the mine workers reacted to some particularly pungent priestly exhortation by ostentatiously refusing
to attend church and began to hold unauthorized services of
their own. When the Deferegger expulsion got under way, the
Dürrnberg dissident leaders and lay preachers were dismissed
from their jobs in the mines and ordered to leave Bavarian or
Salzburg territory. By 1691 some sixty or seventy people had
left—the children kept back as in the Defereggental—settling
mainly in places along the Swabian-Franconian confessional
border. The Evangelical mine worker and popular lay preacher
Joseph Schaitberger settled in Nürnberg, from which magis-
terially Lutheran bastion he then issued, until his death in
1733, a stream of fliers, letters, and pamphlets addressed to
"his Salzburg countrymen and other good friends." These were
collected, edited, and published under his name, and entitled
Evangelischer Send-Brief (Evangelical Missive). Their message
was mainly devotional or informational in character, but often
urged readers to follow the example of the author: that is, to
use love and to shun violence, but to confess and openly to
practice their faith; and where some benighted rule or ruler
forbade this, to leave that land for a godlier place, seeking
thereby peace in spirit even at the cost of one's bit of earth.[33]

---

[33] Joseph Schaitberger, *Evangelischer Send-Brief, Darinnen vier und zwantzig
nutzliche Büchlein enthalten, geschrieben an die Lands-Leut in Saltzburg und andere*

The language is shot through with pietistic pathos, yet the *Send-Briefe* still convey unusual appeal. In various forms they became very popular throughout German Protestant devotional circles and also became a main item of literary contraband reaching the Salzburg mountain farmers to the south.

German Protestantism possessed also an official organization in the Empire, and this too was stimulated and its attention drawn to Salzburg by the Deferegger emigration of the 1680s. The *corpus evangelicorum* was the permanent caucus of Protestant representatives to the Imperial Diet at Regensburg, the Reichstag. The constitutional basis of the corpus was a provision of the imperial constitution which ordained that when confessional issues arose, rather than rule by majority, the Reichstag would divide into Catholic and Protestant bodies and reach separate decisions, thus immunizing imperial German Protestant transactions from Catholic participation and founding a special Protestant forum for imperial religious affairs. The corpus evangelicorum was the regular Protestant agency for this very important and constitutionally very problematic procedure. Naturally, the standing delegations from the Protestant principalities and towns of the Empire which composed the corpus at Regensburg were on the alert for religious issues of a constitutional nature, or that could be so construed, so as to activate their authority. Members of the corpus, an actual group of accredited delegates which met regularly in the Reichstag building in Regensburg, also represented powerful German princes such as the rulers of Prussia, Saxony, and Braunschweig-Hanover, and towns like Nürnberg, Frankfurt am Main, and Hamburg. They were subject to instructions from those courts and councils. But the lawyers and diplomats who resided permanently in Regensburg actually constituted a

---

gute Freund . . . (Nürnberg, 1702, 1732, 1733, 1736, and other editions with varied titles and content); Hermann Clauss, "Josef Schaitberger und sein Sendbrief," *BBK* 15 (1909), 105–23, 153–66; Ortner, *Reformation*, pp. 172–78.

corporation of their own, which zestfully fed confessional issues and disputes back to their sponsor governments.[34]

In 1685 the corpus evangelicorum seized upon the Deferegger case: in July they made formal protest to the archbishopric of Salzburg in defense of the rights of the Defereggen Protestants, declaring that by terms of the Peace of Westphalia, the latter were entitled either to free private devotions, or, failing that, then to the three years' grace time specified in the Peace for free and orderly disposition of their property, and freedom to take their children with them into emigration. The archbishopric replied that these Deferegger were not real Protestants, with constitutionally endowed emigration rights, but rather a "neue zu *dato* ganz unerhörte Secte"; (a new and heretofore wholly unheard-of sect) they were "ärgerliche *Sectarii* und *Novatores*" (trouble-making sectarians and innovators). The corpus, however, was by now fully supported by most of their sponsor states, led by the electorate of Brandenburg, which was then also in the process of arranging the settlement of exiled French Protestants in Berlin and the Mark. The corpus insisted that the Deferegger dissidents were good Lutherans, protected accordingly by German constitutional law, and that the archbishop of Salzburg had deliberately set them up as a pretext for subverting "the religious freedom which has been achieved in Germany at the cost of so much turmoil and blood-

---

[34] On the corpus evangelicorum generally, Heinrich W. v. Bülow, *Über Geschichte und Verfassung des Corporis Evangelicorum* ([Regensburg], 1795); Ulrich Belster, *Die Stellung des Corpus Evangelicorum im Reichstag* (Tübingen, 1968). For the *ius eundi in partes* in particular, Johann S. Pütter, *Historische Entwickelung der heutigen Staatsverfassung des Teutschen Reichs*, 2d ed., vol. 2 (Göttingen, 1788), pp. 391–408; Klaus Schlaich, "Maioritas-protestatio-itio in partes-corpus Evangelicorum. Das Verfahren im Reichstag des Hl. Röm. Reichs Deutscher Nation nach der Reformation," *ZRG Kan* 63 (1977), 264–99, and 64 (1978), 139–79. Formal actions of the corpus are recorded in Eberhard C. Schauroth, *Vollständige Sammlung aller Conclusorum, Schreiben und anderer übrigen Verhandlungen des Hochpreisslichen Corporis Evangelicorum*, 3 vols. (Regensburg, 1751–52) and successor collections.

shed," the freedom that it was the special duty of the corpus to defend.[35]

The public dispute between corpus and archbishopric over the Deferegger went on for some five years, past the immigration of the Huguenots, past the death of the Great Elector of Brandenburg, and the consecration of another archbishop of Salzburg. It was too late then to do much for the emigrants; by the time they were allowed to retrieve their children, most children preferred to stay where they were, or so it was credibly reported. But the public and official intervention of the corpus evangelicorum in favor of the Deferegger at the Reichstag in Regensburg had made its mark. The assertion of the corpus of its role as sponsor of the emigration rights of German Protestants, including even those who lived in a Catholic prince-bishopric, now had its place in the constitutional lore of German Protestantism, even as Joseph Schaitberger's Salzburger *Send-Briefe* had their place in its devotions.

[35] Moser, *Landes-Hoheit im Geistlichen*, pp. 830–58, and *Teutsches Staats-Recht*, vol. 10 (Leipzig, 1743), pp. 297–303; Dissertori, *Deferegger Protestanten*, pp. 57–82.

CHAPTER ONE

THE ARCHBISHOPRIC

The cathedral chapter of Salzburg met at the end of September 1727 to elect a successor to the late archbishop Franz Anton Fürst von Harrach, an indolent and extravagant prince who by these qualities had achieved very considerable popularity, but under whose rule the archbishopric had suffered visible loss in political prestige and ecclesiastical authority. The leading candidate to succeed him was the incumbent dean of the chapter, Sigmund Felix von Schrattenbach, who was believed to enjoy the support of the emperor. Of the twenty electors, however, ten were stubbornly opposed to Schrattenbach. For three days and six successive ballots the dean failed by one vote, unable "somehow or other," writes the chronicler of the event with mild irony, *nescio quo*, to capture the miter; but neither was the narrow chapter opposition able to agree on any of their own number instead. On the fourth day the chapter rested, meeting only to pray. The following morning, October 4, they convened again, and just after nine o'clock "God so moved the urn" that to the surprise of all, Leopold Anton, Freiherr von

Firmian was chosen.[1] The gossip Baron Pöllnitz, who visited Salzburg in 1730, thought he knew the reason, one common enough in ecclesiastical annals, and in 1734, after the expulsion crisis, he published it: the deadlocked chapter had picked Firmian as a stopgap, Pöllnitz explained, because he was believed to be in ill health and unlikely to live for long.[2]

The chapter may have surprised itself by electing Firmian, but not because he was unknown to them: a dozen years before he had been their dean. Leopold Anton, son of a Tyrolean family long active and prominent in state and ecclesiastical service, had been born in 1679 in Munich, where his father was imperial ambassador to Bavaria; his mother was a Countess Thun. When a boy he had been sent to Salzburg as a protégé of his mother's brother, Archbishop Ernst Graf von Thun. At the Salzburg court he distinguished himself as a student, and at age fifteen was named capitular and sent to study with the Jesuits at the Collegium San Appolinaris at Rome. There he found further distinction as a scholar, being particularly attracted to Italian literary classics; and in 1707, shortly before the death of his uncle the archbishop, he was appointed to give the inaugural sermon at the new University Church in Salzburg. In 1713 he was made dean of the Salzburg cathedral chapter, which suggests that at one time he held the chapter's confidence or at least its tolerance; but in 1718, oddly and nescio quo, he became bishop over the rustic, poor, and remote diocese of Lavant, an appointment usually associated with failed ecclesiastical careers.

In 1724, however, Firmian was made bishop of Seckau in

[1] Marcus Hansiz [=Hansitz], *Germania Sacra*, vol. 2, *Archiepiscopatus Salisburgensis* (Augsburg, 1729), p. 915. The contemporary account by the Jesuit historian Hansiz is the main source for this election (pp. 911–18); but for added detail see also Gärtner, *Chronik*, pp. 3–4.

[2] Charles-Louis [=Karl Ludwig] Pöllnitz, *Mémoires, contenant les observations qu'il a faites dans ses voyages*, vol. 2 (Liège, 1734), p. 87. But "these gentlemen [of the chapter] were mightily deceived . . . this prelate lost all his infirmities upon arriving at the episcopate, and promises to survive most of his electors."

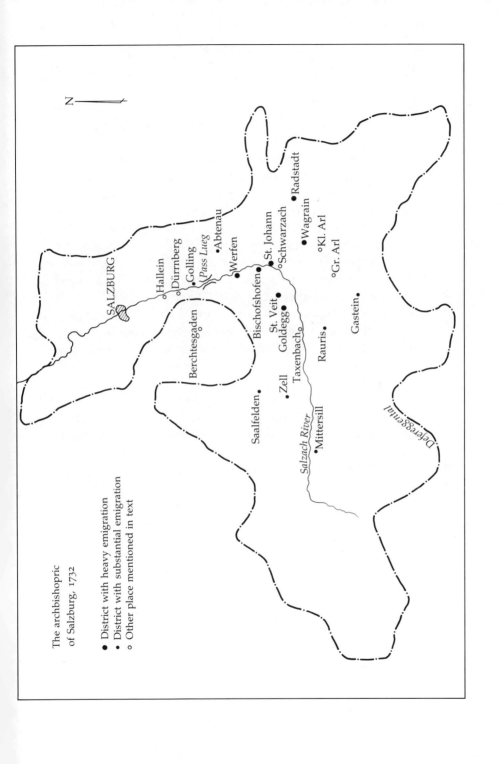

The archbishopric
of Salzburg, 1732

● District with heavy emigration
• District with substantial emigration
○ Other place mentioned in text

N

SALZBURG

Hallein
Dürrnberg
Golling
Pass Lueg
Abtenau
Werfen
St. Johann
Schwarzach
Radstadt
Wagrain
Kl. Arl
Gr. Arl

Berchtesgaden
Bischofshofen
St. Veit
Goldegg
Taxenbach
Rauris
Gastein

Zell
Saalfelden

Salzach River

Mittersill

Defereggental

Styria, and he took up residence at Graz, then a lively strong-hold of the Society of Jesus. Three years later the emperor named him bishop of Laibach, in Carinthia-Slovenia; but when Firmian was elected at Salzburg he turned down that post, and it was the defeated Schrattenbach who then went to Laibach.[3] After Firmian's election the imperial ambassador at Salzburg got a douceur of a thousand new Salzburg ducats, his secretary fifty, and so on down the line; and 32,000 scudi went to Rome for the consecration in February 1728. These figures are proba-bly not unusual. The townspeople of Salzburg wanted a public celebration and an illumination of the city, but the new arch-bishop "expressly forbade this vain display." His predecessor had left him an unexpected 45,000 fl. (gulden) in debts.[4]

Firmian's background and career up until the confrontation with the Salzburg farmers thus mirrors the pattern of the en-dogamous Tyrolean nobility who flowed into the ecclesiastical hierarchy of the alpine church between Bolzano and Passau, and who supplied a large proportion of the archbishops of Salzburg.[5] The personality of Archbishop Leopold Anton has been obscured by his historical notoriety as scourge of the Prot-estants, and also by his own insociability especially in his latter years; but close attention to the early years of his reign yields a fair impression of the man. Contemporary Protestant charges of corruption and sexual misbehavior, such as those collected by the Prussian official Dreyhaupt in 1734, are certainly unre-liable and probably quite false; and the commoner charge of religious fanaticism, adopted by Protestant historians such as Arnold and readily accepted by others, are hardly more

[3] For Firmian's early career: Franz Martin, *Salzburger Fürsten in der Barockzeit 1587 bis 1812*, 4th ed. (Salzburg, 1982), pp. 175–76; Hans Widmann, *Geschichte Salzburgs*, vol. 3 (Salzburg, 1914), pp. 384–85; Gärtner, *Chronik*, pp. 4–6; Hans Wagner, "Politische Aspekte der Protestantenaustreibung," in *REP*, pp. 92–93.
[4] Gärtner, *Chronik*, pp. 4–10, 20.
[5] Johann Sallaberger, "Die Trientiner Familien Firmian und Cristani di Rallo," *SMB* 42 (1981), 1–3, 10–12.

Archbishop Leopold Anton, Freiherr von Firmian. From Hansiz,
Germania Sacra, vol. 2, p. 915.

instructive or even accurate.[6] His attachment to the Jesuit culture he had learned at Rome and had cultivated as bishop in
Graz is apparent, and the Jesuit connection proved to be a critical one for his career and his reputation. But for a prelate of
Firmian's background and training, in a German archdiocese,
this association signified breadth of learning and ecclesiastical
sophistication, rather than black obscurantism. Indeed the first
authoritative history of the archdiocese, a wholly admirable
work by the Jesuit ecclesiastical historian Marcus Hansitz, published in Augsburg in 1729 with a dedication to Firmian, displays an engraved portrait of the archbishop (Illus. 1) in simple
clerical garb set among putti of whom the two most prominent
are equipped with serpents, mirrors, seeing eyes, and books,
signifying learning and wisdom, while a third, holding a cross,
peeps out shyly from a shadowy background.[7] He was an active
supporter of the university, where he introduced the study of
German public law, imperial history, and natural law. These
innovations and his Jesuit leanings brought him into conflict
with the Dominican establishment in control at the university—there was no other Dominican university in the Empire,
or in any Habsburg territory—and on one occasion Firmian
forced the rector's resignation (in this instance probably no
counterintellectual deed). On another occasion he broke a student strike (it was a town-gown affair of honor) and forced the
reopening of the university; in 1731 he forbade—with certain
prudent exceptions—the practice of alchemy in Salzburg.[8]

[6] Herbert Breiter, ed. *Johann Christoph Dreyhaupt: Anecdotes de Saltzbourg oder Geheime Nachrichten von dem Erzstift Salzburg* (Salzburg/Braunschweig, 1977); Carl F. Arnold, *Die Ausrottung des Protestantismus in Salzburg unter Erzbischof Firmian und seinen Nachfolgern*, 2 vols. (Halle, 1900–1901).

[7] Hansitz, as note 1 above. The engraving is signed "G. G. Sedelmayr sculp. Vienna."

[8] Mattias Rumpler and Johannes Hochmuth, *Geschichte des Salzburgischen Schulwesens*, 2d ed. (Salzburg, 1832), p. 154; Gärtner, *Chronik*, pp. 17–19, 417–18; Fritz Klein, "Die Einwanderung der Berchtolsgadener Exulanten in Kurhan-

These encounters with chapter, orders, and university suggest Firmian's differences with influential quarters of the archdiocese, beginning early in his reign. His relations outside
Salzburg, however, brought even greater aggravation. Vienna
and Rome seemed to be in league to humiliate him. Directly
after Firmian's election, Pope Benedict XIII, at imperial instigation, exempted the historic diocese of Passau from Salzburg's
jurisdiction and brought it under direct papal authority; the effect was to take Passau away from Salzburg and hand it over to
imperial Vienna's ecclesiastical sphere. Firmian fought against
this mortifying incursion: he argued at Rome, at Vienna, and
even at the Reichstag at Regensburg, where his diplomats tried
to persuade the three ecclesiastic electors of the empire, Firmian's brother archbishops of Trier, Mainz, and Cologne, to
make common cause with him against Rome. But even the
German archbishops turned their backs, and in 1730 the new
Pope Clement XII, at imperial request, issued a new bull expressly forbidding the archbishop of Salzburg to list Passau as
one of his bishoprics.[9]

For these reasons and probably also because of his own tem-
perament, Archbishop Leopold Anton by the year 1730 appeared a beleaguered figure. In public appearances and personal contacts his air was haughty, embarrassed perhaps, or
irascible; he pursued an interest in astronomy, which, it was
insinuated, provided him an excuse for avoiding evening ceremonies and celebrations. His only pleasure appropriate to his
station was the hunt, which he followed passionately but with

nover 1733," HG 34 (1980), 161; Wagner, "Politische Aspekte," p. 100. Ironically, the emigration of 1731–32 is said to have damaged the educational system of Salzburg because many argued, and many parents believed, that
overeducation had led to the kind of religious error and heresy that had caused
the emigration. Rumpler and Hochmuth, Geschichte, p. 155.

    [9] Gärtner, Chronik, pp. 12–16; Widmann, Geschichte Salzburgs, 3:386; Anton
Faber [=Christian Leonhard Leucht], ed., Europäische Staats-Cantzley, vol. 57
(Nürnberg, 1731), pp. 665–81.

the smallest possible retinue, and many grumbled about his penury and solitude. Of administrative engagement or political relish, the record gives no sign; probably he found the regular business of governing the archbishopric to be tiresome and distasteful. "This prince has a severe and proud air," Baron Pöllnitz confided to his diary and to Europe; "he avoids greeting people and talks with them even less . . . he is almost always alone, and dines alone. In summer, he goes to the country and is very hard to reach. He lives there without a suite and without company."[10] One wonders about the summer of 1731. By that time, Firmian's distant and unfriendly relations with his ecclesiastical court and administration had led to the conditions and crises that produced the emigration of 1731–32, and so blackened Firmian's reputation and ruined his career. But there is little trace of his personal presence in the surviving records of that fatal episode.

The weakness of Firmian's support within the archdiocese (in contrast with the popularity of his indulgent predecessor), and outside it too, obliged him to demonstrate his authority in a convincing manner, if he was to rule at all. Yet it made it very difficult for him to do this through routine channels. Within months after his installation as archbishop, Firmian ordered an investigation into the moral and religious condition of Salzburg. This was not an unusual opening to a reign, but instead of the normal general visitation by archdiocesan officials, he appointed for the purpose a special mission of Jesuit priests, to be led by the Bavarian Pater Andreas Prösl, who was widely known outside Salzburg for his skill and zeal in the work of vitalizing the faith and of conversion. Opposition by the Salzburg religious establishment to this intrusion was all but universal. The cathedral chapter itself was flatly against it. Spokesmen for the Benedictines, the Franciscans, the Capuchins, and the Augustinians in Salzburg protested that there was no need for outsiders to look into their affairs (though the

[10] Pöllnitz, Mémoires, 2:87; Martin, Salzburger Fürsten, pp. 175–76.

Dominican abbot of St. Peter's seemed to think it not a bad idea). Firmian was obliged in the end to instruct the mission to go easy on the capital.[11]

All the more reason, then, to show firmness in the mountain districts, although opposition among officials there, with the exception of a few lickspittles, was even stronger than it was at the capital. Provincial pastors and deacons urged Salzburg to give up the idea. Collecting the mountainfolk into crowds to hear hellfire sermons was no way, they argued, to investigate or to advance the condition of the faith; this could only complicate the work of the regular confessors and stir up trouble. In their experience it was best to deal with the families one by one, a procedure which of course was more than the Jesuit flying mission of four priests could accomplish. In competition with the Jesuit mission, provincial church officers themselves began house-to-house interrogations, beginning with persons whose loyalty to the faith had been impeached, commonly by information from Catholic innkeepers or smiths or other townsmen who had everyday contact with the mountain peasantry.

Suspects under interrogation responded as they always had: with protestations of their loyalty and determination to live and die in the Catholic faith. A few examples may stand for many. Leonhard Rospacher of Gut Högenpichl [Hölzenpichl] in the district of St. Johann (who later emigrated) asked why they'd picked him for questioning. Because he'd slandered an official of the church, he was told. Well, then, he must have been drunk at the time (a favorite excuse). He was a true Catholic, and he could not read. Hans Reinpacher of Gut Tauerlechen, same district, was confronted with a copy of Haber-

[11] The best general histories of the mission—both of them Catholic but both disapproving—are Ortner, *Reformation*, pp. 207–14; and Johannes Baptist Caspari [= Giovanni Battista Caspari di Nuovomonte], *Aktenmässige Geschichte der berühmten salzburgischen Emigration*, trans. Franz X. Huber (Salzburg, 1790), pp. 1–23; see also Arnold, *Ausrottung*, 1:37–49.

mann's Prayerbook, the immensely popular "Habermändl,"
which had been found on his premises.

What was it doing there?
Why, it had always been there, and Reinpacher didn't know
there was anything wrong with it.
If you didn't know anything was wrong with it, then, *why did
you hide it under the stable floor?*
Well, I didn't *hide* it there, I just *left* it there.
Why didn't you tell the inquisitors about it?
Well, I'm too simple.

In the catechism that followed, Reinpacher vowed his soli-
darity with signal points of Catholic dogma: the seven sacraments, the reality of hellfire, the ability of the believer at will to
obey God's commandments. (Reinpacher too emigrated with
his family in 1732.)[12]
It was apparent, then and now, that the mountain folk knew
how to talk like Catholics (or like simpletons) in examinations,
but they did not act like Catholics: they did not regularly attend church or take communion, for example. Sulkiness, indifference, and erroneous notions persisted, examiners found,
behind the calculated verbal screen of conformity. To demonstrate and to cement loyalty to the church, the mission decided, suspects would have to offer specific proofs of it in their
everyday as well as their ceremonial behavior. In particular,
oaths of religious conformity had to be followed by declara-
tions of willingness to join a religious confraternity, by the
daily wearing of the scapulary (a religious garment fitting over

[12] KAS 11/66h: Reformation. St. Johann i. Pg. Verhöre 1727–1730, December
1 and 11, 1730. Reinpacher emigrated with his wife, who died on the journey, and with a son and two small daughters, and settled in Stehlischken in
East Prussia. Rospacher emigrated with his wife and five children, two of
whom died that year, as did Rospacher himself in Königsberg in 1733. Herbert
Nolde, "Alphabetisches Register der Personennamen in den Salzburgischen
Emigrationslisten" (typescript, Göttingen, 1972), pp. 141, 149; Hermann Gollub, *Stammbuch der ostpreussischen Salzburger* (Gumbinnen, 1934), pp. 138, 146.

the head, which covered the upper chest and back), and by public recitation of the rosary—recitation en masse, in congregations and in processions.[13] All these measures became the subjects of sermons and interrogations; and the mountain people muttered and grumbled.

Muttering was nothing new, but now pressure for conformity, instead of being piecemeal and desultory, was applied across a broad front. It was exerted first by a task force of counter-reforming specialists who meant business, who then were joined by competing local authorities: old brooms, mobilized to show that they knew the corners and could do the job better than the outsiders. One new element that seems to have caused peculiar irritation was the introduction of the *englischer Gruss*, the "angelic salutation," wherein every believer was to use the greeting *gelobt sei Jesus Christus*, "Jesus Christ be praised," to which the proper response was *in Ewigkeit*, "in eternity," *Amen*. Pope Benedict XIII had ordained this practice in 1728 and it carried a hundred days' indulgence, thereby tripping signals that had marked the Lutheran revolt two hundred years before. Mountain men found it especially discomforting, tinged with sacrilege, to take Christ's name in vain when they entered the tavern to drink and to gamble, their commonest social occasion.[14] The angelic salutation was a constant provocation because any doubter, at every human encounter, risked blasphemy with use of the greeting but risked betrayal to religious prosecutors for not using it. But most of all, perhaps, it

---

[13] Ortner, *Reformation*, and Caspari, *Aktenmässige Geschichte*; see also the reports in KAS 11/69c: Reformation. Reform der Kleidertracht, Abstellung des Lasters der Unkeuschheit aus den Gebirgen, Pars I, 1729–1731.

[14] On the introduction of the englischer Gruss and its effects, Theophilander [=Christoph Gottfried Franckenstein], *Historische Nachrichten von dem neuen Grusse: Gelobt sey Jesus Christus! Warum die Evangelischen Salzburger, als sie noch im Lande waren, solchen nicht haben annehmen wollen, sondern sich ein Gewissen darüber gemachet. Ingleichen von dem Rosen-Crantze, oder sogenannten Pater Noster in der Romisch[sic]-Catholischen Kirche* (n.p., 1733). Catholic historians (Caspari, Clarus, and Ortner) generally agree with Franckenstein's contemporary account.

was one thing to make such avowals to priests, another to make them before one's peers. Confessional perjury before priests and police had long been an accepted practice in alpine Salzburg and did not degrade the person using it; false witness in face of an equal meant shame and personal dishonor. The angelic salutation went beyond a submission to official conformity, to conformity of conscience. Presumably it was meant to do so.[15]

If left to itself, the missionary campaign might possibly have succeeded, despite these obstructions and shortcomings. More likely, if it had been contained wholly within the archbishopric, it would have ground down to the usual standoff. This seemed the likely outcome early in 1731, when the Jesuit mission retired, with some parting shots at the permanent Salzburg clergy. Such a standoff would have meant resumption of the traditional tacit agreement between the establishment at Salzburg and the mountain peasantry to have as little to do with each other and spend as little candor on each other as possible.

Considering his precarious political position, though, a return to the status quo would have signaled a humiliating defeat for Archbishop Firmian on all fronts, not least among his enemies entrenched in church and chapter. Having gone this far, he could not accept a standoff. His sovereign authority thus became captive to the confessional issue. In March 1731, Firmian reorganized his government. He appointed Hieronymus Christani von Rall—or Gerolamo Cristani di Rallo, a local judge from the smaller nobility of the Trentino, near the Firmian family seat—as *Hofkanzler*, to take over the whole business.[16] Once

---

[15] Peter Putzer, "Das Wesen des Rechtsbruches von 1731/32," *MGSL* 122 (1982), 309, similarly remarks, though without reference to the englischer Gruss, that the conversion campaign peaked when the authorities demanded not only outer but also inner conformity.

[16] For earlier connections between Firmian and Rall, see Sallaberger, "Trientiner Familien"; for the meager information on the background and genealogy of the Cristani family, Ernst H. Kneschke, ed., *Neues allgemeines Deutsches Adels-Lexikon*, vol. 2 (Leipzig, 1929), p. 360.

again Firmian had gone outside his archbishopric to represent his purposes within it. But not only Firmian had this option. For meanwhile, the mountain dissidents also had acquired confessional advocates and allies outside the archbishopric, stronger or at least more committed allies than Archbishop Firmian had. Like Firmian's, these allies were unwilling to let matters follow their own course. The corpus evangelicorum from Regensburg now entered the Salzburg confessional scene; and their entry, together with Firmian's appointment of the newcomer Rall—or Rallo—as Hofkanzler, built a broader confrontation that led directly to the emigration of 1731–32.

The corpus had been eyeing the situation in Salzburg since the missionary program began. In January 1730, certain Salzburg subjects who had declared themselves to be Protestants and fled or been expelled from the archbishopric—the circumstances are not clear, but apparently they had shouted "I am Lutheran!" at a public exercise attended by religious officials— approached representatives of the corpus evangelicorum at the Reichstag in Regensburg to ask for help in filing legal claim for the free emigration of their families and free disposition of properties left behind in Salzburg. The constitutional standing of this claim is equivocal and is not crucial here, but the petitioners Hans Lerchner and Veit Bremer surely had at least a presentable case: a change of confession established a right to emigrate, ultimately with property and family, including minor children. The authority of the corpus to enter the matter is more dubious; but as regular representative of the Protestant states of the Empire, it had come to consider itself and also to act, often without instruction from the constituent governments, as defender and advocate of the rights of German Protestants everywhere. It was currently engaged with confessional disputes in a number of the states and towns of the Empire, and it was not loath to incorporate the plight of Salzburg Protestants into its position. On February 17, following some internal discussion and debate, the corpus addressed a memorandum to the generally respected Salzburg ambassador in

Regensburg, Sebastian Zillner von Zillerberg, in the interest of the two Salzburg petitioners. Zillerberg rejected the corpus note on the grounds that it constituted illegal interference in the internal affairs of the Salzburg archbishopric; and besides, the two peasants in question had not got into trouble simply by becoming Protestants, which might indeed have invoked the constitutional protection claimed, but rather by being publicly provocative and noisy about it. Such civic misbehavior was not protected and particularly in the case of the archbishopric amounted to rebellious behavior.[17]

The corpus soon fired back, adding other dramatic instances of mistreatment of Protestant subjects by Salzburg officials. Ursula Pilzin, the declared Lutheran wife of (I believe) the still-Catholic Michel Burgschweiger of Taxenbach, had been put across the border and denied re-admission and custody of her children. Georg Frommer, now a Regensburg citizen but born in the Pongau (probably Werfen), had revisited Salzburg on business and had been arrested there for selling Lutheran books; he was imprisoned for fifteen weeks and charged 74 gulden for his keep, which he later sought to recover from the Salzburg official who had collected it (but who by then apparently had spent it to buy a title).[18]

As the controversy grew, both sides made selected documents public, and these were extensively reprinted—as literally thousands of pages—in the political press, most notably in Anton Faber's *Staats-Cantzley*, then regularly published in Nürnberg, and in Johann Jakob Moser's *Reichs-Fama*, issued at

---

[17] Texts of these exchanges appear in most documentary accounts, and in Johann J. Moser, *Teutsches Staats-Recht*, vol. 10 (Frankfurt/M., 1732), pp. 391–404.

[18] For the Pilzin and Frommer case see Gärtner, *Chronik*, pp. 20–51; [Christoph Sancke], *Ausführliche Historie derer Emigranten oder vertriebenen Lutheraner aus dem Ertz-Bisthum Saltzburg*, 2d ed. (Leipzig, 1732), pp. 31–43; Faber, *Staats-Cantzley*, vol. 59 (1732), pp. 138–52. Michel Burgschwaiger emigrated, with three daughters, in 1732, and died in Schluissen in East Prussia in the following year: Nolde, "Register," p. 35; Gollub, *Stammbuch*, p. 39.

Frankfurt am Main.[19] The argument relied on the claim by the corpus, for its part, to represent the constitutional rights of Protestants anywhere in the Empire, over and against Salzburg's claim to constitutional authority to govern its own ecclesiastical affairs and to prosecute rebellion. The Salzburg affair was only one of a number of confessional issues which dominated these political journals in 1730–31, and which also included such matters as the procedures of Protestant princes with respect to Catholic properties and installations within their territories, or confessional differences between princes and estates, as well as rights of other Protestants in other Catholic principalities and towns. But after the middle of 1731 the Salzburg controversy became the dominant issue, the most dramatic by far. For in June of that year appeared perhaps the most important, and surely the most curious, document of this story: the "Petition of the 19,000."

The petition was addressed to the corpus evangelicorum and is dated June 16, 1731. It was submitted on behalf and "at the urgent request of the 19,000 persons, not counting children, presently residing in the seven districts, namely Radstatt, Wagrain, Werfen, Bischofshofen, St. Johann, St. Veit, and Gastein, and suffering from an almost unbearable burden," inasmuch as those among them who reject the confessional monopoly of the Roman Catholic faith must "without fail and immediately, change and quit their *locus Domicilii* with wife and child and turn their backs on what is theirs; and among other things, to wit: . . ," and then a list of grievances which began with the obligation to take the sacrament in one kind only, to wear

---

[19] For these events, see the documentation published in the named journals in 1731–32, and in Johann J. Moser, *Akten-Mässiger Bericht von der jetztmaligen schweren Verfolgung derer Evangelischen in dem Erz-Bisthum Salzburg* (Leipzig, 1732), and *Das Neueste von denen Salzburgischen Emigrationsactis. 11 Stücke* (Frankfurt/M., 1732–33). Subsequent accounts are based on Ortner, *Reformation*, pp. 217–20, and the earlier secondary accounts cited therein. There is additional material in SLA EA 97/120: Von der hf. Gesandschaft in Regensburg eingelaufene relationen . . . etc.

scapulary and rosary, to invoke the saints. Also, petitioners were fined 2 gulden if they missed mass just once. "Ja und was noch das meiste," not only that: both native Salzburger and strangers were forbidden to eat meat on fast days, owing to the worldly dogmas, the *Menschen-Satzungen*, of the Roman church, and violators were heavily fined. When they went to church they were preached at mainly about indulgences, confraternities, hellfire, and the sacrifice of the mass, to the distress of their spirits. These measures and conditions made clear for all to see, the petition continued, how "it is completely impossible to continue living thus *in Ecclesia pressa*"; and the petitioners begged their excellencies of the corpus evangelicorum to intervene with the archbishop of Salzburg, to persuade him to allow his subjects freely to choose their faith and to let a Protestant pastor be placed in each of the named districts. "Or failing these, let him without further use of force allow us freely to depart with our families from the territory of Salzburg, and let him buy up our property in land, as much as we have paid for it, in cash money, thus wholly to liberate us from further such pressures and anxieties, etc."[20]

The origin and history of this document are cloudy, and seem likely to remain so. Most critical historians use cautious and noncommittal language when they consider its background, but none (so far as I have discovered) has directly challenged the validity of the petition, nor has scholarly caution extinguished more vivid constructions, drawn by more ardent spirits, of peasant leaders trudging about the Pongau, collecting the 19,000 signatures.[21] At this range we can afford to be

---

[20] Texts are in (among many other places) Johann J. Moser, *Reichs-Fama*, vol. 9 (Frankfurt/M., 1732), pp. 424–30; Faber, *Staats-Cantzley*, 59:160–65; Gärtner, *Chronik*, pp. 52–55; Gerhard G. Göcking, *Vollkommene Emigrations-Geschichte von denen aus dem Ertz-Bisthum Saltzburg vertribenen und in dem Königreich Preussen grössesten Theils aufgenommenen Lutheranern*, vol. 1 (Frankfurt/M., 1734), pp. 774–76.

[21] Among the former, Josef Mayr, *Die Emigration der Salzburger Protestanten von 1731/32: Das Spiel der politischen Kräfte* (Salzburg, 1931), p. 10; Ortner, *Refor-*

more forthright. Clearly there never were 19,000 signers of this document, or anything approaching that number, if indeed the document that surfaced in Regensburg and was circulated from there bore any signatures of any Salzburg Protestant peasants. No historian claims to have seen the original, physical text of such a petition—though to be sure none remarks that he has not. Neither do I find any contemporary description of an original; it exists only in copies. No such collection of petitioners' names or signatures has come to view, and efforts to trace back the sources cited for the existence of one dissolve into nothing.

But the text itself does not actually claim to include such a list of signatories: the presenters of the petition call themselves, rather, *Abgeordneten*, "representatives" of the 19,000 oppressed adult inhabitants of the seven alpine districts. The version ultimately released by the corpus evangelicorum, and commonly published thereafter, lists six names as presenters of the petition, and the text describes them as "subject persons now again resident in the Archbishopric of Salzburg, upright adherents of the Augsburg Confession." But not one of their six surnames, let alone full names, appears among all the twenty-some thousand names on the emigration lists from the seven districts, nor, indeed, anywhere else in the emigration materials, so far as I can determine. The names attached to the petition therefore quite certainly are not the names of Salzburg peasants; they might be names of real persons, past or present Regensburg residents, perhaps, who were not otherwise con-

---

mation, pp. 220–21; among the latter the most scholarly is Gerhard Florey, as in "Die Schwarzacher Versammlungen der Salzburger Protestanten im Jahre 1731," *MGSL* 114 (1974), 246. The near contemporary, near official Prussian account of the petition reads, "Man schickte . . . etliche von den verständigen Bauern. . . . Man hatte ihnen Vollmachten gegeben, welche von vielen unterschriben waren, damit die Sache in aller Namen konnte getrieben werden, und in denselben hatte man zugleich die ohngefehrige Anzahl der Evangelischen ausgedrückt." Göcking, *Emigrations-Geschichte*, 1:153. Carl F. Arnold, whose scouring of relevant archives around 1900 remains unmatched, makes no mention of any list of peasant petitioners and hints at the work of unnamed Regensburg lawyers (*Ausrottung*, 1:51).

nected with the mountain districts or the emigration. More probably they were inventions, added to lend the document credibility by naming names—retroactively—while incriminating nobody.[22] In neither case do they show us who was responsible for the petition and who submitted it; nor do the names suggest whether the document ought to be regarded as a petition—or as a threat.

Ambassador Zillerberg at Regensburg thought he knew, and chances are he was close to the truth. Since early in 1731, draftsmen of the corpus evangelicorum had been preparing petitions on behalf of Salzburg subjects regarding emigration and property rights—the *beneficium emigrandi*—or to contest fines levied on family members for the possession of Lutheran books; and these had passed through Zillerberg's embassy on the way to Salzburg.[23] On June 24, a week after the date on the petition, Zillerberg obtained a copy. He promptly denounced it as another in a series of corpus calumnies directed against Salzburg, this one aggravated beyond measure by its accusation of mass persecution on the part of the archbishopric, and by its invocation of mass disquiet among its population. Where had it come from? The copy Zillerberg obtained was unsigned, except for two small stylized letter p's, thus: $\rho\ \rho$ at the end of the text where signatures normally would appear. This symbol was everyday German chancellery script of the time, normally signalizing the Latin term *perge*, "and so forth," inserted like "etc." where formal salutations or other redundant language had been omitted from a copy or a draft. Zillerberg thought he saw through that, though. "The slanderous authors [*calumniantische delatores*] do not even sign their names; but neverthless they give away their identities with that dual *etc. etc.*" Three days later he reported that he knew exactly who the perpetrators were, and he was sending separately and in proper form

---

[22] The names listed are Jörg Losleben, Hanns Kautz, Joseph Drexler, Matthias Auhammer, Ludwig Trofzer, Veit Biberger.

[23] SLA EA 97/120, February–March 1731, passim.

the real names of ρ and ρ, so that if either one of them should
show up in one of the seven districts he could promptly be arrested. Meanwhile Zillerberg was preparing a defense against
the storm that the petition was raising at Regensburg and in
Protestant Germany. The most politic defense would be to de-
nounce any agitation of this nature in the mountain districts, or
its instigation by others, as unlawful sedition. And meanwhile,
asked Zillerberg, would those priests in the mountain mission
please preach more about the faith, and less about fasting and
hellfire and so on? For the Protestants snatched at every chance
they had with a thing like this, and soon they'd be pestering
the emperor himself about it.[24]

Zillerberg's enclosure naming the culprits is missing from the
file preserved in the Salzburg state archive, but the ambassador
probably thought ρ and ρ were Peter Wallner, a weaver's as-
sistant (*Weberknapp*) from St. Johann, and Peter Reinbacher,
cottager and weaver (*Webermeister* and *Häusler*) from Werfen,
both of them about fifty years old.[25] To complete this part of the
story: Peter Wallner, called Troi-Peterl, was a known scourge
of the Catholics in the districts, and he was arrested and inter-
rogated at St. Johann on June 30. It is not apparent whether the
interrogators, a town official and a joiner-innkeeper, knew
about the petition or not; but they knew Troi-Peterl, and knew
he had been in Regensburg, and they wanted to hear about
that. Wallner testified that he had been sent there by "the
whole peasant community [*Bauern-Gemeind*] of St. Johann" and
had traveled with a man representing Werfen. They had car-

[24] SLA EA 97/120, fols. 44–55 (June 25–28, 1731). But Zillerberg may have
changed his mind about the authorship later on: see note 29 below.

[25] This is the conclusion also of Gertraud Schwarz-Oberhummer, "Die Auswanderung der Gasteiner Protestanten unter Erzbischof Leop. Anton von Firmian," *MGSL* 94 (1954), 15. Wallner and Rainbacher appear in Gollub, *Stammbuch*, pp. 138 and 185, as immigrants to Prussia from the Mittervormarkt, a
suburb of St. Johann, and the Fuxlueghäusl at Aschberg, Gericht Werfen, respectively. Note that neither was a peasant or landholder. They are listed with
the notations "im Arrest" and "arretiert" in the emigration list compiled from
Salzburg sources by Nolde, "Register," pp. 141 and 186.

ried with them a letter telling how the peasants were being persecuted for their religious beliefs and fleeced of their money by Salzburg officials. When the interrogators asked who had written that letter, Wallner turned reticent: he had got it from a peasant in Werfen, somebody he didn't know. But the interrogators had better leave him alone, Wallner said, or there would be trouble. For he had been to the Saxon and Hanoverian embassies in Regensburg; they had "slapped him on the back, congratulated him, called him 'a good old Christian witness,' and encouraged him, saying that if [Salzburg Protestants] were allowed to practice their own faith, and were not arrested or penalized for it, they should be content with that; but if not, then all they had to do was let them know about it in Regensburg, and they would stand up for them." Had Wallner gone to the *Salzburg* ambassador? he was asked. No; the Protestants said they would take care of that. Did Wallner know what perilous ground he was on? "I am only a poor man, and ready to offer my life at any time; I owe only one death." More Wallner would not say, but so much as he did say for the record rang true.

As for the other ρ, the parish priest at Goldegg and St. Veit reported on July 11 that Peter Reinbacher passed through on his way back from visiting Regensburg with Troi-Peterl; Reinbacher told his listeners that Regensburg had promised to send 80,000 soldiers to support them, if needed, against the archbishop, so nobody had to pretend Roman allegiance any longer.[26] Two days after this report, on July 13, the first assembly of the Salzburg dissident peasants would meet at Schwarzach.

The Salzburg government subsequently released both these reports, the Wallner interrogation and the priest's account of

---

[26] Moser, *Reichs-Fama*, vol. 10 (1732), pp. 245–48, 266–67. The manuscript protocol of the Wallner interrogation, which agrees with Moser's published version, is in SLA EA 75/99: Kommission im Gebirge, Jul. 1731, 7–8v (copied by courtesy of archive director Dr. Friederike Zaisberger).

Reinbacher's message, to show Protestant interference from Regensburg in the confessional affairs of the archbishopric. Zillerberg publicly and repeatedly denied the accusations made in the petition, calling them slandrous and treasonous lies. But neither the government in Salzburg nor Zillerberg ever claimed publicly that the petition itself was fraudulent, even though Zillerberg, at least, clearly believed that in the main it was. Nobody was ever challenged, so far as the record shows, to produce the thousands of signatures whose purported existence validated the petition and lent it credibility, nor did anybody ask how so massive a subscription campaign could have been mounted without any Salzburg official or priest having caught wind of it. There is one quite plausible reason for this reticence. The language in the petition, like that which the corpus had used for individual cases, asked for immediate permission to emigrate, a posture most helpful to the archbishopric if it should come (as it eventually did) to the expulsion of dissidents, and particularly to the three years' grace period allowed by the Peace of Westphalia to religious émigrés. For if the peasant petitioners asked to be *allowed* to go, how could the archbishop be accused of driving them out? Also, they had no legal right to demand the installation of Protestant pastors, which the petition posed as the alternative to emigration; consequently it could be argued that subscription to the petition was a rebellious and self-incriminatory act. Thus it was not unequivocally in the Catholic interest to argue that this text was fraudulent. In fact, Catholic historians often have invoked the flawed legal language of the petition in extenuation of the expulsion; Protestant writers have deplored the language as an awful mistake on the part of the 19,000, who by signing the petition both incriminated themselves and asked permission to depart.[27]

---

[27] Thus Peter Putzer, "Der konfessionelle Hintergrund der Salzburger Protestantenemigration 1731/32," *ÖAK* 33 (1982), 13–34; Ortner, *Reformation*, pp. 220–22; and Gerhard Florey, *Geschichte der Salzburger Protestanten und ihrer Emigra-*

Meanwhile the Protestant side, both corpus and historians, have for reasons of sympathy preferred to take the petition at face value—or rather, to take it at the greater value that has been placed upon it by the uneasy allowance of 19,000 unnamed peasant subscribers instead of the six named but ghostly representatives. Neither the legal jargon ("in Ecclesia pressa") nor the emotional appeals ("zur innersten Gemüths-Kränckung") that appear in the text tell us much about the authors. It is not an elegant document, but neither is it a primitive one: writing it would have been well within the powers of an embassy clerk in Regensburg or any trained Protestant pastor, or of Wallner and Reinbacher themselves, with a few technical tips. A final reason why the authenticity of the petition has not been directly challenged, though many historians are patently uneasy about it, is that number: 19,000. Nineteen thousand is almost exactly the number of Protestants—but counting children—that Rall himself found later in the summer, and it is not far from the number that ultimately emigrated. Nineteen thousand is also almost exactly the *total* population, *not* counting children, of the named districts,[28] just as in the language of the petition: "the 19,000 persons, not counting children, presently residing in the seven districts . . . and suffering from an almost unbearable burden."

Whatever anybody thought or thinks about its authenticity, the publication of the petition by the corpus evangelicorum set off an explosion of public controversy which brought the situation of the Salzburg peasants to national attention. Zillerberg in Regensburg launched a counterattack in the press, denying the slanders of the petition and impugning the motives of its sup-

---

tion 1731/32 (Vienna, 1977), pp. 87–88. In addition to the failure to mention the triennium, the use of the term "in Ecclesia pressa" is cited to show that the petition cannot have been drafted by skilled lawyers, since there was no established Protestant church and therefore the term was technically incorrect. See Wagner, "Politische Aspekte," p. 95.

[28] Compare the figures in Arnold, *Ausrottung*, 1:73.

posed authors.[29] The government in Salzburg issued a statement pointing out that the petition's claim to free public religious exercise of a confession that was not recognized in the archbishopric was both unconstitutional in imperial law and contrary to territorial law. So this claim constituted a rebellious and seditious demand—as did any invitation to foreign intervention, notably from Saxony and Brandenburg-Prussia as leading members of the corpus evangelicorum, in the religious affairs of the archbishopric of Salzburg. Such an invitation would violate the constitutionally fundamental religious peace of the Empire.[30] Firmian meanwhile commanded a new commission of lay officials to go out into the mountains, summon the inhabitants, hear their grievances especially against local priests and officials, and find out what really was going on out there; heading the commission was Chancellor Rall himself.[31] But before the commission could arrive, the repercussions from Regensburg had reached into the mountains; and peasant resistance, which the missionary campaigns had set off, now turned to initiatives launched, apparently, from among the mountain peasantry themselves. A series of assemblies was held over a period of three weeks at Schwarzach, a settlement on the Salzach in the Goldegg district, a more open place than most, where the mountains recede from the stream, centrally located among the seven districts affected. Three meetings at

[29] SLA EA 97/120, passim; but I cannot assign exact dates to Sebastian Zillerberg, *Die bisshero unter dem Deck-Mantel einer Religions-Bedrückung verborgene, Nunmehro aber . . . Entdeckte Bosheit einig. Saltzburgischen Emigranten* (Stadt am Hoff, 1731), or to Zillerberg, *Manifest, worinn die Seditions-Facta und andere in grosser Menge verübten Insolentien der aufstandenen Saltzburgischen-Unterthanen im Gebürg . . . vorgeleget . . . wird . . .* (Stadt am Hoff, 1731). In the *Deck-Mantel*, p. 2, Zillerberg seems to be saying that the "nichtswertige Charteque" of the 19,000 was fabricated by the otherwise unidentified Salzburger Philipp Stöckel and Johann Schartner. Unlike the six names attached to the corpus version, these could be Salzburg peasant surnames, but I cannot identify the individuals.

[30] SLA EA 97/120, July 12, 1731.

[31] The order constituting the commission is dated July 9, 1731. Ortner, *Reformation*, pp. 223–24; SLA EA 74–75/98–99: Kommission im Gebirge, Juli 1731.

least were held there: one just before the arrival of Rall and his commission in the mountain districts, another while the commission was holding its hearings, and then one soon after the commission left.[32]

The return of Wallner and Reinbacher from Regensburg seems to have prompted the first Schwarzach meeting. Reinbacher, as noted, had appeared in Goldegg/St. Veit early in July to report on the results of their mission; and Peter Wallner turned up in Gastein, where he urged his listeners to attend a meeting to be held at Schwarzach on Friday, July 13.[33] Rall's commission from Salzburg was due to arrive at Werfen on the following Sunday and to begin its hearings on Monday. About a hundred and fifty peasants came from the districts to the Friday Schwarzach meeting. Peter Wallner again reported on his visit to Regensburg, and the farmholder Rupp Frommer from Werfen read out a "note", a *Zettel* from Regensburg. The exact contents of Wallner's report and of this Zettel from Regensburg are not known; but all accounts agreed that the message received by the meeting was that Salzburg Protestants could count on support from the Imperial Protestant Council at Regensburg, and maybe from the emperor, but only if they made open confession to the Lutheran faith. After these announcements there followed prayers, hymns, and scripture readings, and a resolution to declare and to abide by their faith, and to remain in their homes, relying on the counsel from Regensburg. At this meeting the celebrated *Salzlecken* apparently took place, where several of the peasants dipped their fingers into a box of salt and then licked them, in witness of their common commitment to this defiant course.[34] Around that time, begin-

---

[32] Florey, in "Die Schwarzacher Versammlungen," has made the most thorough study of these meetings; I am relying mainly on his careful and sober accounts, largely reconstructed from the subsequent interrogations of participants, as well as on the secondhand official reports more commonly cited.

[33] Schwarz-Oberhummer, "Gasteiner Protestanten," pp. 15–16.

[34] Efforts to show a ritual or scriptural meaning for this gesture are voluminous but have reached no conclusive results. Certainly it was no ancient folk

ning just before the Schwarzach meeting but mainly during the following week, meetings in several of the districts passed by acclamation public confessions of their Evangelical faith, explicitly relying on imperial protection, and sent these resolutions to local officials. On the Sunday following that meeting, the priest at Gastein, southernmost of the districts, told a meeting of countrymen that if they persisted, he would withhold the sacraments: communion, marriage, baptism, burial in holy ground. At this the farmers were furious: they retired to the tavern and sang Lutheran hymns loudly out the open windows.[35] On that day, Rall's commission arrived at Werfen in the northernmost of the districts.

The commission swept through the affected region at an extraordinary pace, holding hearings and questioning officials in nine districts in the course of two weeks' travel, accumulating in that time some six hundred pages folio of material for its report.[36] It heard a great many substantial complaints from provincial townsmen about commercial regulations and fees, too many peddlers, and the like. Such complaints have encouraged some historians to claim that the trouble in the districts was

---

custom; there are many solemn allusions to salt in scripture, and this was Salzburg after all. But although some such gesture seems to have been made, what it was intended to signify was certainly obscure to most of the participants and it remains so. This detail became so famous, however, that almost every account tries to interpret it (beginning with the Pfleger's at Werfen on August 1, 1731); King William of Prussia, on the way to Gastein in 1865 for the meeting with Austria that put him on the road to being German emperor, is said to have made a special excursion to Schwarzach to view relics of this ceremony. For recent efforts to decipher the Salzlecken and a critique of earlier ones, begin with Florey, "Die Schwarzacher Versammlungen," pp. 252–54, 261–66; and Ortner, *Reformation*, p. 226.

[35] The most eloquent and perhaps best known of these *Bekenntnisse* is probably the one resolved at the Gastein meeting on July 15; there is a facsimile copy in Ortner, *Reformation*, pp. 228–29: "Unt wan die Herschafft wolt hart unt gestreng verfahren mit uns, so haben wir uns schon auff den hohen rath angefragt ob uns mocht geholffen werten, Welches uns gott sey lob und dankh schon ist versprochen worten." See also Schwarz-Oberhummer, "Gasteiner Protestanten," pp. 17–18.

[36] SLA EA 74–75/98–99: Kommission im Gebirge, Juli 1731. Vols. 1 and 2.

mainly fiscal and economic, not, at bottom, religious. But these townsmen were reliably Catholic subjects, and once that had been ascertained, the commission was no longer interested in them. They wanted to find out who the lawlessly Protestant troublemakers were, and how many they were. Some of the peasants who had recently declared themselves Protestant at the assemblies, now told the commission that they were really Catholic, having succumbed at the meetings to threats and pressure from the militant Protestant majority. Nevertheless, most abided by their declared "Evangelical" or Lutheran confessions, or else were identified as Protestant by local officials. Moreover, Rall himself was wholly unwilling to follow the traditional practice of tacit mutual deception, a practice that since the Petition of the 19,000 in Regensburg and the mobilization of the peasants, seemed all but untenable anyhow. In two weeks' work, the commission collected lists that identified—by name—over twenty thousand Protestants in the mountain districts of the Pongau.[37]

Such results must have come as a shock to Archbishop Firmian, whose direct involvement had been minimal; his hand and his instructions almost never appear in the administrative materials. Probably the numbers were a surprise also to Chancellor Rall as he compiled them, if in fact he did. Surely nothing in the prior history of confessional relations of prelates with

[37] Lists in SLA EA 74–75/98–99, though I do not there find the summary "Finalbericht" that the title of the bundles seems to promise, nor any summary count of the names of Protestants listed for the several districts. The figure 20,678 has been conventional ever since 1731, however, and probably is not far off the mark; more striking is the absence of any contemporary analysis of these masses of raw data. Ortner, *Reformation*, pp. 230–34, minimizes the force of the Protestant commitment on the part of the peasantry in favor of economic concerns, through his emphasis on townsmen's, Catholic, and apologetic testimony before the commission; similarly, the figures in Schwarz-Oberhummer, "Gasteiner Protestanten," pp. 19–20, showing unexpected Catholic loyalty before the commission, should be qualified by the disproportionate number of nonpeasants in that mining and recreational center, a fact that is also reflected in Gastein's low ratio of emigrants to population, lowest of all the Pongau districts.

peasants could have prepared the government for a confrontation on this scale. Moreover, it was taking place in the full glare
of publicity generated at Regensburg and spreading through
the courts and capitals of the Empire and even Europe. Thus it
amounted to an unacceptable provocation. From now on, in
the view of the prince-archbishopric, the heretic peasants were
in a condition of open rebellion—the position that Zillerberg in
Regensburg had recommended and that the government at
Salzburg had adopted in mid-June, at the time of the petition.

But it really did look like a rebellion now. On July 30, the
Monday after the commission's return to the capital, Rall issued a ban on popular assembly, pending official determination of the matter, and a warning against *Hin- und Herschwär-
men*, "swarming around." A contingent of soldiers went to the
Lueg Pass, the precipitous narrows of the Salzach which sepa-
rates the broader valleys around the city from the mountains to
the south, with orders to allow no more than two peasants to
pass through at a time, in either direction. Additionally, a defense was set up around the armory at Radstatt.[38] A merchant
from St. Johann town reported on August 1 that the mountain
farmholder Wolf Bramberger had told him that the peasantry
had nothing to fear from the archbishop, who had no soldiers,
nor would the emperor ever send him any; so if the prince
made a move they had only to send off a letter and Brandenburg-Prussia would send in the 80,000 men, and the Swiss
would join in too.[39] On August 3, the Salzburg War Council

[38] Gärtner, *Chronik,* pp. 59–60; Ortner, *Reformation,* pp. 236–37; Florey,
"Schwarzacher Versammlungen," p. 261.
[39] Moser, *Reichs-Fama,* 10:251. This report was released by the Salzburg government along with others meant to show outside interference, so it is not
unimpeachable. But the Protestant Moser accepts it without comment, and it is
quite consistent with the kind of talk—notably the 80,000 figure—that was
current among the Salzburg Protestant peasantry around this time. That,
oddly, is the number conventionally used by historians to quantify Frederick
William's army at peak strength in 1740 (for example, see Eugen von
Frauenholz, *Entwicklungsgeschichte des deutschen Heerwesens,* vol. 4 [Munich,
1940], p. 35).

ordered the districts to submit lists of all young males capable
of bearing arms, including "peasant sons, farmhands, and
other young bucks [Burschen]." It is not apparent whether this
census was meant to identify potentially dangerous elements,
or to prepare for conscription, bringing such elements under
military discipline while preparing to suppress a rebellion. Returns from the districts, from safely Catholic areas and from
towns as well as from the affected districts, implied either or
both, and probably the authorities had all these options in
mind.[40] On the following Sunday, August 5, peasants from all
the Pongau districts met again at Schwarzach, probably between 150 and 400 of them, in defiance of Rall's prohibition.

A conference of leaders and activists some days before this
(referred to as the second Schwarzach meeting, held July 25)
had proclaimed a boycott of church services and priestly sacraments. Some priests were refusing to administer them anyway,
and the purported note or Zettel from Regensburg had said
that support from the Reich could be provided if, but only if,
the peasants were publicly committed to the Lutheran faith.
The boycott seems to have been generally observed. But depri-
vation of clerical services caused much uneasiness, despite
some lay preaching and baptizing and some garden burials.
And instead of help from Regensburg, so far the peasants had
got only Rall's inquisition from Salzburg. The sense of the August 5 meeting seems to have been that the religious provisions
of imperial law, taken together with the peasants' own large
number—the large number established, ironically, by the Rall
commission—would oblige the archbishop, if he could be sub-
jected to appropriate political pressure, to appoint Protestant
pastors in the districts. They decided that a delegation of
twenty-four should go to Regensburg to invoke the help of

[40] SLA EA 81/105: Spezifikationen der Schutzen, Wehrhaften Bauern, deren
Söhnen und Knechten und anderen Burschen, 1731. The order is dated August
3, and the response was immediate: returns are dated August 4–6. Reporting
officers emphasized the mustering of single males who could be brought
promptly to the towns.

Protestant forces there, and possibly to the emperor's seat at Vienna as well. Two days later such a delegation set out north-ward, reportedly bearing lists that identified some 18,000 Prot-estants by name: lists probably generated, if indeed they ex-isted, by the hearings of the Rall commission. As the delegates crossed the border into Bavaria they were arrested and the lists were seized. Three members of the delegation, who had valid passes, were allowed to continue (Peter Höllensteiner of the Werfen district, Nikolaus Forstreiter from St. Johann, and An-dreas Gapp from Radstatt). The others were transferred from Bavarian to imperial jurisdiction at Linz, and then returned, together with their lists, to Salzburg; there they remained un-der arrest until May 1732.[41]

These midsummer efforts to enlist the relief expected from the Protestants in the north clearly had backfired. With the Schwarzach meetings and the hapless mission to Regensburg, the mountain peasantry succeeded only in putting themselves into a posture of disobedient and seditious assembly, and pos-sibly of treason. The archbishopric had claimed all along that the issue was not religious oppression but rebellion; and inso-far as that proved to be the case, they had no legal claim, or realistic hope, for serious intervention in their favor from out-side. The corpus evangelicorum continued to issue ardent manifestos and memoranda. But no German prince with force at his disposal had any liking for rebels; and Salzburg during the late summer of 1731 made every effort to show that its Pon-gau peasantry was indeed in a state of rebellion, having "under

[41] Florey, "Schwarzacher Versammlungen," pp. 261–68. But again, I find no sign of the "signatures" or "petitions" that Florey mentions. The bundle SLA EA 79/103: Eingeschickte Beschreibungen der evang. erklärten Unterthanen, die bei den vom Kaiser extradierten Salzburger Bauern verzeichnet gefunden (1–10 Oktober 1731) contains instead lists in official form of names and proper-ties, arranged by district. Archival confusion may be at work here, and Ortner too (*Reformation*, pp. 234–37) is skeptical about these lists and their provenance. So is Arnold, who traces the story of the lists to an Austrian official at Linz (*Ausrottung*, 1:71).

the pretense and disguise of religious oppression," as Firmian informed the emperor, "made riotous assembly, taken weapons in hand, threatened with fire, robbery, and murder."[42] The archepiscopal government's fear of violence getting out of hand was not merely a pretense or a misapprehension. The reports coming into the capital that summer and fall from the districts show, however skeptical the reading, grounds for genuine alarm. An official hand, probably Rall's, underlined and bracketed the most lurid passages in the reports for publication. Efforts like these to influence opinion outside the archbishopric, however, further fed fears of lost control within it, raising the specter of a collapse of civic order with all the costs, humiliation, and political calamity that might entail.

This escalation in turn lent a shrill and panicky note, even a tone of fanaticism, to the archbishopric's efforts to manage opinion. But at the same time, the reports arriving at the capital at Salzburg from the mountains were, and remain, singularly uninstructive, an administrative jumble of sensational but undigested anecdotes leading only to Rall; there is no sign in the record that anybody ever tried to evaluate or to summarize it. It served to stir up and to alarm the government, without producing any considered suggestion of how to proceed. Indeed, Rall's government in August and September showed no sign of any policy toward the dissidents other than a general intention to prevent or suppress rebellion. Meanwhile restlessness in the Pongau continued, but without any apparent goal or program on the part of the inhabitants there either, since the failure of the mission of the twenty-four. Tension rose sharply, however, when on the night of Wednesday, September 26, Salzburg police arrested thirty-three persons identified as Protestant ringleaders and sent them to the Hohensalzburg fortress to join members of the August delegation already imprisoned there, and to await trial. News of this aroused vocal indignation and protests among the Protestant peasants. Around this

[42] Message dated August 26, 1731, in Moser, *Reichs-Fama*, 10:34–36.

time a contingent of Austrian troops, which during the weeks preceding had been taking up positions at the border, crossed into Salzburg territory at the archbishop's request.[43] But the first sign that the government had turned its mind to something more than punishing individual rebel activists came on the following Monday, October 1. On that day Rall ordered the districts to supply reports on the circumstances—social estate, tax liability, family circumstances—of all those who had been identified as Protestants. The irregular replies were impossible to summarize and probably were not carefully examined. The order signifies, though, that the archbishop and his government were now contemplating, tentatively at least, removal of the mountain Protestants from Salzburg territory.[44]

During the month of October, Salzburg jurists worked on an order to command and to justify the expulsion of Protestant dissidents. When finished it was dated October 31 (All Hallows' Eve, and thus the anniversary of Luther's Ninety-five

[43] Mayr, *Emigration*, pp. 23–27. Since the end of July, a high-level Salzburg delegation led by Hannibal Graf von Thun, dean of the cathedral chapter, had been at Vienna to combat influences from the corpus evangelicorum, endeavoring to convince a skeptical Prince Eugene and other personages there of the danger of an alpine peasant rebellion and the need for imperial political and military support: SLA EA 84/108: Korrespondenz mit dem Kaiser . . . Ankunft des kaiserlichen oö. Geh. Rates von Gentilotti . . . Beschwerde des Corpus Evangelicorum . . . 25 Juli [1731!]–2 Oktober 1732, pp. 5–9, 18, 40, 65–68, 106–7, 135–136.

[44] Ortner, *Reformation*, p. 238; SLA EA 79/103. As best I can tell, no summary analysis of this material has ever been made, and perhaps no realistic one is possible. Meanwhile, Ortner's hopeful proposition (p. 255) that it shows the Protestants to be poorer and of lesser estate relative to Catholics, and that their emigration was thus economically motivated and socially selective, will not stand casual inspection. Actually these irregular materials allow for no realistic confessional comparison except perhaps in the case of Saalfelden, a highly unrepresentative district in the Pinzgau which minimizes both the degree of Protestant infection and the capital wealth at risk; also, many persons still designated as Catholic (and well-to-do) on these lists of summer 1731 turn up as emigrants in spring 1732. Informal inspection of all districts shows that some of the wealthiest peasants are acknowledged or suspected Lutherans, and so are some of the poorest.

Theses). The edict was not released then, probably to avoid offending Vienna, for the emperor had notice of it only on October 26, and an official copy only on November 9. Preparations were not complete in Salzburg, either: on November 2, soldiers in the critical districts were sent to search houses and barns and seize all weapons in Protestant possession; they had collected about two thousand by November 10.[45] On November 11 the emigration edict was announced, declaring Archbishop Firmian's intention to "extirpate and uproot these unruly, seditious, and rebellious folk wholly and henceforth"—*diese unruhigen seditiosen und widersässigen Leut nunmehro gäntzlich und von der Wurtzel ausvertilgen.* The undomiciled part of the population, the *Nichtangesessenen,* were to leave "with bag and baggage"—*mit tragender Pack und Sack*—within one week. Householders had up to three months to leave, depending on where they were ranked on the tax lists: the lowest were to go first.[46]

It is not certain how the archbishop or his government expected the mountain Protestants to respond to this. The purpose of the edict was clearly not, however, to induce declared Protestants to recant and affect Catholicism again, so as to avoid emigration; at least, that was not Rall's own expressed intention, and the edict contained provisions explicitly designed to prevent such behavior.[47] More probably, the govern-

[45] SLA EA 80/104: Emigrationspatent; Entwaffnung, Verzeichnisse. 2 Nov.–31 Dez. 1731, pp. 2–5 and passim. About half the seized weapons were firearms; the rest were swords, knives, pikes, and maces. The Protestant peasantry had been ordered to surrender firearms two weeks earlier (Ortner, *Reformation,* p. 238), but authorities were not satisfied with the compliance achieved.

[46] The undomiciled are here designated as "Innwohner, Beysassen, Taglöhner, Arbeiter, eingelegte Personen, Knechte oder Dienstboten, beider Geschlechte, welche das 12. Jahr erreicht." All published documentary collections print the emigration patent. KAS 11/69e: Reformation. Emigrationspatent 1731. Verkauf der Emigrantengüter im Beisein des preuss. Gesandten. Verzeichnis der Güter 1734–38, etc., contains a handwritten copy bearing the signatures of Archbishop Leopold Firmian and of Court Chancellor Cristani di Rallo. For a summary, see Ortner, *Reformation,* pp. 240–43.

[47] Hans v. Zwiedineck-Südenhorst, *Deutsche Geschichte im Zeitraum der Gründung des preussischen Königtums,* vol. 2 (Stuttgart, 1894), p. 644, remarks that

ment hoped and perhaps even believed that the Protestants would take the opportunity to depart in peace; the administrative provisions of the edict suggest this; and after all, that was what the petition of June had asked for. As for what the mountain Protestants themselves thought: like others of their time and condition they were used to stern commands and manifestos that never got effectively carried out, not least in the history of their own intermittent encounters with the authorities at the court, and they seem to have paid no special attention to this one when it appeared. A week passed; then another. On November 24, the soldiers stationed in the districts began rounding up the undomiciled for escort across the border and out of the territory.

In Chapter 4, on the peasants' experience of the migration, there is more to be said about who the *Nichtangesessenen* were— although not a great deal more, because of the lesser trace they have left on the written record.[48] To their elders and employers they were, however, valuable farmhands and servants: a week after the edict, the so-called Unanimous Peasants' Committee of the St. Johann district petitioned the archbishop, with apologies for their own past "extreme rudeness [*gehöbte Grobheit*]," asking permission for the undomiciled to stay until spring at least, so as to get on with the work and make financial arrange-

---

Firmian made the edict so tough in the hope that the Protestants would recant once again; this is tempting but, for once, Zwiedineck-Südenhorst seems to be wrong. The emperor may have hoped this would happen, but Salzburg repulsed an imperial suggestion to this effect, saying it had no intention of returning to the old system: Gärtner, *Chronik*, pp. 238–48. To that extent, the Salzburg expulsion suits the "confessionalization" theme developed especially by Heinz Schilling in *Konfessionspolitik und Staatsbildung . . . Lippe* (Gütersloh, 1981), and elsewhere; but to put the Salzburg case as a confrontation between the early modern state and a putative village communal society (R. Po-Chia Hsia, *Social Discipline in the Reformation: Central Europe, 1550–1750* [London, 1989], extrapolating from Ortner (*Reformation*), seems off the mark.

[48] Their names are collected and reported, by Gericht, in SLA EA 92/116: Marschrouten der Emigranten durch das Reich in das kgl. Preussische . . . von den Pfleggerichten eingeschickte Spezifikazionen der emigrirten Personen, in lists that still await analysis.

ments.[49] But since the undomiciled were in large part unmarried young men, to the archbishop's government and the military contingents the undomiciled represented the security factor they had had in mind with the August survey of "peasants' sons, farmhands, and other *Burschen*," and the best thing to do was get them out as smoothly and as quickly as possible. In fact the expellees made very little fuss, considering the haste with which they were collected and deported, and lamentations by family members never went far beyond that.[50] About four thousand of them left, in seven columns, without any known destination until the very last contingent, which was picked up by Prussian officials in late winter.[51] There they enter into the context of the kingdom, in the next chapter.

As the first columns of the undomiciled began their march down the Salzach and through the passes to the north, Firmian agreed to soften application of the edict so as to allow the household families to stay until St. Georgi: April 23, 1732. Their undomiciled children still in Salzburg could remain too, as long as they came home and stayed there. And farmholders could retain title to their landed property until September 1734, provided they themselves and their families left bodily by April 1732 and provided they left their properties in the hands of dependable Catholics.[52] This was a partial concession to demands from outside the archbishopric that the Protestants be allowed the Triennium, the three years' grace for orderly disposal of property, promised by the Peace of Westphalia to reli-

[49] Dated November 17, 1731: Moser, *Reichs-Fama*, 10:34–35. This list may have been inspired by archepiscopal officials, though I have no evidence that it was.

[50] Curiously it is Gärtner, *Chronik*, p. 223, who makes the most of peasant resistance to the expulsion of the Nichtangesessenen. The treatment in Ortner, *Reformation*, pp. 244–46 seems generally right.

[51] Wolfgang Menger, "Die Salzburger Emigration nach Ostpreussen in den Jahren 1731 und 1732. Eine medizinisch-geschichtliche Studie zum Umsiedlungsproblem," *MGSL* 98 (1958), 91–93.

[52] Order of November 29, 1731; text in Moser, *Reichs-Fama*, 10:91–94.

gious émigrés, but only a partial concession, for it did not allow the exiles physically to remain during that term or actually to control their farms. To be sure, the claim of the archbishopric all along had been that the peasants were not legitimate religious converts, but rebels, to which the provision of the Triennium did not apply. On the other hand, the rebel argument was awkward for Salzburg, because while religious dissent made provision for expulsion, rebellion did not. Neither imperial law nor politics sanctioned the deportation of one prince's rebellious subjects to another prince's territory.

Thus the archbishop's government was caught in an odd constitutional position, and a politically most unhelpful one as well. It could not invoke religious grounds for the expulsion without invoking the Triennium, which by its provision for delay risked the spread of dissent and rebellion throughout the principality—and particularly among the salt miners who earlier had shown disaffection but had been passive in 1731 thus far. But it could not invoke grounds of rebellion and still avail itself of the constitutional rights to enforce religious uniformity and to expel dissidents from its territory onto somebody else's. So, in effect, failing either basis, it used both: civil rebellion as grounds for prompt action, religious dissent as grounds for expulsion.[53] As for the intentions of the peasants' Protestant advisers, or whoever may have been the source of the Zettel from Regensburg: it is hard to imagine that their advice to the peasants to profess allegiance to Lutheran doctrine could end anywhere but with massive emigration, inasmuch as the archbishop could not realistically be expected or constrained, or even requested as a matter of law, to install Protestant pastors in his archbishopric. That the peasants were entitled to free

[53] The best modern discussion of this situation is by Putzer, "Das Wesen des Rechtsbruches," pp. 295–320. Putzer defends the legal position of the government except for its denial of the Triennium, which he deems unconstitutional but politically founded on the danger of massively expanding emigration and rebellion.

private devotions inside their homes could at least be constitutionally argued, but they clearly did not have a legal right to
public religious exercise and Protestant pastors.

The legal considerations are not empty ones, for quite apart
from their rhetorical uses, they are not far away from confessional and political realities in the Germany of the time. But
they did not guide the actions of Archbishop Firmian or his
fellow Tyrolean, Chancellor Rall. Rall as chief executive officer
of the archbishopric had gone forcefully ahead with the policy
of clearing the mountains of heresy. Firmian himself seems to
have had no clear idea or, at the beginning, even much real
interest in what he might be getting into, with the missionary
expedition into the Pongau. The treasonous *Religions-Eyfer* that
this mission encountered, the religious passions that it had unleashed, seemed to him spiteful and strange.

The whole episode had turned out to be a "wasp's nest," as
Firmian called it retrospectively in his penitential sermon of
1734, signifying the sort of calamity one stumbles into and gets
badly stung for it. This sermon, his one surviving public reflection on the matter, summarizes the archbishop's experience of
the affair. It was an exercise characteristic of the genre and of
this prince of the church. Firmian opened fashionably with
classical allusions, beginning with the story of Plato's student
Trochilo, who dared to go out upon the sea and got caught in a
terrible storm. Shipwrecked, Trochilo barely saved his life; and
when he got home he had all his windows walled up so that he
couldn't see the ocean and be tempted again. Firmian, after
toying with that whimsical choice and predicament for a bit,
went on to the homiletic lesson of the gambler's temptation: "A
player, when he is apart from all society, thinks not on the
game," but when he sees the others shuffling the cards and
throwing the dice, he has to play too.

By scriptural association Florian's penitential sermon turned
to Christ alone on the mountaintop and the temptations of
power; and then the tone shifts to the history of the church: to
the heresy of the Albigensians, and the story of the holy Domi-

nic, standing alone against their heresies, *singulare adversus haereses*. Finally Firmian came to those wolves of his time who had disguised themselves as sheep: his own treacherous subjects who had taken the holy sacraments falsely and without scruple, perjuring, until through the rosary he had found the one faithful support, *singulare adversus haereses*. "Thanks be to *thee*, dear city of Salzburg: that thou hast stood by us . . . thanks to thee have we been so happily freed of this nest of hornets." Finally Firmian turned to Gospel: "By their fruits shall ye know them, *ex fructibus eorum cognoscetis eos*. . . . But as we are now united in faith, *dimittes Domine Servum tuum in pace*."[54] O Lord, now lettest Thou Thy servant depart in peace. This was the archbishop's story. By the end of 1731, initiative in the matter of his Protestant subjects had fallen to other hands.

[54] [Firmian], *Buss- und Fasten-Predigt von dem Reichs Fürsten Leopoldo Antonio Eleutherio, Ertz-Bischoffen zu Saltzburg* (Salzburg, 1734), pp. 1–15.

CHAPTER TWO

THE KINGDOM

Peter Heldensteiner from Werfen and Nikolaus Forstreiter from St. Johann, members of the delegation of twenty-four which had set out in August 1731 to find allies against the archbishop's government in the Protestant north, held legal travel passes, and with these they escaped the arrest and extradition that dispersed the rest of the group. After failing to find help or hearing in such capitals as Regensburg and Kassel, in mid-November they arrived finally in Berlin, northern- and easternmost of German capitals. There they were heard, and with close attention: Two Prussian consistorial councillors examined the Salzburger on articles of faith and doctrine and pronounced them "true Evangelical fellow-Christians": doctrinally correct on the point of salvation by faith and not by works, on infant baptism, on Holy Writ as the literal true word of God, and on communion in both kinds. These were no subaltern ecclesiastics, either: Johann Gustav Reinbeck was an eminent Prussian churchman of rationalist tendency and a trusted adviser to King Frederick William on religious affairs, and Michael Roloff was a favorite preacher at the court, sometime chaplain to the regiment the king had commanded as crown prince. Ques-

tioned on the just authority of secular rulers, further, the Salzburger testified that "this is appointed by God, and we must
obey it, be it queer or kind [*sie sey wunderlich oder gelind*]."[1] A
transcript of the hearing and the theological ruling by the
churchmen was included in a cabinet report on the Salzburg
situation submitted to Frederick William early the following
year, and the king noted in its margin, "Let him [Firmian] turn
out all the Protestants, as many as he wants, out of his country, in the space of a year, and send them to my country; I will
be most obliged."[2]

The certification of Heldensteiner and Forstreiter in Berlin
and the king's comment were Prussian royal counterparts to
the clap on the shoulder and to the Zettel that the two Peters
Wallner and Reinbacher had got in Regensburg the preceding
spring, where Protestant officials of the Empire had recommended public Evangelical confession to the Salzburg peasants
as the condition for free migration. But the November hearing
at Berlin was also a reminder of an earlier intervention of the
corpus evangelicorum, led by Brandenburg-Prussia, on behalf
of the Deferegger Protestant exiles in 1685. For a royal context
to the theological examinations at the Hohenzollern capital in
1731–32, we may return first to the last days of this king's
grandfather whose name he bore: Frederick William, already
called the Great Elector.

The great event and lasting achievement of that elector's late
years, half a century before, had been his invitation of French
Huguenots to Prussian territory when they were expelled by

---

[1] Johann J. Moser, *Reichs-Fama*, vol. 10 (1732), pp. 95–98. The transcript and
report were publicly distributed and widely reprinted.

[2] Johann G. Droysen, *Geschichte der preussischen Politik*, vol. 4, part 3 (Leipzig,
1869), p. 159, n. 2. "Sollen alle die Protestanten, so viele er sie aus Lande
[haben will], in Zeit von einem Jahr [entlassen] und dann nach meinem Lande
schicken, ich werde ihnen höchstens obligiert sein." Bracketed insertions and
spelling changes are Droysen's. Historians of technical bent tend to call Frederick William I "King *in* Prussia," but contemporaries ordinarily used "of" and
so shall I.

the government of Louis XIV in 1685. Fifteen or twenty thousand French Huguenots had come, settling mainly in and around Berlin, to the great advantage of the relatively backward economic and cultural conditions of Brandenburg. The old elector won lasting fame thereby for his Protestant piety and his economic shrewdness, and especially for his perception, anticipating the tuitions of Max Weber, of how well these two went together.

The invitation of the Huguenots has also won for the Great Elector a place in a later history of religious toleration, inasmuch as the Reformed or Calvinist Huguenots were promised free religious exercise in formally Lutheran Brandenburg-Prussia (the elector himself was Reformed). After the Thirty Years' War and especially after the migration of the Huguenots, prudent accommodation to religious differences became an important element of the population policies of a number of German princes. A demographic history of Germany in the seventeenth and eighteenth centuries, if one is ever written, will have to pay close attention to the issues of religious discipline or indifference. Religious difference was accepted grounds, politically, legally, and culturally, for emigration from one territory to another, for resettlement and sometimes for expulsion. Religious exiles were especially welcome for purposes of colonization and economic development because, unlike more casual wanderers who followed subsidies and other economic advantages, they ordinarily could not go back home when they were disabused of their hopes or had spent their benefits.

Fiscally inspired confessional indifference, however, bore an aspect of unchecked sectarianism, giddy enthusiasms, and reckless rebellion. These were condemned by all right-thinking authorities. For that reason the Great Elector's invitation of 1685, in the Edict of Potsdam, had been explicitly directed to "co-religionists of the Evangelical-Reformed faith."[3] So also

---

[3] Bernhard Erdmannsdörffer, *Deutsche Geschichte vom Westfälischen Frieden bis zum Regierungsantritt Friedrichs des Grossen 1648–1740*, vol. 1 (Berlin, 1892), pp. 708–10.

Salzburg authorities at that time and in their own interest had named the Deferegger "trouble-making sectarians and innovators." Only those dissidents who could be shown to be theologically sound in one of the orderly and recognized German confessions, the Salzburg government had ruled, could be allowed to take out of the territory their minor children and the proceeds from orderly sale of their property.

That view had been accepted by the Protestant princes and the corpus evangelicorum, and the position in 1731 was unchanged.[4] This was a main reason for the carefully staged interrogation of Heldensteiner and Forstreiter by Prussian officials in Berlin in November 1731, and for the wide publicity accorded the happy results. Ecclesiastical endorsement authorized the reception of immigrants from another territory without taint of subversion and validated the property and family rights for Protestant emigrants from Catholic territories, as provided by imperial law to genuine adherents of the Augsburg Confession. Confessional loyalty and fiscal advantage could also work together, as the precedent of 1685 had shown.

But the invitation and settlement of the Huguenots had been more than a clever stroke of cameralist political economy, and more than an act of piety too, though certainly it was both of these. It was also a calculated and highly dramatized effort to represent the Brandenburg-Prussian house as a leader, protector, and champion of German Protestantism, if not of European Protestantism, at a critical juncture of confessional politics. This was no accidental or implausible role for a prince whose uncles included such Protestant champions as the elector Frederick, Winter King of Bohemia; and, by marriage, Gustavus Adolphus of Sweden and even Bethlen Gabor of Transylvania; and who was himself uncle to William, prince of

---

[4] See the materials printed in Gerhard G. Göcking, *Vollkommene Emigrations-Geschichte von denen aus dem Ertz-Bisthum Saltzburg vertribenen und in dem Königreich Preussen grössesten Theils aufgenommenen Lutheranern*, vol. 1 (Frankfurt/M., 1734), pp. 96–118.

Orange. In the year of the Huguenot expulsion Charles II of England had died, as had the elector Palatine. Both were succeeded by Catholics, which in the latter case produced a Catholic majority of five to two in the electoral college of the empire. It was a time for Protestant champions.

The prince of Orange, poised to become king of England in an action to thwart the presumed designs of the king of France, had already urged the elector Frederick William of Brandenburg-Prussia to undertake—as Leopold von Ranke put it in his account of the affair—"some kind of spiritual mission which would put him at the point [*Spitze*] of Protestantism: an invitation, which suited the profound ambition that this Prince [Frederick William] nourished in his soul." A counselor to the elector had advised him that the break with Louis XIV of France which this Protestant policy entailed would be costly in the short run but well worth the price in the long: "You lose subsidies, but you win *Reputation*." Moreover, this was a Protestant gesture that would not alienate the emperor, who at that time had his own traditional as well as immediate reasons for hostility toward France, as Ranke also noted.[5] A judicious Austrian historian contemporary to Ranke, Hans von Zwiedineck-Südenhorst, put it, similarly but more acidly, that King Frederick William I in 1731 saw the same chance his grandfather had seen in 1685: to make of himself the greatest Protestant leader since the fabulous Gustavus Adolphus.[6]

To be leader of German Protestantism was surely an ambition to which the notably pious, not to say superstitious, King Frederick William I was especially accessible. Competition between Prussia and Hanover for this role in confessional politics had narrowed and intensified since the conversion of the

[5] Leopold v. Ranke, *Zwölf Bücher Preussischer Geschichte*, 2d. ed., vols. 1–2 bound as one (Leipzig, 1878), pp. 353–77; the quotations are from pp. 356 and 358. See the similar view of Otto Hintze, *Die Hohenzollern und ihr Werk*, 5th ed. (Berlin, 1915), pp. 253–54.

[6] Hans v. Zwiedineck-Südenhorst, "Geschichte der religiösen Bewegung in Inner-Österreich im 18. Jahrhundert," *AÖG* 53 (1875), 467.

Saxon August the Strong to Catholicism in 1697.[7] And as in his grandfather's exemplary case, it was a role that also suited Frederick William's fiscal and demographic needs. Indeed it fit wonderfully well, especially if achieved in a way that also offered blessed relief from one of the king's worst headaches, the depressed and depressing condition of East Prussia.

Since the beginning of his reign, Frederick William had been struggling with the problem of East Prussia and particularly of Prussian Lithuania, here meaning the far border region of East Prussia, east of Königsberg and including the general districts of Memel, Tilsit, Ragnit, and Insterburg. This area had been wasted by wars and Tartar invasions in the seventeenth century, and the royal domains at the end of the Great Elector's reign had only a third of the peasant workforce they had had in 1610. Heavy taxation around the turn of the century, without growth in productivity, had not helped matters. Worst of all, the population was devastated by plague in 1708–10, which probably killed about a third of the population of East Prussia as a whole, but as many as three-quarters of the population of Prussian Lithuania, where it was most severe: possibly one hundred-fifty thousand people may have died there. Over eight thousand peasant holdings were left unoccupied, untilled, and turning to waste—insofar, that is, as they were not taken over by local nobility and/or their own surviving dependent peasantry, which effectively removed them from the royal economy and fisc. Most of these farms were still listed as empty when Frederick William became king in 1713.[8] The den-

[7] Erdmannsdörffer, *Deutsche Geschichte*, vol. 2 (Berlin, 1893), pp. 378–79.

[8] Wilhelm Sahm, *Geschichte der Pest in Ostpreussen* (Leipzig, 1905), pp. 76–96; August Skalweit, *Die ostpreussische Domänenverwaltung unter Friedrich Wilhelm I. und das Retablissement Litauens* (Leipzig, 1906), pp. 246–47; Rudolph Stadelmann, *Friedrich Wilhelm I. in seiner Tätigkeit für die Landeskultur Preussens* (Leipzig, 1878), pp. 32–35. But official sources upon which these accounts rely are based on dismal reports by local fiscal officers likely to exaggerate their own difficulties whenever possible: James L. Roth, "The East Prussian Domänenpächter in the Eighteenth Century: A Study in Collective Mentality" (Ph.D. diss., University of California at Berkeley, 1979), pp. 37–38.

sity of the population of East Prussia then was about 600 to the square (German) mile; in the 1870s, by comparison, though the area was still overwhelmingly rural, the density was 2,700 to the square mile.[9]

This condition engaged the king's attention from the beginning of his reign, attention that grew to anxiety and sometimes amounted to obsession. From the start, it also brought him into conflict with the German nobility that was thinly scattered about the region. The East Prussian nobles not only appropriated as many of the empty lands as they could for their own exploitation, they also absorbed the scanty peasant labor force into the serf economy, a process that, as Frederick William complained already in 1714, "badly hinders the *Peuplierung* of the country." Meanwhile the royal domain lands—about a third of the territory of East Prussia and the most by far of the Prussian-Lithuanian part—brought in hardly any income at all.

The king worked hard, and on many fronts, to reverse this tendency and turn these conditions to the crown's advantage. In 1721 he abolished the "indigenous" court system through which the local nobility had controlled justice and administration in East Prussia, and replaced it with fiscal officers sent and directed from Berlin. In 1723 the new General Directory effectively ended local self-government in the region, and the city of Königsberg was placed directly in the jurisdiction of the war ministry. A war and domains board [Kriegs- und Domänen-kammer] was set up in Gumbinnen, in the Lithuanian district, to see to the settlement of the empty lands there—as royal domains.[10]

For the administration and exploitation of these domains, the crown established a lease-holding system, in which the domain

[9] Gustav Schmoller, "Die Verwaltung Ostpreussens unter Friedrich Wilhelm I.," *HZ* 30 (1873), 47. The German mile of the time equaled about five present U.S. miles, by which measure the equivalent densities would be about 24 and 108.

[10] Schmoller, "Verwaltung Ostpreussens," pp. 44–45, 58–62; Stadelmann, *Friedrich Wilhelm I.*, pp. 32–33.

leaseholders, or *Pächter*, were simultaneously crown officers, *Amtmänner*. In this system each domain Pächter directly operated the one or two central farms, or *Vorwerke*, in his district, each with its own mill, tavern, brickyard, brewery and such services, and a dozen or so resident families. He was also responsible for collecting the rents and services due from the domain peasantry settled on the surrounding crown lands. For this office, for this enterprise, and for these incomes the Pächter paid to the crown treasury a lump sum that was fixed periodically, after detailed inspection and analysis, by a royal assessment board. His profit could come only from raising his production above, or lowering his costs below, the levels posted as annual cash values of rents and services by the assessors. Prussian nobles were generically ineligible to become Pächter, and most leaseholders were professional estate managers with backgrounds in royal service.[11]

The "Retablissement" of the East Prussian domains began in earnest in 1721, with a plan for economic recovery organized by Count Heinrich Truchsess von Waldburg, himself of an East Prussian noble family but an energetic and trusted senior official in royal service.[12] The plan included a restoration of domains, organization of markets, construction of new Vorwerke to carry out administrative and technological improvements, the clearing of river transport, and many other projects. This ambitious and enormously expensive program for a relatively poor kingdom cost over five million thaler before it was done, as much as a quite respectable regional war might have cost.[13]

---

[11] Roth, "Domänenpächter," is a good study of a complex and treacherous subject; see pp. 54–106 for a general description of the system. For background, Hans-Helmut Wächter, *Ostpreussische Domänenvorwerke im 16. und 17. Jahrhundert* (Würzburg, 1958); and Gerhard Czybulka, *Die Lage der ländlichen Klassen Ostdeutschlands im 18. Jahrhundert* (Braunschweig, 1949).

[12] The best general accounts are Fritz Terveen, *Gesamtstaat und Retablissement: Der Wiederaufbau des nördlichen Ostpreussen unter Friedrich Wilhelm I.* (Berlin, 1954); and Skalweit, *Domänenverwaltung*.

[13] About four million of this was spent in 1722–28, on the first settlement

Its success depended on improving the productivity of the land by increasing the agricultural workforce on the domains, thus enabling the leaseholder to produce a return on this heavy investment, meanwhile holding off further encroachments by surrounding nobility. A *Peuplierungpolitik* was always at the heart of the enterprise.

French-speaking Swiss Calvinists had been invited to the area as early as 1711, but not many came, and those who did were not experienced farmers, were malcontent and restless; and their settlement was deemed generally unsuccessful.[14] In 1719 the king formally abolished serfdom throughout East Prussia in favor of heritable peasant freeholds, to make immigration safer and more attractive, and not incidentally to spite the nobility.[15] Then a special royal patent was addressed to German settlers in 1724, offering them favorable conditions on East Prussian domains, where the crown expected them to be more productive than the ethnic Lithuanians already settled in the area. During 1723–25 some four thousand peasants from northwest Germany, Hessen, and the Palatinate were settled in the Lithuanian districts of East Prussia, and perhaps as many more were recruited from various other territories of the Prussian crown. By 1726 about seventeen thousand non-Lithuanians, almost all German, had been brought into the Lithuanian districts. Then immigration stopped; and this total, as it happened, was roughly the number of Germans on the land, settled among a Lithuanian majority, when the Salzburger began to arrive in 1732.[16]

---

wave, and just under one million in 1731–34, the time of the Salzburger immigration: Skalweit, *Domänenverwaltung*, p. 350.

[14] On the Swiss, Gerd Wunder, "Die Schweizer Kolonisten in Ostpreussen 1710–1730 als Beispiel für Koloniebauern," in *Bauernschaft und Bauernstand 1500–1970*, ed. Günther Franz (Limburg/Lahn, 1975), pp. 183–95; Horst Kenkel, *Französische Schweizer und Réfugiés als Siedler im nördlichen Ostpreussen (Litauen) 1710–1750* (Hamburg, 1970).

[15] Stadelmann, *Friedrich Wilhelm I.*, p. 76.

[16] Estimates of the numbers responding to the several immigration cam-

Efforts to attract emigrants had lapsed in 1726–27 because of strong symptoms of discouragement and collapse in the program. Poor management and financial chicanery were one cause of this, and Frederick William sent out an investigating commission with orders to purge the administration, to "hunt the fox out of his hole, say who is guilty." But despite repeated efforts, he seemed unable to establish control in East Prussia. The west German settlers turned out to be less productive than the native Lithuanians; they complained constantly about their treatment; and they failed to pay their assessments. New immigrants ceased to arrive in East Prussia, and as the program soured, the livelier officials in the government at Berlin and Potsdam shifted their interests toward industrial development, especially textiles, in less remote and primitive parts of the realm. There seemed little credit or satisfaction to be won in Prussian Lithuania.[17]

Bad weather too came to East Prussia in 1726; there was famine that winter, and even the plague threatened to return. Many settlers died, and cattle were slaughtered by the thousands; seed-grain stocks were eaten up, extending famine into the future. That spring, the king agonized over his wasted efforts and the failing condition of the country. In May 1727 he wrote to his closest friend, Prince Leopold of Anhalt-Dessau, that "the situation in [East] Prussia is miserable. The deathrate is unbelievable. If God does not give us a good year the plague is sure to come this winter: God forbid. . . . In the end I can only trust in God. . . . The good God has helped me so amazingly out of so many bad situations, he will help me again, I trust in that. . . . If he does not, then I deserve no better. . . . I am moralizing; well, I have good reason to." Two months later

paigns before 1727, and especially the response to the 1724 patent, vary widely, and I am unable to resolve the differences; but the total seems about correct. See Stadelmann, *Friedrich Wilhelm I.*, pp. 32–39; Skalweit, *Domänenverwaltung*, pp. 256–62; and Wunder, "Schweizer," p. 191.

[17] Stadelmann, *Friedrich Wilhelm I.*, pp. 45–46; Skalweit, *Domänenverwaltung*, pp. 269–70; Roth, "Domänenpächter," pp. 45–50.

his moralizing had taken another and more resentful turn, as he wrote to Anhalt-Dessau again: "What is happening in Prussia is not our fault! We can give directions but the Lord God has to give his blessing, and if he refuses to give it, that is not our fault!"[18] Indeed in the king's own context of the Salzburg episode, the Deity plays a substantially larger or at least a more immediate role than it did in the archbishop's. For the theologically more sophisticated Firmian, even in the penitential sermon of 1734, the theodicean position was more remote and more complex than it seemed to Frederick William.

"*Anfein* I'll make another *Disposicion* of my *afferen*," wrote the king then to Anhalt-Dessau. The failure in Prussia made him ashamed to show his face, he wrote; "I prostituted myself there before the world." He had learned his lesson, he told his ministers; "I am now an *Indifferentissimus* when it comes to [East] Prussia," he told them. "I'll give away all my domains and strike 400,000 Thaler out of the budget; it's all gas and wind"; and from 1727 until the summer of 1731, Frederick William refused to put any more money into the Retablissement program.[19] But still this failure, with its unrealized investment of more than four million thaler already, rankled and troubled him profoundly, whosever "fault" it was. For Frederick William identified himself almost indistinguishably with Prussia, his weal with Prussia's and his justification with Prussia's justification; and he presumed that God did, too; so more was at

---

[18] Otto Krauske, ed., *Acta Borussica: Die Briefe König Friedrich Wilhelms I. an den Fürsten Leopold zu Anhalt-Dessau, 1704–1740* (Berlin, 1905), pp. 372–73, 375–76. Anhalt-Dessau had accompanied Frederick William on an inspection tour of the Insterburg district in 1721 and at the king's urging had bought up huge tracts of agricultural land there, over whose forests, roads, and peasantry Frederick had given him full economic and juridical authority, at the time when the crown was trying to wrest control of the province away from the local nobility. J. F. Goldbeck, *Vollständige Topographie des Königreichs Preussen. Erster Theil welcher die Topographie von Ost-Preussen enthält* (Königsberg, 1787; repr. Hamburg, 1966), p. 42.

[19] Skalweit, *Domänenverwaltung*, pp. 102–15. "Flatulence" was a term favored by Frederick William to express fiscal dissipation.

issue here than the four million Thaler, even. It was divine favor, God's auspices. In 1730 came the terrible crisis with Crown Prince Frederick: the Lieutenant Katte affair, with its awful intimations of homosexuality at work in the Prussian royal succession itself.

The king had Katte executed before young Frederick's eyes, and put the prince to work at an administrative board in Küstrin, learning how to lay out Vorwerke and domains. But that did not free Frederick William of anxiety, or, behind his customary bluster, a certain shame about his failures and misfortunes. People noticed, early in 1731, that the king seemed oddly ill. He grew enormously fat, stopped hunting, fell asleep at queer times.[20] Then corruption struck again, this time as open peculation in the administration of Prussian Lithuania, and Frederick William went out personally to Königsberg and Gumbinnen, to see to it. In that summer the confessional troubles broke out in Salzburg and the Petition of the 19,000 appeared in Regensburg.

In Prussia the king thought that he really had got the fox out of his hole this time. A commission investigating rumors of graft at Gumbinnen had ordered the arrest of a number of officials, including War and Domain Councillor Schlubhut, who was accused of theft from public funds, including some earmarked for settlers from the Palatinate. A criminal court in Berlin had found Schlubhut guilty and sentenced him to several years' imprisonment. The judgment was locally disputed, and so the king went out to Prussia to see for himself. After looking into the matter he told Schlubhut that what he really deserved was the gallows. Schlubhut, with astonishing imprudence, retorted that one did not hang a Prussian nobleman. At this Frederick William caused a gallows to be built in the courtyard of the chamber at Königsberg.

[20] Georges Pariset, *L'État et les églises en Prusse sous Frédéric-Guillaume Ier, 1713–1740* (Paris, 1896), pp. 75–76; Friedrich Förster, *Friedrich Wilhelm I., König v. Preussen*, vol. 1 (Potsdam, 1834), pp. 384–92.

The next day being Sunday, the king went to church, where he heard a sermon on the text, "Show mercy, that you shall know mercy," at which the king wept copiously and, no doubt, unfeignedly. On Monday he summoned the rest of the council to watch Schlubhut hang.[21] That having been done, and being in the neighborhood, the king and his official party took the occasion to make a tour of the Lithuanian districts. This tour of inspection took place in June and July of 1731, while Salzburg's Chancellor Rall and his commission were pursuing their inquiries among the alpine valleys of the Pongau and uncovering astonishing numbers of Protestants. Oddly, the volume then current of Faber's *Staats-Cantzley*, an important review that periodically published at Nürnberg documentary materials on German and European politics, had as its frontispiece a portrait of a remarkably slim and genial-looking Frederick William I of Prussia; this volume also first brought wide public attention to the religious conflicts in the mountain regions of Salzburg.[22]

The coincidence of timing joins history of the Salzburg confessional with the crisis of the Retablissement in Prussia, and links the archbishop's story with the king's. After the hanging of Schlubhut and the tour of Lithuania, Frederick William's mood changed markedly for the better. The king reversed his views on the settlement program, and took a new and hopeful interest in the development of the East Prussian domains. During that summer this coarse, brutal, and violent sovereign became a counterpart to the scholarly and remote, the fastidious in the way of indolence, the sequestered ecclesiastical prince in Salzburg.

At the end of July Frederick William issued from Königsberg

[21] Droysen, *Politik*, 4:158; Förster, *Friedrich Wilhelm I.*, 1:323–324; David Fassmann, *Leben und Thaten Friderici Wilhelmi, Königs von Preussen*, vol. 1 (Hamburg, 1736), pp. 422–23.

[22] Anton Faber [=Christoph Leonhard Leucht], ed., *Europäische-Staats-Cantzley*, vol. 56 (Nürnberg, 1730). The documentation, pp. 141–161, concerned the Bremer-Lerchner case.

a "Housekeeping Regulation for the Domains of the Prussian Kingdom," a law to standardize and enforce the central farm and lease-holding system already mentioned. The regulation commanded all domain Pächter to introduce the so-called Magdeburg System of farming, whereby each Vorwerk was to be cultivated wholly by implements and animals belonging to it, operated by cottagers [*Gärtner*] permanently settled on it or by paid wage labor, rather than by contributions of labor and animal power from tenants on the outlying domains. New emphasis was to be put on animal husbandry, particularly dairying, and thus on heavy manuring and deep plowing. The tenant farm families were to work individually, intensively, and exclusively on their own holdings. What the king contemplated for East Prussia was a pattern of independent, effectively heritable family farms, clustered around the central royal Vorwerke whose leaseholders would provide regional processing services, collect fixed rents, and organize markets and revenues.[23]

There is little doubt that Frederick William had his eye on the Salzburg Protestants as early as midsummer 1731: the time of both the Petition of the 19,000 and the "Housekeeping Regulation for Prussia." But there is no direct evidence whatever that he connived at the religious disturbances in the Pongau or encouraged peasant resistance there. If he did, he hid it well enough to escape the scrutinies of suspicious Salzburg officials then and of diligent Catholic historians ever since. Quite certainly he had nothing directly to do with the rumors that swept through the Pongau peasantry that summer, of the eighty thousand Protestant or Brandenburg soldiers ready to march to their aid. Even Peter Wallner at his interrogation as recorded by Salzburg officials in June had mentioned the Saxon and Hanoverian embassies at Regensburg, and not the Prussian.

But there were implicit links between Potsdam and the Pongau, and these were activated through the corpus evan-

---

[23] Roth, "Domänenpächter," pp. 43–54; Stadelmann, *Friedrich Wilhelm I.*, pp. 132–36, with the text of the Reglement on pp. 333–38.

gelicorum at the Reichstag. As between corpus and king, any initiative seems to have passed from Regensburg to Potsdam, and not Potsdam to Regensburg. To be sure, the force of the situation made direct initiative from the king superfluous. Early in August the Prussian ambassador at the Reichstag , in a report to the king, raised the possibility of accepting religious refugees from Salzburg, and the king set a copy of the report before the General Directory on August 21 with the notation: "Very good, even if he can get only 10 families, if he can get 1000 or more, good. F. W." Accordingly, an order went to the Prussian embassy at Regensburg at the beginning of September to recruit as many families—"families," the order specified—as possible.[24]

Throughout September, while the Salzburg authorities seemed undecided what action to take, the Prussian government fell noticeably silent. Potsdam's support for the *corpus* in its memoranda war with Salzburg was perfunctory; or rather, perhaps, it was markedly circumspect. Tell Salzburg, wrote Frederick William to his ambassador in Regensburg in late October, that Prussia expects the *emperor* to do his duty in this matter. Prussia might carry out the usual legal measures in German confessional disputes, reprisals against Catholics in its own territories (known as *Repressalien*, or *retorsio juris iniqui*), but only if other Protestant princes of the empire did do so "together in one *Tempo*."[25] Whether the king knew of the expulsion order then being drafted in Salzburg or not I cannot tell; chances are he had at least an inkling. But for that moment he seemed inclined, if to anything, to dampen the confessional combativeness of the corpus.

During the autumn months of 1731 Prussian confessional

[24] Ortner, *Reformation*, p. 240; Carl F. Arnold, *Die Ausrottung des Protestantismus in Salzburg unter Erzbischof Firmian und seinen Nachfolgern*, vol. 2 (Halle, 1901), pp. 45–46.
[25] I deem this note of October 23, 1731, to be a grudging response to requests from Regensburg for action against Salzburg. Moser, *Reichs-Fama*, vol. 11 (1732), pp. 732–33.

belligerency was muted. Even the archbishop's expulsion order, when it was published early in November, aroused no Prussian response that has survived—leaving aside, of course, the examination of Forstreiter and Heldensteiner ten days later, on the twentieth. The expulsion of the undomiciled Salzburger in the last week of November attracted much public attention and sympathy during December and January, as they wandered about southern Germany, living by such charity as they could find in Memmingen, Kaufbeuren, Augsburg. The king, however, showed little interest in them. He abstained entirely from the confessional outrage and vituperation directed at Salzburg which accompanied their passage and sharply rejected a proposal from confessionally belligerent members of his government to restrict Roman Catholic exercises in East Prussia: "I have a lot of Lithuanians in the Tilsit lowlands as colonists, kato [Catholic]," he wrote "If I take away their church services those people will run away. That is the mistake that Louis XIV made, and I will not copy him. I am populating my land, not depopulating it."[26] Frederick William wanted no part in a Protestant crusade at that stage.

The domiciled families were now under orders to leave on St. Georgi, April 23; but nobody was quite sure what would happen then: whether the archbishop would stand firm on his command, or what action might come from the Protestant side, in Salzburg or the Reich. Chancellor Rall and the corpus went on reviling one another. Frederick William finally acted on February 2, twelve weeks before the St. Georgi deadline, with a formal Patent of Invitation. "In Christian-Royal mercy and heartfelt sympathy for Our Evangelical co-religionists," opened the proclamation, "since the aforesaid are being obliged to leave their Fatherland purely and entirely on account of their

[26] Max Lehmann, Preussen und die katholische Kirche, 1640–1740 (Leipzig, 1878), p. 837. But the king added that it would be a good idea to get rid of the Jesuits and install Augustinians or Cistercians [Bernhardiner]. This was not a time of religious strife in Prussia, where the tensions surrounding the 1724 "blood-bath of Thorn" had distinctly slackened (see pp. 404–27, 822–38).

faith, We have decided to extend to them a mild and helping Hand, and to this end to receive them in Our Land, and to preserve and to care for them in certain districts of Our Prussian Kingdom." The archbishop of Salzburg was "requested in friendship . . . to consider and treat them, as many of them as wish and intend to go to Our Lands, henceforth as Prussian subjects," entitled by law freely to dispose of their property and to take the proceeds out of the archbishopric. The royal proclamation made no mention, however, of the three years' grace allowed for the disposition of property, something the lawyers of the corpus evangelicorum were still loudly insisting upon.

The Prussian proclamation notified all German princes and towns, through whose territories the Salzburg Protestants might travel on their way to the certain Prussian districts, to accord them the treatment of Prussian subjects and to allow free passage in accordance with that status. Now any further injury done to Salzburg Protestants would bring direct Prussian reprisals, "in full expectation that all Evangelical Powers, if they have not already made such determination, will follow our example." Prussian commissioners at Regensburg and at Halle were prepared, said the proclamation, to provide guidance and transportation to the places of settlement, where the newcomers would enjoy all the freedoms, rights, and privileges of colonists. That meant the provisions of the 1724 colonization law, now republished and redirected by this new proclamation: free arable and meadow land and timber; exemption from duties and fees for a period of years; draft, meat, and milk animals, and poultry; tools and household goods; seed and edible grains for a year.[27] I shall reserve greater detail of these promises and their fulfillment for the migrants' own

[27] Moser, *Reichs-Fama*, 11:698–707; Stadelmann, *Friedrich Wilhelm I.*, pp. 38–41; Max Beheim-Schwarzbach, *Hohenzollernsche Colonisationen* (Leipzig, 1874), pp. 201–2, and his *Friedrich Wilhelms I. Kolonisationswerk in Litauen, vornehmlich die Salzburger Kolonie* (Königsberg, 1879), pp. 369–70.

story. The immediate effect of the Prussian proclamation of February was to determine the outcome of the Salzburg religious disturbances which until that time was still uncertain. The Protestant families there would leave, and would go to the Lithuanian domains of the East Prussian Retablissement.

For although the corpus at Regensburg had been the center of agitation, Potsdam, replying to Salzburg, was the place of decision (Vienna's role will be a matter for the next chapter). Only two weeks after his February invitation to the Salzburg Protestants, Frederick William noted his "obligation" to Archbishop Firmian for his new colonists on the ministerial report certifying their orthodoxy. Two weeks after that notation, the king publicly threatened specific reprisals against Catholic clergy and clergy in his own Brandenburg-Prussian territory if the emigration of the Salzburg Protestants should be interfered with. Moreover, the threat of sanctions against the Prussian Catholic establishment was made on the same day, March 1, 1732, that the king refused to restrict Catholic exercises in East Prussia, this being "die *fautte* die Luis 14. gethan." The momentum of Frederick William's confessional policy seems clear: to assert leadership in defense of the religious weal and the material interests of German Protestants, while prudently adapting German confessional strife to Prussian economic advantage.

This was surely a wholly defensible initiative and a quite reasonable confessional policy. Its import contains, to be sure, yet another vector. Three weeks after his invitation to the Salzburger, the king cleared up the problem of the East-Prussian Mennonites, rather in the manner of Archbishop Firmian, by expelling them from the realm. These were people who had been exiled from the region around Bern in Switzerland twenty years before; some had found their way to Hamburg and had come to East Prussia at the invitation of the then King Frederick I, the present king's father, with a promise of exemption from military service, conceded to the civil beliefs of the sect. Some had settled in Königsberg, where they became merchants and distillers, being excluded from the crafts and retail trades ostensibly on account of the guilds' fears of sectarian contamination. Other Mennonites, reputedly good Swiss cattle farmers, settled on the Tilsit lowlands. Their refusal of military service meant friction with Frederick William I, however, when he succeeded to the throne. "Such people are good enough for *Partikulier*," he grumbled in 1718: that is, for the lesser class of princes, "but not for great rulers." Despite the earlier promise of immunity he began military conscription among the Mennonites in 1723. His own officials protested this breach and the king exploded, "I will not have such a tribe of weasels [*Schelm-Nation*], who will not be soldiers!" On February 22, 1732, the king ordered all Mennonites to leave Prussian territory within three months. The terms and language of the Prussian expulsion order resembled Firmian's order of the preceding November, except that Frederick William's added that those expelled were to be replaced by "good Christians who do not think it forbidden to be a soldier."[28] That condition excluded the Mennonite sect but not members of the three established confessions.

The response of the Salzburg farmholders to Frederick William's invitation was all but overwhelming; but he knew and he named its ultimate auspices. "Very good!" the king noted on a panicky commissioner's report that there might be many more than the five or six thousand colonists first contemplated. "What grace God does the House of Brandenburg! For this certainly comes from God!" And when the first column of domiciled families approached Berlin in June, he went out to Zehlendorf to meet them, chatted with them, and directed them to sing a favorite hymn of his which seemed right for their condition too: "In my deep need I put my trust in God"— *Auf meinen Gott trau' ich in aller Noth*. When the colonial officer

---

[28] Erich Randt, *Die Mennoniten in Ostpreussen und Litauen bis zum Jahre 1772* (Königsberg, 1912) is an excellent account; my quotations are from pp. 20, 33, and 54.

guiding the procession reported that the Salzburger did not know that one, the king led off with it himself, the Salzburger then picked it up after all, and sang it out lustily, the story goes, as they passed by in review.[29]

The Prussian special immigration commissioner, Johann Göbel, set up shop in Oetting in Bavaria, just across the Salzburg border near where the Salzach enters the Inn. As Salzburg officials counted the emigrants and their cash out, on one side of the border, Göbel counted them in, on the other side. Administratively the transmigration process seem to have gone smoothly all around. Force was not needed. Göbel dispatched to Prussia twenty-six columns of about eight hundred souls apiece between the beginning of April and mid-August, most of them during June and July. About twenty thousand people were sent through Franconia and Saxony to Halle (where they were supplied with young aspirant pastors) and Berlin. Between sixteen and seventeen thousand of these eventually reached Berlin or Frankfurt an der Oder, the rest having dropped out or died—especially the elderly—along the way overland. From Berlin they were sent to Königsberg: About ten thousand reached Königsberg by water in sixty-four shipments via Stettin, of whom about five hundred died, most of them children, who suffered a deathrate of 14 percent on this seaborne part of the journey alone. About five thousand reached Königsberg by land, in eight hundred wagons with twelve hundred surviving Salzburg horses. Among these last overland columns about three hundred persons died, again most of them children.[30]

[29] Beheim-Schwarzbach, *Hohenzollernsche Colonisationen*, pp. 203–5. This was the second column to reach Berlin. The first had been mainly remnants of the final group of Nichtangesessenen, who were picked up by Commissioner Göbel around the end of January: Wolfgang Menger, "Die Salzburger Emigration nach Ostpreussen in den Jahren 1731 und 1732. Eine medizinisch-geschichtliche Studie zum Umsiedlungsproblem," *MGSL* 98 (1958), 93.

[30] Beheim-Schwarzbach, *Hohenzollernsche Colonisationen*, pp. 203–7; Menger, "Salzburger Emigration," pp. 96–98; Göcking, *Emigrations-Geschichte*, 1:500–501. There are complete itemized lists in Göcking, 2:654–888.

In Prussian Lithuania the Salzburger were spread out among the Swiss and German settlers that had arrived earlier and the still earlier and majority Lithuanian population. A survey made in 1736, for example, showed 770 Salzburger families settled on domain lands, among 2,957 Swiss and other German farmsteads, and 8,367 Lithuanian.[31] There had turned out to be fewer actually empty farmsteads [*Wüsten*] than existed in the king's imagination, or more likely, fewer than the figures filed by local officials had led some to suppose; so that actually about four-fifths of these new colonists were put not on empty land but on farms already under cultivation, replacing elderly or unproductive occupants, or taking over farmsteads vacated by deaths.[32] But by the end of 1734 about twelve thousand Salzburg colonists were officially accounted for, about ten thousand of them settled on the land.

The financial consequences of the transaction for the Prussian economy are not easy to ascertain. The Salzburger had taken cash in the amount of some 800,000 Prussian thaler (as 1,200,000 gulden imperial) out of the archbishopric, an amount that was reduced by the 10 percent emigration tax levied by the archbishopric at the border. A substantial part of this, perhaps half, seems to have reached Prussia with the migrants, the rest having been spent en route or hidden from Prussian authorities and accounts. The Salzburger legally exchanged silver coins in the amount of 160,000 thaler for currency acceptable in Prussia; but nobody knew or knows how much other money they had, how much they held back, or how much they spent on the way. About sixty Salzburg families promptly, and some two hundred more over the next dozen years, were able to buy properties outright from the crown, usually for about two hundred thaler apiece in cash. These then were subject to a regular

[31] Beheim-Schwarzbach, *Hohenzollernsche Colonisationen*, pp. 272–73. He provides detailed ethnic breakdown by locality (pp. 276–312).
[32] See the figures for the Insterburg District in Göcking, *Emigrations-Geschichte*, 2:233; also Skalweit, *Domänenverwaltung*, p. 274.

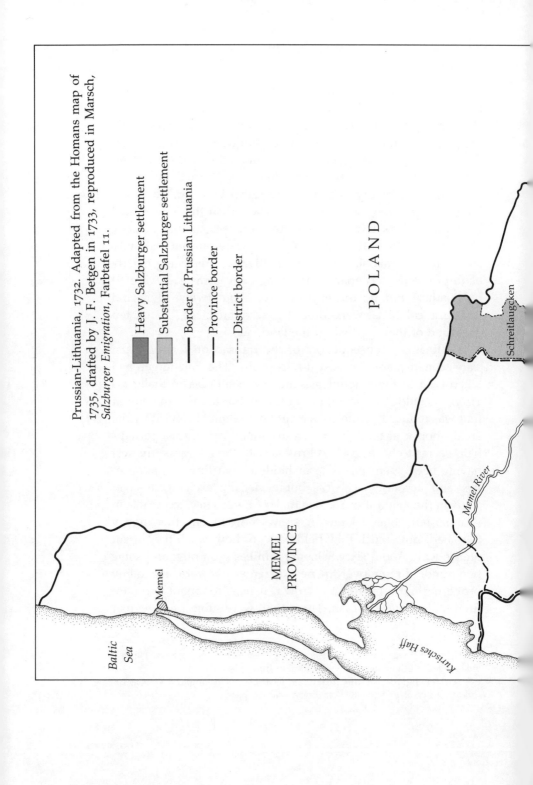

Prussian-Lithuania, 1732. Adapted from the Homans map of 1735, drafted by J. F. Betgen in 1733, reproduced in Marsch, *Salzburger Emigration*, Farbtafel 11.

Heavy Salzburger settlement

Substantial Salzburger settlement

Border of Prussian Lithuania

Province border

District border

POLAND

MEMEL PROVINCE

Memel

Baltic Sea

Kurisches Haff

Memel River

Schreitlaugcken

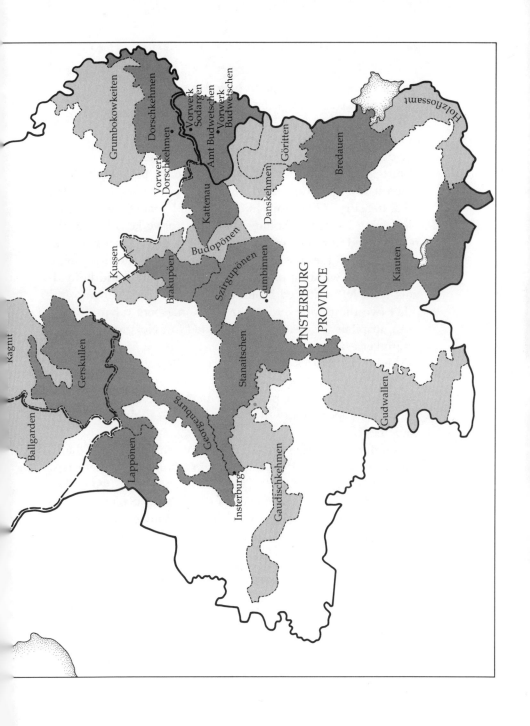

land tax when the exemption period expired. What these sums represented will soon become somewhat clearer.

Another seven hundred or so families were settled on crown domains at royal expense and became liable for rental and labor dues to the Vorwerke, about twelve thaler a year for each farmstead. These amounts were added to the price of the lease when it was next calculated, in 1734, and so ended up in the royal treasury. About four hundred people, mostly young couples, were located as cottagers on the Vorwerke. Most of the rest worked for hire or by contract on the farmsteads, and about half of these were established on two hundred more family farms within a few seasons. About a thousand individuals were left scattered around the ten provincial towns. Another two thousand were still in the Königsberg urban district, or in hospitals, or dead or unaccounted for. Next to none were on Junker estates.[33]

The official figures for Salzburger families settled eventually in the Lithuanian Retablissement program are shown in Table 1 (with total number of persons in parentheses), as the immigrants were located and the royal accounts caught up with the settlement.

In order to describe the administrative structures and the financial proceeds that were the crown's immediate interests, I begin by examining the Vorwerk Sodargen, one of two central domain farms and service centers (the other, smaller and presumably older, was called the Vorwerk Budwetschen) in the Budwetschen district, an area where many Salzburg colonists

[33] For the preceding figures: Skalweit, *Domänenverwaltung*, pp. 271–75; Beheim-Schwarzbach, *Hohenzollernsche Colonisationen*, pp. 208–9; Beheim-Schwarzbach, *Friedrich Wilhelm I.*, pp. 190–91; Otto Kerschhofer, "Die Salzburger Emigration nach Preussisch-Litauen," *MGSL* 116 (1976), 190–91; Paul Dedic, "Nachwirkungen der grossen Emigration in Salzburg und Steiermark," *JGPÖ* 65–66 (1944–45), 79–84. Totals from varied sources do not agree, and to pretend greater precision would be fraudulent; the proportions I have given here are probably 90% accurate. There will be more detailed figures in Chapter 4.

Table 1. Resettlement of families

Households	1734		1744		%, 1744
On purchased farms	55	(346)	237	(1,578)	17.3
Crown tenants	658	(3,836)	862	(5,406)	59.4
Cottagers (on Vorwerke)	129	(405)	105	(458)	5.0
Total households	842	(4,587)	1,204	(7,442)	
Wage or contract		(3,232)		(1,654)	18.2
Total located		(7,819)		(9,096)	100.0

Source: Skalweit, Domänenverwaltung, pp. 274–75; Menger, "Salzburger Emigration," pp. 122–23; Beheim-Schwarzbach, Friedrich Wilhelm I., pp. 165–66.

were settled. As shown in Table 2 sixty-four people lived on the Vorwerk Sodargen in 1734, including fifteen families and an unmarried bookkeeper.

Table 2. Composition of households, Vorwerk Sodargen, 1934

Occupation	Husband/ Wife	Children	Manserv.	Maidserv.	Infirm	Total
Amtmann Hasfordt	2	4	4	5		15
Secretary/tutor	2					2
Accountant	1					1
Cottager #1	2	2				4
Cottager #2	2	4				6
Cottager #3	2	1				3
Cottager #4	2					2
Cottager #5	2	1				3
Cottager #6	2	1				3
Cottager #7	2					2
Cottager #8	2				1	2
Herdsman	2	2				4
Brewer	2					2
Carpenter	2	2				4
Innkeeper	2					2
Miller	2	5		1		8
Total	31	22	4	6	1	64

Source: GStA PK XX. HA Pt Budweitschen, II: Prästationstabellen 1734, p. 188.

That tabulation offers a notion of the allocation of labor on a relatively elaborate but not unusual royal farm. All but one of the children were under twelve years old. Cottager #8 was Simon Former, who bore a common Salzburg name and supported an elderly male relative—I cannot identify him further; but none of the others was a Salzburger, affirming royal policy of placing Salzburg colonists on tributary family farms rather than the Vorwerke. No butcher or baker is mentioned; probably the innkeeper [Krüger] had these functions insofar as they were specialized (or possibly the servants in the Amtmann's household).

Table 3. Assessed incomes of the Vorwerk Sodargen, 1734

Tillage:	Area	Rent		
Fallow	144 M.	0 thlr.		
Meadow	0	0		
Wheat	8	24		
Rye	176	186		
Barley	64	96		
Oats	80	47		
Total arable	432 M.		353 thlr.	
Husbandry:				
90 milch cattle @ 3 thlr.		270		
30 calves @ 45 gr.		15		
Pigs and poultry		25		
Garden		3		
		313		
Gross total rents			666 thlr.	
Less expenses:				
Church tithe	3 thlr.			
Clerical costs	50			
Wages, forage, and taxes	137			
			190	
Net income			476	

Source: GStA PK XX Pt Budweitschen, II: Prästationstabellen 1734, pp. 165–66. For conventional area equivalents to Hufen and Morgen, see Chapter 4, note 34, below.

The eight cottager [*Gärtner*] families worked 432 *Morgen* or 14.4 *Hufen* land that were part of the Vorwerk itself (112 ha = 277 U.S. acres), averaging 1.8 Hufen per family, a third of it regularly in fallow. Since the average sharework or tenent farmer [*Scharwerkbauer*] settled on a family farm in the Budwetschen district worked 1.4 Hufen, the Vorwerk's arable land was presumably cultivated mainly by its own residents, without much need for outside labor, so that service dues could be collected in money, as the Magdeburg System provided; some occasional labor was hired, as shown in Table 3. This is a summary representation of the assessed incomes [*Arrende*] of the Vorwerk itself, the central farm, not counting revenues from sharework peasants or freeholders settled elsewhere in the Amt Budwetschen.

Table 3 shows the domestic economy of Sodargen, central farm of the Amt, or District, Budwetschen. Ninety milch cattle seems a good many (almost a dozen for each cottager family plus one Amt servant), especially in the absence of any meadowland on the Vorwerk itself; but note the substantial sum deducted for forage, labor, and crown obligations. In any case, the proportion of cattle to cottager family is about the same as at other Vorwerke in the area.

The greater part by far of the total revenues of the Amt Budwetschen, however, came not from the two central Vorwerke themselves, but from the obligations both of the freeholders and especially of the sharework peasants settled on the domain lands under the Amt's jurisdiction, as shown in Table 4.

Table 4, a condensation of the one prepared by royal commissioners, shows that sharework peasants in the district were assessed at about 17 thlr. per family, on holdings that averaged 1.5 Hufen (Salzburger families in 1734 had substantially smaller holdings and lesser dues). That amounted to about 100 thlr. annually from each of the 45 "villages" (meaning about six households) in the Amt. Finally, Table 5 summarizes the total assessment for the Amt Budwetschen, one of fifty such districts in the Lithuanian provinces of East Prussia.

Table 4. Income from dues, Amt Budwetschen

Regular dues (excluding Vorwerk income)			
From freeholders (16 households, on 63 Hufen)			
Land tax	97 thl.		
Beer tax	3		
		100 thlr.	
From sharework peasants (266 households, on 377 Hufen)			
Land tax	1,537		
Service dues	1,322		
Cereal shares:			
Rye @ 40 gr.	389		
Barley @ 30 gr.	351		
Oats @ 18 gr.	841		
	1,581		
Total dues from sharework peasants		4,440	
Total regular dues			4,540
Irregular dues:			
Bee tax	9		
Head tax on laborers and artisans	13		
Total irregular dues			22
Total			4,562

Source: GStA PK XX Pt Budweitschen, II: Prästationstabellen 1734, pp. 3–7, 144–148. One thaler = 90 groschen.

It includes essential services, rents, and licenses not included in the preceding tables, plus the revenues of the other Vorwerke in the Budwetschen district.

Table 5 shows the annual sum for which Amtmann Hasfordt of Budwetschen was held responsible to the royal treasury. These figures represent administrative approximations and aspirations, but for Frederick William's Prussia they are probably not far off the mark. To reach an overall estimate of the financial proceeds of the Salzburger resettlement program is a chancier matter still, but worth a try. The king's treasury spent about half a million thaler on the whole operation; and although any affectation of accuracy in the matter would be absurd, such calculations as I am able to make suggest that the crown was able to recover about a third of that sum directly,

Table 5. Total assessment, Amt Budwetschen

Revenues:			
Rental income			
Vorwerk Budwetschen	487 thlr.		
Vorwerk Sodargen	476		
District brewery	262		
Windmills (4)	420		
Fishponds	10		
Taverns	34		
Untilled fields	14		
Brickworks	20		
Total rental income		1,723	
Regular dues		4,540	
Irregular dues		22	
Total revenues, Amt Budwetschen			6,285
Expenses:			
Personnel			
Amtmann and leaseholder	150		
Constable	50		
Chimney sweep	3		
Peasant elders (10)	125		
Total personnel		348	
Writing materials and bindings		10	
Total expenses, Amt Budwetschen			358
Annual cash sum to be rendered to the royal treasury			5,927

Source: GStA PK XX Pt Budweitschen, II: Prästationstabellen 1734, pp. 8–9.

from sale of freeholds and from tenant dues capitalized at the standard rate of 5 percent, and two-thirds of it by the end of ten years.[34] It is impossible to guess how much more may have

[34] This assumes (following official figures) an average purchase price of 190 thaler for each two-Hufen Köllmer holding and 12 thaler annual tax thereafter; and 12 thaler annual dues on each one-Hufe share tenancy. It would be possible to work up a more precise figure from the calculations of the domain lease assessment commissions, beginning at the Zehlendorf Prussian archive with GStA PK 162A: Findbuch, für die Prästations-Tabellen; but I doubt that the more finicky numbers would be appreciably more accurate. My estimate is based on these assessment inventories, combined where possible with the lists

reached crown coffers from other cash that immigrants brought with them in 1732 or later received from sale of their Salzburg properties, transfers that brought at least another half-million thaler in urgently needed cash to the Prussian economy. Taken altogether, and projected into the future, this seems better-than-fair return.

The invitation to the Salzburger and their resettlement south of the Memel was on the whole, therefore, sound business practice for Prussia, performed quickly and efficiently. But still, it had its shortcomings. Almost none of the Salzburger had sold their home farms before leaving the archbishopric. Moreover the king, for all his insistence on the rights accorded religious emigrants by the Peace of Westphalia to sell their properties and bring the proceeds with them, had never brought up the matter of the three years' grace the law allowed for that purpose. Frederick William wanted the Salzburger farm families in Prussia, wanted them in Prussia just as fast as Firmian and Chancellor Rall wanted them out of Salzburg, and the migration was essentially completed by the end of that summer of 1732.

The properties the migrants had left behind, however, nearly two thousand of them, were valued at almost two and a half million Prussian thaler (four million gulden imperial), and as soon as the families were safely resettled, the Prussian government set about recovering whatever it could of that. It could not recover much, though the Salzburg government offered full cooperation, publishing a list of properties up for sale and taking Prussian commissioner Baron Christoph von Plotho on an extended tour of the Pongau in 1736. Plotho was able to negotiate some sales, at a quarter to a half the assessed value, the latter being normally the price recorded at a property's latest previous sale. Very little even of that discounted price was

of Salzburg settlers in Horst Kenkel, *Amtsbauern und Kölmer im nördlichen Ostpreussen um 1736* (Hamburg, 1972), and cost estimates by Beheim-Schwarzbach, *Hohenzollernsche Colonisationen*, p. 230, and *Friedrich Wilhelm I.*, p. 380.

in cash paid down, and the balance owed was all but impossible to collect. But in the end, about three hundred thousand thaler, about one-eighth the pre-emigration assessed value of the abandoned properties, followed the former owners to East Prussia; or so Plotho's somewhat questionable books showed. On these transfers the Salzburg government levied the same 10 percent emigration tax that had applied to the cash the emigrants had taken with them.[35]

That cash income was fair business for Salzburg too. And although state revenues from the disturbed areas of the Pongau declined briefly in 1731–32, they had recovered well by 1735, by which time most of the abandoned farms had been reoccupied.[36] The archbishopric circulated the detailed printed lists of properties offered for sale throughout Salzburg, as well as to the Tyrol, Bavaria, the Rhineland, and wherever else Catholic buyers might be found—but avoiding nearby Austrian crown territories, out of deference to the emperor. Preference was given to buyers who would come from outside the principality, even when native buyers were ready to pay more. This was good standard cameralist political economy, surely. But other judgments may have been at work; for it was not easy to

[35] There are summary figures in Kerschhofer, "Salzburger Emigration," pp. 178–79; Dedic, "Nachwirkungen," pp. 79–84; and Beheim-Schwarzbach, *Hohenzollernsche Colonisationen*, pp. 174–78. Most Prussian historians claim that the emigrants inflated the claimed values of their properties, this having been asserted by Plotho as one explanation for his inability to collect more for them; but the owners' claims are wholly consistent with such official assessments and prior prices as I have seen. Of course property values dipped sharply—but briefly—at the time of the emigration. Main primary sources on the Plotho commission are in KAS 11/69e: Reformation. Emigrationspatent 1731. Verkauf der Emigrantengüter im Beisein des preuss. Gesandten. Verzeichnis der Güter 1734–38, etc.; SLA EA 69: Kommissionsakten der von F. Baron Rehlingen mit dem preuss. Gesandten Frh. v. Plotho vorgenommenen Bereisung des Gebirges 1736; and GStA PK: Rep. 5 Tit. 21 Nr. 15, vols. 1–3: Acta, wegen Liquidation der von den Salzburgern in ihrem Vaterlande zurückgelassenen Forderungen . . . 1735–38.

[36] Gerhard Ammerer, "Funktionen, Finanzen und Fortschritt; zur Regionalverwaltung im Spätabsolutismus am Beispiel des geistlichen Fürstentums Salzburg," *MGSL* 127 (1987), 367–89.

find the right buyers near at hand, since the local population of experienced farmers had been drastically reduced. Some buyers were innkeepers and artisans from the capital and provincial towns, even hatters and smiths and carpenters, ready to pick up bargain investments in land.

Archepiscopal officials especially were in good position to profit from forced sales. Some buyers who came actually to work the land had come from the more barren alpine areas of Salzburg, where emigration had not occurred in 1731–32: they were sons and daughters of poor peasantry there. But wherever they came from (and the scanty records are unclear), the new owners, when not speculators, seem often to have been people who could not have aspired to the status of independent mountain peasant under normal economic circumstances: "former soldier," skinner, forest worker, guard, schoolmaster. There is almost no overlap of surnames between the lists of emigrated sellers and the lists of new buyers of the Pongau farms, as though these two sets, wherever they hailed from, were members of wholly separate cultures or tribes. It is most unlikely that the archbishopric looked upon its resettlement program as a social welfare project for its poor, or as a bonus for religious loyalty among the better off; but the population transfer worked to the benefit of many Salzburger anyway and attracted capital investment to the vacated lands which offset the sums Plotho's commission was able to remit to Prussia.[37]

The economy of the mountain districts, though, had never seriously affected archepiscopal policy there or its response to the Protestant problem. In Salzburg, this had assuredly been more a problem of religious and civil order, and a proud (but indolent) prelate's humiliation if he should be unable to sustain either and both. The source of revenues represented by the

[37] In addition to the manuscript sources mentioned in note 35 above, see Josef Brettenthaler, "Die Wiederbesiedlung," in REP, pp. 172–79; and Gertraud Schwarz-Oberhummer, "Die Auswanderung der Gasteiner Protestanten unter Erzbischof Leop. Anton von Firmian," MGSL 94 (1954), 66–68.

population that actually emigrated was slight and was readily restored. But on the other hand, the fiscal consequences might have been serious if the Pongau infection had been allowed to spread massively, especially to the susceptible salt-mining districts near the capital. Any religious disorder posed a threat to that important and emblematic resource, salt, and fear of this was undoubtedly an important reason for the haste with which the expulsion was carried out and for Firmian's one clearly illegal act in this affair, the denial of the Triennium. In the end, the evacuation and reoccupation of the emigrants' farmsteads probably had little economic effect on the archbishopric one way or the other, and the themes of both processes were not fiscal but confessional.[38] Getting free of that aggravating, embarrassing, and dangerous Protestant bone in his throat was the main profit Archbishop Firmian had from the transaction with the king of Prussia.

But Frederick William's purposes and profits were not all material. Indeed, it might be argued that his financial gains from the Salzburg immigration were relatively slight, inasmuch as the Salzburger made up only a small minority of the population even in the places where they were most thickly settled, and their contribution to the Retablissement program was proportionally small. But theirs was a highly dramatic contribution, and the immigration elucidated the king of Prussia's Protestant leadership in the context of his program for the economic development of East Prussia. The Salzburg colonists came to symbolize this fiscal program and to confessionalize it. The expulsion and the dramatic migration of the Salzburger across Germany produced an immediate explosion of publicity from Protestant sources of which the chief victims were German Catholicism and Archbishop Firmian, and the chief beneficiaries were Prussia and especially Prussia's king.

[38] Compare on this point R. Po-Chia Hsia, *Social Discipline in the Reformation: Central Europe, 1550–1750* (London, 1989), pp. 63–70, generally following Ortner, *Reformation*.

Some early samples will suggest the nature of this publicity. Probably the most widely distributed and reprinted contemporary account of the expulsion—also the earliest and in most respects quite accurate—was written by Christoph Sancke, pastor at the Thomaskirche at Leipzig (where J. S. Bach was musical director).[39] Sancke ended the first installment of his history, published in the summer of 1732 while the emigrant column were in passage, with a tribute and appeal to the king of Prussia, without whose intervention, wrote Sancke, Firmian's expulsion of the Salzburger portended an imperial crisis, one that might have exploded the German Reich itself. "Surely he wins thereby far greater fame, than he might have done by winning great battles, conquering impregnable fortresses, or by the taking of whole kingdoms. His memory will live so long in Grace, as the Evangelical Church exists on earth: that is, until the great Day of Judgment overturns everything."[40]

There were many such paeans, to which I shall return in a concluding chapter. *Emigranten-Lieder* were popular forms, and following are some verses from one of these songs, probably composed in Augsburg in that summer of 1732:

> Du König Himmels und der Erden,
> erhöre unser Bitt und Flehen,

[39] Characteristic of the legendary magnetism already gathering about the Salzburg emigration is the story that J. S. Bach's cantata "Brich dem Hungrigen dein Brot, and die, so im Elend sind, führe ins Haus," called the "Flüchtlings-kantate," was inspired by the Salzburg expulsion and was introduced before an audience of emigrants by the Thomasschule choir at Leipzig in June 1732. This was not the case: S. Jost Casper, "Johann Sebastian Bach und die Salzburger Emigranten—eine unheilige Legende," *MGSL* 122 (1982), 341–70. I owe the reference to Tanya Kevorkian.

[40] [Christoph Sancke], *Ausführliche Historie derer Emigranten oder vertriebenen Lutheraner aus dem Ertz-Bisthum Saltzburg,* 2d ed. (Leipzig, 1732), p. 224: "Gewiss er erlanget dadurch einen viel grössern Ruhm, als wenn er grosse Schlachten gewonnen, unüberwindliche Vestungen erobert, und gantze König-reiche eingenommen hätte. Sein Andencken wird so lange in Seegen stehen, als die Evangelische Kirche auf Erden bleibet, d.i., bis der grosse Gerichts-Tag alles über einen Hauffen treibt."

Dass wir so bald so glücklich werden,
   und unser lieben König sehn,
Der uns, durch seine starcke Hand,
Verschafft ein neues Vaterland.

Beglücke Sein Erlaucht Regieren,
   und gib Ihm ferner Muth und Geist,
Das Werck mit Seegen anzuführen,
   das alle Welt merckwürdig heisst:
Erhalt Ihn und sein Haus gesund,
So rühmt und preisst Dich Hertz und Mund.[41]

Frederick William could hardly expect a more brotherly relation with the God the King, with whom such language commonly identified him and with whom he shared fatherhood
over the Salzburg pilgrims; and pictorial representations of the
migration state the theme more dramatically still. Illustration 2
shows an engraving that accompanied "Dialogue between a
Salzburger and a Waldensian," published at Magdeburg in
1732:

Though leave I must my parents, children, friends, and house
   and farm,
Yet the Lord will take me in his arms.
He holds me fatherlike at his right hand,
And leads me well content to Frederick William's land.[42]

The columns of marching and singing Salzburger entered
graphically—and iconographically—into the tradition of the

[41] "O King of heaven and of earth, Hear Thou our prayer and plea, That we
may soon in rapture be, And our beloved King may see, Creating, with His
mighty hand, For us a newer Fatherland. Thy blessing on His noble reign, And
keep in Him the soul and nerve, That blessed labor to sustain, That draws the
eyes of all the world; Preservest Thou Him and his house, Then hear our praise
in heart and voice." *Kurtze und wahrhafftige Nachricht von denen Salzburgischen
Emigranten . . . 1732 . . . Arnstadt angekommen* [Arnstadt, 1732], pp. 27–29.
[42] *Die Zweyte Unterredung Im Reiche der Lebendigen, Zwischen einem . . . Saltzburger Und einem . . . Waldenser . . .* (Magdeburg, 1732).

King Frederick William I holds out his hand to the Salzburg Protestant exiles. From *Zweyte Unterredung Im Reiche der Lebendigen.*

House of Hohenzollern. In this story's manifest parallels and reminders of the biblical Exodus, Prussia figured as land of promise, and Prussia's king as God's instrument or indeed collaborater—symbolically even his incarnation—in the work of deliverance. God's hand must have been present from the start, in cloud and in flame, from the plagues and famines in East Prussia, to the mountain awakening of the evangelical spirit, and from the persecutions by Chancellor Rall in Salzburg, to the fructifying of the Lithuanian plain. Frederick William, king of Prussia, no mere gross and miserly drillmaster as some might have supposed, had turned tragedy into triumph, a demonstration of God's marvelous ways, bearing marks of God's favor.

This was far the greater gain for the king. In this he had overreached his father and lived up to his famous grandfather. He had advanced the royal work of peopling his land, and done it with God's oppressed children. Firmian, said the archbishop, had been "happily freed of this wasp's nest." Frederick William, said the king, had heartfelt cause to be "most obliged."

CHAPTER THREE

THE EMPIRE

The migration of the farmsteaders from alpine Salzburg to Prussian Lithuania suited both archbishop and king so well as to offer circumstantial reasons for supposing them to have been objects of a trade, a mutually advantageous and agreed transaction between those two princes. There is, however, no evidence of direct intervention by the king of Prussia in the relations between Archbishop Firmian and his subjects, let alone any evidence that Salzburg ever solicited Prussian cooperation in their removal. If this was a trade between them, it was not a conspiracy on either of their parts but a transaction negotiated at more than arms' length and without direct contact between principals.

Such a transaction implies a broker: a medium through whom tacit understandings may be developed and who underwrites their terms. And there was one: Charles VI, Holy Roman Emperor of the German Nation, whose office was in fact mainly that of a broker and guarantor of the relations among members of the Empire. Moreover, among the terms of any contract, tacit or explicit, are the rules and conventions operative in the public context of relations where the principals find themselves. Both principals in this instance were important princes of the Holy Roman Empire, and very conscious of it.

It can be argued, and it has been, that Firmian would never have carried out the expulsion without clearance from Vienna, including assurance that Prussia would accept the exiles; but it may be argued also that without imperial encouragement, Frederick William would never have invited them.[1] This line of speculation reaches further: that were it not for a particular conjuncture of imperial politics in 1731, the Salzburg mountain Protestants would not have come to declare themselves, or even if they had, that the passes to the north would then have been blocked, rather than opened, and they would have been more or less forcibly returned to the discipline and doctrines of the Roman Catholic Church.[2]

The imperial political stage in 1731–32, as reflected, for example, in the pages of Johann Jakob Moser's documentary chronicle *Reichs-Fama*, was dominated by three major issues. One of these was a proposed imperial law to control and police the industrial trades, a measure pursued mainly by Prussia; the second was the guarantee by the imperial German estates of the succession rights of the House of Habsburg, the so-called Pragmatic Sanction, this project pursued mainly by the emperor. The third was the expulsion of his Protestant subjects undertaken by the archbishop of Salzburg. Taken together, these three constitute an instructive example of the working of

---

[1] Most recently on Salzburg's behalf by Peter Putzer, "Das Wesen des Rechtsbruches von 1731/32," *MGSL* 122 (1982), 312, and Hans Wagner, "Politische Aspekte der Protestantenaustreibung," *REP*, pp. 92–100. Note that by placing responsibility on Vienna and Berlin, the burden on Salzburg is accordingly reduced. For the Prussian part, Droysen is scornful of imperial ambassador Seckendorf's report to the king (December 26, 1731) that "der Kaiser hat *permission* ertheilt [! comments Droysen] dass die salzburgischen Unterthanen . . . mit Sack und Pack abziehen können." Johann G. Droysen, *Geschichte der preussischen Politik*, vol. 4, part 3, (Leipzig, 1869), p. 157, n. 2. I find Seckendorf's language less remarkable than Droysen did.

[2] Thus Hans v. Zwiedineck-Südenhorst, "Die Anerkennung der pragmatischen Sanction Karls VI.," *MIÖG* 16 (1895), 322.

German imperial politics—not drastically different from the political workings of many other political systems, certainly, but different enough to cast lights and shadows. The Trades Ordinance centered on the relation between imperial politics and the domestic economic development of German states. The Pragmatic Sanction raised central issues of the imperial constitution, the nature of imperial authority, and the affirmation or denial of the traditional imperial rôle of the Habsburg dynasty in central Europe. These were the German imperial contexts, political and economic, for the confessional confrontation of 1731–32 in and over Salzburg.

The Trades Ordinance was pushed through the Imperial Diet, the Reichstag, by the Prussian government in January 1732: during the period, that is to say, that lay between the Salzburg expulsion order of November and the Prussian invitation order of February, though its history reaches back at least a decade. This legislation had been designed in Prussia to assist the state-sponsored development of Prussian industry. It had a double connection with the Salzburger affair, for not only did the trades law and the migration fall together in time and in politics, but also, Prussia's invitation to the Salzburger in 1732 was an extension of economic programs begun in 1723 and 1724, though these had been directed mainly to increase the industrial development of Prussian towns.

Prussia in those years had issued orders designed to encourage immigration from all over the empire, promising free citizenship and master's certificates to qualified workers, building materials, and tax exemptions to skilled artisans who would settle in Prussian towns, especially in the western and middle parts of the monarchy. Weavers were a special target, linen being an important article of commerce, and woolen cloth a military staple; so weavers were offered free looms and interest-free loans to get started. Parallel offers had been made to rural settlers, and these have helped to bring about Swiss and Hessian immigrants of the mid-1720s, mentioned in the foregoing chapter on the kingdom. From the beginning, Prussian economic development programs postulated maximum separation of town from country, of industrial from agricultural production, so as to organize economic activities in their proper locations. Rural cottage industry was discouraged, to enforce concentration in the countryside on agricultural production, and to centralize manufactures and commerce in the towns where they could be adequately policed.[3] The rural settlement part of the program had been a disappointment, partly at least because so many of the colonists were townspeople, unaccustomed to farming, disdainful or for other reasons not amenable to the kind of domestic self-discipline required for the family-farm organization of agriculture contemplated by the Magdeburg System and the Retablissement.

The Prussian government's program of industrial development in the 1720s also had run into immediate trouble because, as development officers believed or declared, they could not police industrial practices outside Prussia's own borders; and that problem led to the Imperial Trades Ordinance of 1731. For in order to assert real sovereignty over commerce and manufacture within its own borders, the Prussian state had to seek Empire-wide legislation, because important features of German economic activity functioned in the sphere of the German Empire as a whole, and Prussia's borders within the Empire were long and complex. More particularly, the guild organization of labor, in Prussia as elsewhere in Germany, depended on journeymen who came during their wander-years from other parts of the Empire. An expanding Prussian industrial workforce and productive capacity must depend on them all the more. Meanwhile journeymen's organizations in other places, in competing territories with looser economic controls such as

[3] The best account is Gustav Schmoller, "Das brandenburgisch-preussische Innungswesen von 1640 bis 1800," in his *Umrisse und Untersuchungen zur Verfassungs-, Verwaltungs- und Wirtschaftsgeschichte besonders des preussischen Staates im 17. und 18. Jahrhundert* (Leipzig, 1898), pp. 382–404; but see also Moritz Meyer, *Geschichte der Preussischen Handwerkerpolitik*, vol. 2, *Die Handwerkerpolitik Königs Friedrich Wilhelm I.* (Minden, 1888), pp. 23–72, 251–354.

Saxony, Silesia, Poland, Hanover, and the autonomous imperial towns had developed considerable bargaining power for themselves. Locally advantageous conditions of work, tenure, and civic status in their native places, made it harder to attract journeymen to work at Prussian looms and under Prussian economic discipline.

The resulting disadvantage in the labor market also reduced the Prussian masters' productivity. Moreover, Prussian officials found their attempts to control the organization of domestic industrial labor handicapped by the artisan guilds' own disciplinary instruments, the imposition of ostracism and blacklisting, *Auftreibung* and *Beschimpfung*. These sanctions operated across territorial boundaries, and many journeymen, who might be only temporarily in Prussia, feared them more than they disliked Prussian state discipline as such. For if as workers in Prussia they once accepted that discipline, the consequent taint of dishonor and betrayal might be invoked against them elsewhere and at any time, but especially when in future they might seek entry to any German guild as a master or try to install journeymen of their own.[4]

Directly at issue in this situation was the German guilds' control over internal discipline and thus over their membership. But control over membership by journeymen's associations and by masters' guilds meant their control over labor supply and over markets, respectively. These very factors were at the heart of the Prussian program of industrial immigration and development. Masters, too, risked dishonor and ostracism if they accepted state regulations and prohibitions drafted to open up and to increase production. Any guild that relinquished its authority to such public regulation could be tainted and so taint anybody associated with it. Thus the guild system of ostracism and blacklisting which inhibited economic expan-

---

[4] To the Schmoller, "Innungswesen," and Meyer, *Handwerkerpolitik*, accounts, add Mack Walker, *German Home Towns: Community, State, and General Estate: 1648–1871* (Ithaca, 1971), pp. 93–97, 435–51.

sion could not be defeated in one place or one jurisdiction while it still functioned and flourished in nearby places in another jurisdiction. And the German guild system functioned, as Gustav Schmoller conveniently located it, "from Bern to the Memel"—from the Alps to the Baltic shore.[5]

So Prussian officials committed to industrial development, particularly in textiles, became convinced that they could not improve present productivity, let alone attract new journeymen and master artisans, unless there were uniform rules and effective controls for industrial regulation which operated also in the neighboring territories with which they must compete for labor, skill, and industrial reputation. Economic legislation at the imperial level, however, had achieved next to nothing in the past, and as the industrial development program began Prussian officials believed, and they argued, that "nothing can be done at the Reichstag, by starting negotiations at Regensburg, on account of the regular opposition, for centuries, from the College of Imperial Towns," the free cities where the guild system's political influence was most strongly represented.[6] So first they tried to establish common economic rules for the German north and east through negotiations among the several governments there: Poland and Saxony, Silesia, Bohemia, Hanover. But all through the 1720s Warsaw (for Poland and Saxony), Vienna (for Silesia and Bohemia), and Hanover (ruled jointly with England) dragged their feet. Probably lethargy and lack of interest had as much to do with their hesitation as active resistance. Anyhow these courts—and note that all three, like Brandenburg-Prussia, were imperial electors—seemed content with their own existing arrangements, or at least were unwilling to subject themselves to Prussia's.

At this Frederick William himself grew interested and took a hand. In 1730, after an economic summit conference planned for Leipzig had been buried by Saxon procedural muddling,

[5] Schmoller, "Innungswesen," p. 340.
[6] Ibid., p. 387.

the king turned to the Reichstag at Regensburg after all, with a draft of an imperial law to "remedy abuses among the guilds." He now meant business, read the instruction to his ambassador: "the General Directory desires nothing other, than that imperial endorsement take place, the sooner the better."[7] And behold, it happened. The imperial vice-chancellor Friedrich Karl von Schönborn, from Vienna, intervened at the Reichstag in September 1730 to promote enactment of the imperial trades legislation proposed by Prussia. Wheels then began to turn at Regensburg; but at first very slowly and reluctantly. This is getting us nowhere! wrote an impatient Frederick William to his Reichstag ambassador; we need action, now, "which would be quite easy for His Imperial Majesty to bring about." The Reichstag colleges, after some further spinning of procedural wheels, grudgingly approved the Prussian draft in June, and the emperor signed in mid-August 1731.[8] That was just the time Frederick William was first showing interest in the possibility of an immigration of Salzburg Protestants, and the peasant delegation from Schwarzach was on its way to seek support from the emperor and the Empire's Protestant estates. This was also the time when, as will appear, the emperor himself intervened directly in the matter of the Salzburg Protestants.

The emperor's conversion at this time to imperial regulation of guilds and his support for Prussia's program were not inspired by interest in industrial conditions or in imperial economic policy for their own sakes. His own Austrian and Bohemian territorial governments, in fact, sent the Reichstag text back to Vienna unopened, on the grounds that the imperial chancellery had no authority over them in such matters. Eventually the text was published in those places as territorial but not as an imperial law.[9] What the Emperor Charles VI did care

[7] Ibid., p. 394.
[8] Meyer, *Handwerkerpolitik*, pp. 61, 250–51, 255.
[9] Schmoller, "Innungswesen," pp. 395–96.

about, though, more than anything else in this world—or maybe the next—was what would happen to the imperial succession when he died. For Charles of Habsburg, *imperator ac semper Augustus*, bore a heavy burden: no less than five hundred years' tradition of imperial and Austrian authority in the House of Habsburg of which he now was temporal head, a tradition crystalized in the cumulative pages of historic attributes, titles, vows, and exhortations which introduced every official declaration he signed. This patrimony stood in peril because of his inability to produce a son, and the peril grew with every passing year. To sustain the heritage he would have to deliver it intact to his daughter Maria Theresa; and to bring this about he needed the support of the Protestant electoral princes to the north, and most particularly, that of the elector of Brandenburg, king of Prussia. That problem of the Pragmatic Sanction, to use its quaint constitutional name, was the emperor's context for the story of the Salzburg expulsion.

Technically, the sanction was a dynastic agreement by members of the House of Habsburg that all its rights, duties, and titles, as now were severally embodied in Emperor Charles IV, would in the event of his death without male issue pass undivided and unchallenged to, and through, an heiress, presumptively his eldest daughter, Maria Theresa: a matter serious enough for the family patrimony. But this was far more than a dynastic issue within the House of Austria only; it was a serious constitutional matter for the whole Empire. For the constitutional understanding, upon which the Empire was founded and which had been tested more than once over the centuries, was that the emperor was expected to exert force enough to carry out a protective function in central Europe, and to adjust and adjudicate relations *among* its contentious members, but not force enough to dominate them altogether, so to violate the "German liberties." But the family agreement, by binding together the whole Habsburg heritage into a permanent indivisible block, threatened to overturn that imperial constitutional tradition and understanding, redoubling the re-

sistance and apprehensions surrounding Maria Theresa's presumed succession.

The problem would probably have arisen in one way or another even without the genealogical accident of Maria
Theresa's place in the line of descent; but that circumstance
had made the matter unavoidable by 1731, when the emperor
decided he must seek endorsement of the sanction by the Empire itself, at the Reichstag in Regensburg.[10] This step, com-
mented the constitutional historian Heinrich von Bünau at the
time in a memorandum for the Saxon government, "may be
deemed the greatest imaginable political coup [Staatsstreich] on
the part of the House of Austria, but more than that, the slip-
periest step the Reich could take." It threatened to "change and
disrupt the whole structure of the Reich. . . . If the [Imperial]
Estates guarantee the Sanction, they make the imperial office
effectively hereditary—a marriage portion, like the crowns of
Hungary or Bohemia."[11]

Charles had got the sanction recognized by members of the
House of Habsburg in 1722–23, and after that by sundry individual German princes. But his advisers considered formal
guarantee by the Reich to be essential if the agreement was to
hold up and to hold water. Without Reich approval, the sanction might be challenged as an unconstitutional attack on the
German liberties and as such an open political provocation. But
with a Reichstag guarantee, whoever challenged the sanction
would be violating imperial law and earn an unpleasant name
for rapacity. During the early and middle 1720s, a time of
marked religious tension in the Empire and of Protestant sabo-
tage at the Reichstag,[12] those most hostile to the Habsburg in-

[10] My account will follow that of Zwiedineck-Südenhorst, "Pragmatische
Sanction," pp. 276–341.

[11] Ibid., pp. 292–93.

[12] Andreas Biederbick, Der deutsche Reichstag zu Regensburg im Jahrzehnt nach
dem Spanischen Erbfolgekrieg 1714–1724 (Düsseldorf, 1937); Karl Borgmann, Der
deutsche Religionsstreit der Jahre 1719/20 (Berlin, 1937); Max Lehmann, Preussen
und die katholische Kirche, 1640–1740 (Leipzig, 1878), pp. 404–27, 816–31; Hugo

heritance contract were the chief Protestant princes: England-Hanover on the European scene, but in Germany especially the staunchly Protestant elector of Brandenburg and king of Prussia, who had denounced the sanction as contrary to the "preservation of the Evangelical religion and the European common weal." At the imperial court there ruled, according to a Prussian note to London in 1724, "great ambition and greed for despotic authority in the Reich, in religious as in political matters." Endorsement of the sanction would "establish forever the already predominant power of the House of Austria, and to give over any chance of preserving the freedom of the Estates of the Empire, and the evangelical faith, from slavery and oppression."[13]

In the later 1720s, however, friction between England-Hanover and Prussia (and Frederick William had little love for his cousin George) helped cool religious tensions in the Empire.[14] The Emperor Charles, also, showed himself to be accommodating in a matter close to the Prussian king's heart, namely, the rights of his own house to inherit the Rhenish duchies of Jülich and Berg. For Charles knew well enough that the electors of Bavaria, Saxony, and the Palatinate all had their eyes on parts of the Habsburg inheritance, perhaps even on the imperial orb itself. Court circles at Vienna concluded that Prussian support was indispensable for sustaining the Pragmatic Sanction. "If the Emperor does not have Prussia on his side," went the word from Vienna to imperial ambassador Count Friedrich von Seckendorf at Berlin in June 1728, then "what Elector or Prince of the Empire can be counted on, without the outlay of extravagant sums, to help him? . . . So the closest possible alliance with Prussia is the only means for the preservation of peace in

---

Hantsch, *Reichsvizekanzler Friedrich Karl Graf von Schönborn, 1674–1746* (Augsburg, 1929), pp. 239–64.

[13] Zwiedineck-Südenhorst, "Pragmatische Sanction," pp. 281–83.

[14] Heinrich Schilling, *Der Zwist Preussens und Hannovers 1729–1730* (Halle, 1912).

the Empire and the maintenance of the arrangement for the Succession."[15] In a secret treaty made at that time, Frederick William agreed on Prussia's behalf to acknowledge the Pragmatic Sanction. Another important breakthrough came in March 1731, when England-Hanover also agreed to support the sanction, in return for Charles' renunciation of his plans for a commercial company operating out of Ostende in the Austrian Netherlands.

A secret conference held at Vienna in the spring of 1731 determined that it was now time to take action on the imperial stage, to achieve formal guarantee of the sanction by the Reichstag. But as this began, the French began to organize an anti-Habsburg, anti-sanction party including the electors of Bavaria, Saxony, the Palatinate, and Cologne, all of whom saw opportunities at least for blackmail, surely for territory, maybe for imperial ascent, thus creating a remarkable situation in which these Catholic electors of the empire were aligned against the emperor, who consequently was wholly dependent on the Protestants. The unserious archbishop-elector Clemens of Cologne was bought back that summer; he betrayed his Wittelsbach brother in Munich in return for the emperor's promise of Liège and a permanent annual subsidy beginning with a down payment of 200,000 gulden. But it was clear enough in the minds of high officials in Vienna that without active support from the Protestant king of Prussia, there could be no guarantee of the Pragmatic Sanction and so of the Austrian succession by the German imperial diet and estates. That was the position in the summer of 1731.[16]

The Habsburg succession thus became linked with the religious excitement aroused that summer among Protestants at Regensburg and elsewhere by the proceedings of the arch-

[15] Zwiedineck-Südenhorst, "Pragmatische Sanction," pp. 286–87. The author of this language was probably Count Wurmbrand, then vice-president of the Reichshofrat.

[16] Ibid., pp. 287–88; Martin Naumann, Österreich, England und das Reich 1719–1732 (Berlin, 1936), pp. 166–85 and passim.

bishop of Salzburg and by the Protestant Petition of the 19,000 which turned up in the hands of the corpus evangelicorum in June. But despite the preoccupation of the emperor and his advisers and some political historians with the notorious Pragmatic Sanction itself, the fundamental question it raised for the Empire was a broad constitutional one, and a genuine one: whether a Habsburg emperor, strengthened by this dynastic arrangement, would still carry out his function as broker of German politics, as go-between and accommodator of the interests and the conflicts among the German princes, as defender of the basic laws of the Empire and thus of the German liberties. The emperor needed to show how valuable a function this was, and also, that he could be trusted with it. This was no time to seem a bully, let alone act like one. And in the especially sensitive public area of religous conflict, such as the one provoked by the disturbances in alpine Salzburg, it was no time to seem a bigot, either. It was the time to be an honest broker.

Moreover, although the success of the emperor's dynastic and German policies required keeping the allegiance of the Prussian court, or at least not alienating it, not to antagonize the archbishop of Salzburg was also important, for fear of "driving Salzburg into the arms of the Bavarians," a possibility that seems to have given the councillors in Vienna serious and unremitting concern. At first glance it is not easy to say just why Salzburg mattered to them so much as it seems to have done. To be sure, the archbishop of Salzburg, although the emperor had no more love for him than Frederick William had for his Welf cousin in London, was after all Catholic Primate of Germany, with a claim on the loyalties of the Catholic party at Vienna, personified in the Jesuit father Vitus Tönnemann, confessor to the emperor. The archbishop was also director of the Imperial College of Princes, with very useful procedural powers at the Reichstag.

More important, probably, was a regional consideration; for not only were the Bavarian Wittelsbachs currently the most adamant and most ambitious opponents to the Austrian succession plan: since time out of mind the House of Wittelsbach had challenged Habsburg predominance in the southeastern corner of Germany, and it would do the Habsburgs no good at all to see Salzburg join Bavaria in a territorial bloc—especially one that linked Bavaria by way of Firmian's Salzburg with his native Tyrol and the Italian plain and the Habsburg family interests there. Moreover, the elector of Bavaria was executive secretary—*Kreisauschreibender Fürst*—of the Bavarian Circle of the Empire, and to him therefore Salzburg, as member of that imperial circle, had constitutional recourse in matters respecting its security. Consequently the current religious crisis might well put Salzburg at the disposition of Bavarian interest.

Bavaria and Saxony in 1731 were the main challengers to the Habsburg inheritance plan, as they proved also to be when the emperor died in 1740. Charles had to keep Prussia from turning to Saxony, and Salzburg from turning to Bavaria. This might happen if Reich politics returned to dangerously polarized confessional blocks. The position of Prussia was by far the more important, but also more treacherous, because, although the Roman Catholic elector of Saxony and king of Poland was a leading rival for Maria Theresa's inheritance, the Protestant Saxon government in Dresden and its delegation at Regensburg were titular head of the corpus evangelicorum of the Empire and signed the corpus's official statements, in Saxony's name, at the very top of the list of Protestant princes and electors.[17] Consequently, Prussia's long ambition for Protestant leadership in Germany threatened, by this peculiar link, to undermine its pledge to support the Habsburg inheritance plan, to the degree that religious passions might rise. Where the faith was imperiled, Frederick William could hardly show himself to be less Protestant than the king of Poland.

In so complex and sensitive a position, the religious troubles

---

[17] For this problem generally Adolph Frantz, *Das katholische Direktorium des Corpus Evangelicorum* (Marburg, 1880).

in the Salzburg archbishopric were more than a routine political irritant. They became a serious problem for imperial politics. At first the ministers at Vienna tried to hush the matter up. Salzburg for its part, already ostentatiously in touch with Bavaria about its security problems, demanded support from the emperor. At the end of July a delegation including the dean of the cathedral arrived in Vienna seeking special audience, to ask for an imperial statement denouncing the rebellious mountain peasantry and for imperial military help in controlling them. (Otherwise, it was suggested, might the trouble not spread to the Austrian province of Carinthia?) A privy conference of Austrian state councillors met on August 16 to consider the matter, under the chairmanship of Prince Eugene of Savoy, who was still the most influential figure in imperial politics, possibly excepting the emperor. The conference decided to muster some troops unobtrusively on the border with Salzburg, to prevent the infection of Carinthia from the Salzburg disturbances and to be ready for such other missions as might become necessary. Imperial emissaries at Regensburg were ordered to head off any Salzburg efforts there to enlist Bavarian assistance. And the archbishop of Salzburg was to be warned in tough language that the emperor expected him to meet any and all just complaints on the part of his subjects with open justice, so as to undercut rebelliousness at home and hostile publicity abroad.[18]

Two public imperial proclamations followed directly. The emperor ordered the city council of Regensburg "to direct its citizens and clergy wholly to refrain from interference in and misdirection of foreign subjects," activity that was prohibited by the Religious Peace of 1555 and by the Peace of Westphalia, "lest in the disguise of an anachronistic religious enthusiasm

---

[18] Zwiedineck-Südenhorst, "Pragmatische Sanction," pp. 299–300; SLA EA 84/108: Korrespondenz mit dem Kaiser . . . Ankunft des kaiserlichen oö. Geh. Rates von Gentilotti . . . Beschwerde des Corpus Evangelicorum . . . 25 Juli [1731]–2 Oktober 1732, fols. 5–68.

[*unter dem Deckmantel eines unzeitigen Religions-Eyfers*], events be brought about, from which there could result serious disturbances and even bloodshed." That order called attention to what by now hardly anybody doubted anyway: that Protestants at Regensburg somehow had a hand in the disturbances in the Pongau. At the same time the emperor made a declaration to the subjects of the archbishop of Salzburg, reminding them that it was his, the emperor's, obligation as lord, judge, and keeper of the peace to warn against actions that violated "natural and imperial laws [*die natürlichen und Reichsgesetze*]." They must return to peaceful ways. If they had legitimate complaints against the archbishop, religious or otherwise, they were free to make, and need not fear making, direct written representations (read the proclamation), to *Us*, to the emperor, for rightful remedy.[19]

Such language was clearly not what Salzburg had been hoping for, and the imperial edict was not even published in the archbishopric, to the great annoyance of the government at Vienna. Salzburg continued to send in reports of the bloody rebelliousness of the mountain districts, interspersing these with requests for military assistance. But Salzburg's Chancellor Rall persistently refused to publish the imperial proclamation, telling the emperor's privy conference that publication would encourage the dissidents to reverse field once more and claim they were loyal Catholics all over again; the archbishopric had had enough of that, said Rall, and maybe Austria will have had enough of it too.[20]

Both Vienna and Salzburg, however, held to the position that what was going on in the Pongau was civil disorder, not religious: Vienna so as to suppress the dangerous confessional connotations, Salzburg to refute claims by the corpus and the Protestant courts that the peasants were entitled to the safe-

---

[19] Johann Jakob Moser, *Reichs-Fama*, vol. 10 (Frankfurt/M., 1732), pp. 34–38; Gärtner, *Chronik*, pp. 113–15.

[20] Gärtner, *Chronik*, pp. 238–48.

guards of the Peace of Westphalia, specifically including the right of free emigration and the Triennium, the three years' allowance for the orderly disposition of property. But nobody else was persuaded of this notion, or not enough to say so. The confessional nature of the disturbance, the *ius emigrandi*, and specifically the grace period became the main subject of expostulation at Regensburg and in the Protestant capitals and press. On this issue, Catholic opinion in the Reich was all but silent.

Repeated warnings reached Vienna from Berlin and Regensburg that Prussia was being urged to break ranks on the Habsburg inheritance question and revert to a partisan Protestant position unless the rights of the Salzburg Protestants, and specifically a right to free emigration, were upheld. Saxony was close to winning Prussia over to the enemy camp, reported Baron von Bartenstein, an aggressive court figure perennially at the vortex of Habsburg house politics.[21] The corpus evangelicorum had to be silenced, Prussia's drift toward Saxony had to be halted, and the danger of a confessionally partisan Protestant block must be reduced. But on the other hand, there were mutterings in Catholic political circles that the emperor was acting soft on heresy. To stop all this, insisted the imperial minister at Regensburg to his government, required a clear declaration from Salzburg that the right of emigration would not be refused or diminished.[22]

That conclusion marked the end of Austrian efforts to minimize or to localize the Salzburg problem in the imperial context. At the end of September an Austrian contingent with three companies of dragoons and nine of infantry, some three thousand soldiers in all, entered Salzburg and took up positions in the mountain districts.[23] During October the emigration

[21] For Bartenstein's dismissal as a condition for Maria Theresa's recovery of her inheritance after the Succession War, Mack Walker, *Johann Jakob Moser and the Holy Roman Empire of the German Nation* (Chapel Hill, 1981), pp. 152–60.

[22] Zwiedineck-Südenhorst, "Pragmatische Sanction," pp. 293–306; Moser, *Reichs-Fama*, 10:38–61.

[23] Josef Mayr, *Die Emigration der Salzburger Protestanten von 1731/32: Das Spiel der politischen Kräfte* (Salzburg, 1931), pp. 26–27. There are tables of the Aus-

patent was drafted in Salzburg; the emperor got a copy on the twenty-sixth; it was dated the thirty-first and published on November 11. On November 24, the undomiciled single men and women were rounded up by the Austrian troops to be taken across the border; their long, pitiable, and conspicuous winter trek across Germany began. Then on November 29, the deadline for the Salzburg domiciled families was extended until the following April. The whole problem would have to be alive at least until then. Meanwhile, the resolution for formal endorsement of the Pragmatic Sanction by the estates of the Empire was coming up in December.

The success of this resolution in the Reichstag depended wholly on the support of Brandenburg-Prussia, as the first deliberations at Regensburg showed. Among the important principalities, only Prussia stood firmly behind the emperor and the Pragmatic Sanction. The electors of Bavaria, Saxony, and the Palatinate all flatly opposed the guarantee, and Hanover dithered. At precisely this moment, Frederick William's delegation reintroduced the issue of the Salzburg Protestants, telling the imperial commissioner at the Reichstag that inasmuch as the emperor's warnings to the archbishop had been without effect, he must expect retaliatory measures by Protestant princes against their Catholic subjects, "so that they, too, will have to evacuate in mid-winter without money or the bare essentials of life." The Prussians intimated that a favorable resolution for the Habsburg inheritance might depend, "pro conditione sine qua non," on a positive solution to the confessional confrontation in Salzburg. The emperor's commissioner begged his principals in Vienna to put an end, somehow, to all the outcry generated by the situation of the Salzburg Protestants, which had made his mission at the Reichstag all but impossible.[24]

Now events began to move very quickly, at Vienna, and

---

trian soldiery in Salzburg in SLA EA 84/108, fols. 439–45. The senior officers in this force were all Catholic, junior officers mostly Lutheran.

[24] Zwiedineck-Südenhorst, "Pragmatische Sanction," pp. 312–13.

even at Regensburg. The conference of ministerial bigwigs in Vienna reconvened on December 27 and decided to send a special emissary to Salzburg with more tough talk. By refusing to publish the imperial proclamation of August directed at the Salzburg Protestants, Firmian was to be told, the archbishop had failed in his duty. His abrupt emigration order, by failing to allow for the orderly disposition of property, had violated the Peace of Westphalia and had provoked Protestant hostility at a most unfortunate time. Salzburg must lie low at the Reichstag, must not respond to Protestant abuse in kind, because of the growing danger of confessional polarization there and in Germany at large. But most significantly, Salzburg should "extend its hand to willing emigrants." For, if the Salzburg Protestants were to depart voluntarily, that would take the wind out of the sails of then corpus evangelicorum and other militants.

This demarche was given for delivery to Johann Franz Gentilotti, a former Salzburg court chancellor (from 1716 to 1729), now Austrian privy councillor, who was summoned to a personal audience with Charles VI to receive an additional "oral statement" for private transmission from the emperor to the archbishop (who was peremptorily greeted in Gentilotti's presentation letter as *Hochwürdiger Fürst, Lieber Andächtiger*, rather than the wordier but warmer customary salutation), a message that Gentilotti duly and orally delivered in February. He also made a vigorous speech to the cathedral chapter at Salzburg bearing on all these points, accompanied by some finger waving about the state of pastoral care and attention in the mountain districts.[25]

Meanwhile the Austrian ministerial conference met with its ambassador, Count Seckendorf, who had come from Berlin with a formal messsage from the king. Seckendorf for months

---

[25] For the Gentilotti mission, Gärtner, *Chronik*, pp. 348–51, which follows the chapter protocols; also SLA EA 84/108, materials of January and February 1732; and Georg Loesche, *Neues über die Ausrottung des Protestantismus in Salzburg 1731–32* (Vienna, 1929), pp. 13–14. On Gentilotti's background and qualifications, see Johann Sallaberger, "Die Trientiner Familien Firmian und Cristani di Rallo," *SMB* 42 (1981), 1–3, 10–12.

had been urging Frederick William to bring the Salzburg Protestants to East Prussia, and the meeting at Vienna again linked
that issue directly with the Pragmatic Sanction. Bavaria and
Saxony were lost, they decided, and maybe also Cologne, despite the expensive sweetener that Archbishop Clemens had
got. All these Catholic princes were trying to drive a wedge
between the emperor and the Protestant electors. And now,
this most inopportune hue and cry over the Salzburger was
working for them and ruining chances for the Habsburg inheritance plan. Archbishop Firmian had gone too far; he must
come to terms with the Protestants with respect to the emigration rights of the Salzburger—and in a manner that would
place and keep him under obligation to the emperor. Above
all, Fredrick William of Prussia must not be given the shadow
of a cause to doubt either the emperor's loyal friendship or his
support for the king's own perennial inheritance project, the
Jülich-Berg duchies. The emperor's written comment on the report was "Quoad hoc placet Undt dass nie anderst als durch
Vermitlung geschehe," which I take to mean, Approved, but
this must happen only through our mediation.[26]

The resolution to guarantee the Habsburg inheritance was
brought before the three Reichstag colleges—electors, princes,
and towns—during the second week in January 1732. First it
passed the princes (presented there by Salzburg as director),
then came the electors and the towns. The elector palatine did
not appear at the proceedings at all. Bavaria and Saxony protested, and Bavaria walked out. On the night of January 11–12,
the precious approved text was sent home to Vienna, where it
got formal imperial endorsement dated February 3. On the day
before that, February 2, Charles from Vienna inscribed a personal letter to Frederick William at Potsdam, thanking him for
his indispensable support for the Pragmatic Sanction.

The emperor's letter of appreciation on this score was signed

[26] Zwiedineck-Südenhorst, "Pragmatische Sanction," pp. 314–15. The report
of the conference is dated January 18, 1732; it is not apparent when it took
place. Events were outrunning administrative procedures, in any case.

at Vienna February 2, exactly the day when the king at Potsdam issued his formal invitation to the Salzburg Protestants and declared them under Prussian protection. Ten days after that, Frederick William made his own marginal note of obligation to Archbishop Firmian. Some circumstantial evidence, as Henry David Thoreau said of only one trout in the milk, is very strong. February 23 was another date of circumstance and portent. On that day Francis, duke of Lorraine, Maria Theresa's consort, son-in-law of the emperor and himself now emperor-to-be, arrived in Potsdam as a station on a tour he was making of European capitals and possibly bearing the emperor's appreciative note of three weeks before. For on that day the king read the note. "Answer him," he scribbled in the margin, "much obliged."[27]

And on that busy February 23, the Prussian Mennonites were banished from the kingdom.

Leopold von Ranke, following his notably Prussian political nose through the events surrounding the Reich guarantee of the Habsburg inheritance in 1732, remarked that "a monument to the political arrangement that brought this [guarantee] about was the settlement of the Salzburger in East Prussia." The canny Austrian historian of the sanction, Hans von Zwiedineck-Südenhorst, made a lighter comment, or rather perhaps, a like comment in a more derisory Viennese mode: that the story of this fusion, through imperial politics, of two such categorically different matters as the Salzburg emigration and the Pragmatic Sanction guarantee, belonged under a special heading: "Humor in History." Ranke thought that the main agent for this linkage was Seckendorf, who as Protestant imperial ambassador to Prussia was "one of the most influential men in

---

[27] "Solle sehr obligirt antworten": quoted by Zwiedineck-Südenhorst, "Pragmatische Sanction," p. 317. For accounts of the duke of Lorraine's visit to the Prussian court, see David Fassmann, *Leben und Thaten Friderici Wilhelmi, Königs von Preussen,* vol. 1 (Hamburg, 1736), pp. 426–34; and Salomo Morgenstern, *Über Friedrich Wilhelm I.* (n.p., 1793), p. 134.

Germany at that time."[28] No doubt Seckendorf's agency was at least a catalyst of the arrangement. Hovering about the contexts of all three courts one senses, also, the presence of Prince Eugene of Savoy, aged but impregnably influential, who was idolized by Frederick William, and to whom the achievement of the Pragmatic Sanction was a career's ultimate goal (and who commanded and supplied the Austrian detachments in Salzburg).

In any case the connection among these events was not an accidental one, historically random and arbitrary, or even humorous: not in the imperial context. It was precisely the business of the Holy Roman Emperor to mediate terms of accommodation between interests such as those of the archbishop of Salzburg and the king of Prussia. The issue of the Pragmatic Sanction, in 1731–32, was whether the House of Austria could, and would carry out such business of the Holy Roman Empire.

The displacement of the Salzburg Protestants was therefore effectively settled upon in January and February 1732, between the Reichstag endorsement of the Pragmatic Sanction and the Prussian Patent of Invitation. Now it remained to finish the business as expeditiously and as neatly as possible. The Prussian colonial commissioner Göbel met with the Salzburg ambassador Zillerberg in Regensburg early in February, to make practical arrangements.[29] The main obstacle remaining to swift consummation was the problem of the three years' grace: the Triennium, to which, under all law and in good conscience, the emigrants were entitled, together with the right to take the proceeds of the sale of their property out of the archbishopric. The corpus evangelicorum in Regensburg, constitutional lawyers all, insisted on this right and spoke with the voices of the Protestant countries of Germany and most of Europe, by virtue

[28] Leopold von Ranke, *Zwölf Bücher Preussischer Geschichte*, 2d. ed., vols. 1–2 (= *Sämtliche Werke* 26–27; Leipzig, 1878), pp. 137–40; Zwiedineck-Südenhorst, "Pragmatische Sanction," p. 322; Wagner, "Politische Aspekte," pp. 92–100.
[29] Mayr, *Emigration*, p. 97.

of the territorial and dynastic arrangements of the empire. The archbishop of Salzburg for his part, although since the preceding autumn he had effectively lost all control over the matter, insisted again that his plaguey Protestant subjects were actually rebels, or if not rebels, then radical religious sectarians, who therefore had no claim on these confessional guarantees or the support of genuine German Protestants. But as the April 23 deadline approached, nobody was quite sure what his government would do when it arrived, or what reaction it might provoke in the Pongau. The Austrian regiments, however, were still stationed in the archbishopric.

During February and March, the English, Danish, and Prussian crown representatives in Regensburg and Vienna all emitted bursts of indignation at Firmian's mistreatment of Protestant subjects and what they deemed his stubborn defiance of imperial law.[30] On March 1, Frederick William formally instituted constitutional retaliation, warning the Catholic cloisters and endowments within Prussian jurisdiction to expect serious reprisals if the archbishop of Salzburg persisted in his wrong behavior. Prussian Catholics in response begged Firman to desist.[31] Other Protestant princes followed, and so did the Protestant kings, and then the corpus evangelicorum as a whole.[32] Public opinion, or at least published opinion, grew increasingly excited; no Protestant authority cared now to seem slack in this matter. The emperor publicly urged the archbishop to behave in a constitutional manner. In a private letter to Firmian (without formal salutation and signed "your friendly friend, Carl"), he begged the archbishop to understand that he, the emperor, was feeling a lot of pressure from "foreign and domestic

[30] Moser, Reichs-Fama, vol. 11 (1732), passim.

[31] Gärtner, Chronik, pp. 212–15. To a plea from Catholic Halberstadt, Salzburg replied that the inborn love of justice of the king of Prussia was too well known to allow suspicion that he might mistreat his loyal Catholic subjects. For the indistinct legal status of Repressalien and Retorsionen, see Walker, Moser, pp. 315–19.

[32] Moser, Reichs-Fama, 11:733–67.

powers, princes, and estates; sharper threats from one day to the next." The Protestant reprisals in the making would affect many thousands of loyal German Catholics, wrote friendly Carl, and could bring about "a complete disruption of the domestic peace and other harmful consequences." For these consequences he, Firmian, would be responsible and must expect the blame.[33] Prince Eugene, too, kept letters in the mail to the archbishop about the provisioning, mustering, and exercising of the Austrian regiments stationed in Salzburg.[34] Meanwhile, possibly to the archbishop's surprise and certainly his further annoyance, he got little or no support from his Roman Catholic colleagues of the Empire. For when he asked the three ecclesiastical electors—Trier, Mainz, and Cologne—to support his position at the Reichstag in Regensburg, they mumbled and delayed and finally replied, all of them, that it was best in such sensitive matters to rely on the emperor to do his constitutional duty.[35]

In the last weeks before the St. Georgi deadline, however, a solution to the constitutional snag began to form, and it was the one intimated by the Gentilotti mission. Unlike the corpus in Regensburg, it now appeared, but like the king and the archbishop, the Protestant peasants themselves were not interested in the Triennium. They were ready to go now. Well then, wrote emperor to archbishop, you can allow the Triennium to those who invoke it, which must satisfy the Protestant estates; but where the peasants are willing to leave before then, why, let them go, and above all impose on their departure no conditions "by which the *emigrations-werkh* might now be made more difficult."[36] And so the emigration came to pass—indeed, by

[33] SLA EA 84/108, fols. 403–6. The emperor's letter is private, not countersigned, and uses the informal pronouns "ich" and "Sie." The signature is "Ewr Ldn freundwilliger freundt, Carl."

[34] Ibid., fol. 430ff., from "Ewer Dienstwilliger Freund, Eugenio von Savoy."

[35] Gärtner, *Chronik*, p. 265.

[36] "Wodurch das emigrations-werkh nun wurde beschwerlicher gemacht." SLA EA 84/108, fols. 400–406 (April 7, 1732); similar language characterizes fols. 490–491 (May 16, 1732).

that time, early April, it had already begun. The families lined up peaceably in columns to be counted and to pay their emigration tax to the Salzburg authorities, then to be counted again and collect travel money from the Prussian commissioners, and so to be dispatched to Lithuania. They went so peaceably that the Austrian soldiers could be brought home early, well before the "emigrations-werkh" was finished. That was a saving; they were not needed there now and they might be useful elsewhere (in Poland, say, where a confrontation over the royal succession to August of Saxony was impending). A meeting of the Catholic representatives at Regensburg in June concluded that by his intervention with the archbishop of Salzburg, the emperor had drawn the teeth of the corpus evangelicorum, removing any serious risk of coordinated Protestant retaliations on an imperial scale.[37]

In Vienna, however, anxiety was still in the air, for two main reasons: first, the undiminished importance of keeping the loyalty of the Prussian king, which remained at risk at least until the migrants were resettled, all financial arrangements were complete, and the de facto transaction was ratified by the two principals themselves; and second, the ongoing danger of Protestant infection of Austrian crown lands, and possibly other Catholic territories, by the example of the spectacle of the migrating Salzburger. Complicating and aggravating the situation at court in both respects was a characteristic political division creating stalemate in Vienna, between a party centered in the privy conference around Prince Eugene which thought in terms of secular reason of state, the security of the succession, and the need for Prussian support, and which abhorred religious strife accordingly; and the Roman Catholic party at court represented by Father Tönnemann, the imperial confessor, who warned against the spread of heresy in Austria and the Empire which might result from religious indifference, and

[37] Memorandum dated June 13, 1732, from the "Dominicaner-Kloster": Moser, *Reichs-Fama*, vol. 12 (1733), pp. 443–48.

who corresponded regularly and confidentially with Rall in Salzburg.[38]

The emperor early in July turned from the Austrian court to a constitutional body of the Empire, the Reichshofrat, for a prompt resolution of the confessional issues there, citing the danger of delay, *"ob periculum in mora."* He needed a resolution within two weeks which would smother religious restlessness and offend neither Frederick William nor Firmian. The Reichshofrat committee too stalemated along confessional lines and gave Charles no useful formal guidance, irresolution that may have been the sensible position.[39] But the question of delay did not involve only expeditious and tranquil prosecution of the "emigrations-werkh." The issue was pressing in July because the emperor was to meet with the two principal parties, Frederick William of Prussia and Leopold Firmian of Salzburg, in August and September.

These successive summit meetings exemplified the emperor's intermediatory rôle. With them he concluded an arrangement whose terms, though, had already been largely decided upon, at least so far as the fate of the exiles was affected, and which actually satisfied the concerns of both Father Tönnemann's and Prince Eugene's parties at Vienna. The meetings

---

[38] Wagner, "Politische Aspekte," pp. 98–99. Correspondence from Tönnemann is scattered throughout the Salzburg records of imperial relations in SLA EA 84/108. The murky figure in Vienna who reported to Rall the purported confidential views of Tönnemann, of the papal nuncio, and the privy conference, whom Mayr (*Emigration*, p. 134) calls "den kaiserlichen Minister Deleau" and whom Carl F. Arnold (*Die Ausrottung des Protestantismus in Salzburg unter Erzbischof Firmian und seinen Nachfolgern*, vol. 2 [Halle, 1901], p. 5) calls "den Salzburgischen Geschäftsträger in Wien Theodor de l'Eau," seems to me through orthographic ambiguity and a double play on the name to have been a Graf Seeau, member of the same Traunstein family as the director of the Austrian Salzkammergut mines, and very likely the one who backed the wrong horse in the Austrian succession crisis and was sent "nach Temesvar zur ewigen Gefangenschaft": Const. v. Wurzbach, ed., *Biographisches Lexikon des Kaiserthums Oesterreich*, vol. 33 (Vienna, 1877), p. 302.

[39] The Reichshofrat resolution of July 18 and surrounding materials are also in SLA EA 84/108, passim, so presumably Rall was kept fully informed.

produced no substantial changes; in effect they were public rat-
ifications of the arrangement, reached in separate meetings,
each under direct influence of the emperor. It seemed possible
that Frederick William might be looking for further concrete
rewards in return for his support of the Pragmatic Sanction,
but there is little evidence that he did, and he is sometimes
blamed because he did not. It is hard to imagine, however, that
the matter did not come up.[40] In ceremony and in public report
the two meetings—the one with Frederick William and the one
with Firmian—were strikingly different. The emperor took his
annual cure at Carlsbad during July, and the Prussian king had
been expected to wait upon him formally there; but instead
Charles went to Prague on the twenty-sixth, and first met with
the king informally outside Prague, where he had gone ostensibly to hunt, on the twenty-eighth. Charles then returned to
Prague, and three days later, August 1, Frederick William entered the city, incognito, but accompanied by imperial ambassador Seckendorf, the Netherlands ambassador to Prussia, his
chief foreign policy adviser (and Austrian pensionary) General
Grumbkow, and by a number of other Prussian high court officials.

The king was met by his hero Prince Eugene in a mere six-
horse *Parade-Wagen*, their meeting being incognito, and he remained in Prague for four days, taking his meals as guest of
the emperor. When the king left, the emperor made gifts to all
his entourage, including a solid gold tobacco box, complete
with pipe-packer and -scraper, for Frederick William himself.

---

[40] But here the testimony of Gärtner, *Chronik*, pp. 361–62, is chronologically
confused and probably speculative: "Und indem der Kaiser zur Aufrecht-
haltung der pragmatischen Sanction die Freundschaft und dem Beystand des
Königs suchte, benutzte dieser die Gelegenheit, vom Kaiser zu verlangen, dass
er die Religionsbeschwerden der Protestanten gegen Salzburg nach deren
Wunsche entscheiden möchte. Der Kaiser beschloss, dies Sache einigen seiner
Räthe zum begutachten zu übergeben," and Gärtner goes on to the Reichshofrat discussion, which however had taken place some weeks before the
meeting.

The emperor also awarded him some residuary rights in East Frisia, having to do with the Jülich-Berg inheritance, which were promptly announced at the Reichstag. We are not told what gifts—if any—the incognito king made to his hosts, or what discussions of the Salzburg question, if any, took place.[41]

From Prague the emperor traveled to Linz, and Archbishop Firmian made hurried preparations to meet him there, not incognito but in all pomp and splendor. At the beginning of September he sent three shiploads of his service ahead, with eighty-two persons, eighteen horses, three coaches, and necessary kitchens, confectionaries, and cellars. He himself left Salzburg on the ninth, with his chief courtiers and officers, and on the eleventh drove to his audience with the emperor, accompanied by all three coaches, each drawn by six horses, carrying his court, and a dozen pages and lackeys trotting alongside, a spectacle that seems to have evoked some caustic comments from the citizens of Linz. In the anteroom Firmian asked the court chancellor to be received with the honors due to an imperial elector, which of course Firmian was not, but which Frederick William was, although the king, traveling incognito, had waived these honors. After an initial quarter-hour of politeness with the emperor, including an invitation to hunt the next day, the archbishop was turned over to Empress Elizabeth, a Protestant-born princess of Braunschweig, as it happened, and on top of that, aunt and godmother to the betrothed bride of Crown Prince Frederick of Prussia.

The hunt (both princes dressed in forest green with gold embroidery) was a failure, the stags having broken through the lines of beaters, so that only one beast was driven within range

[41] Fassmann, *Leben und Thaten*, 1:471–79. Droysen, *Geschichte der preussischen Politik*, pp. 162–67, 171, describes this meeting wholly in the context of the Jülich-Berg succession issue and claims that Frederick William was betrayed by the emperor there (which therefore justified the seizure of Silesia by Frederick II in 1740), but Droysen concedes that the king himself did not feel ill-treated at the time.

of the emperor, who graciously invited Firmian to dispatch it. Then to dinner, which after some bows and gestures involving fingerbowls and towels, they took in red velvet armchairs. The "current Salzburg situation" entered the conversation between courses, just before dessert, apparently; but what was said about it I cannot tell. Dessert arrived; there was more stage business over fingerbowls and towels; and then the horns blew, Firmian took his leave, and the emperor rode off to try his luck in the field alone. Another audience with the emperor on the fourteenth lasted a whole half-hour, and the archbishop left the following day, having distributed 2,372 gulden imperial in tips to imperial and local courtiers and officers. Any imperial gifts Firmian or his entourage may have received, apart from that one stag, are not recorded.

Meanwhile Chancellor Rall had been engaged with the Austrian chancellor Sinzendorff, together with the ubiquitous Baron Bartenstein, the latter being present this time, it appears, in his capacity as Privy Officer for Petitions [Geheime Bittschriften-Referent]. Sinzendorff remarked stuffily that since by now Firmian had proved himself to be "schon eifrig genug" in religious matters—quite zealous enough—it might be time for him to remember that he was a prince as well as an archbishop, and to think about the welfare of his state and the Empire and to stop arousing the ire of all the Protestants. Rall retorted that he could hardly act in more statesmanlike a manner than he already had. After more wrangling the chancellors agreed that Salzburg would issue an proclamation affirming the emperor's position on the confessional rights accorded by the Peace of Westphalia and their application to the emigrants' case.[42] This amounted to a rude imperial scolding and an ultimatum to the archepiscopal chancellor.

So much for the contrasting ceremonials, reflecting as they did the political styles of these two contemporary eighteenth-

---

[42] Gärtner, *Chronik*, pp. 371–79.

century courts.[43] Frederick Williams's tight-fisted ceremonial of parsimony was as studied a political representation as Firmian's elaborated extravagance. Whatever Frederick William may or may not have achieved with his penurious incognito imperial attendance, Firmian got little enough for his exhausting and costly one. For while the king of Prussia and elector of Brandenburg still had cards to play and debts to call in imperial politics, the archbishop of Salzburg had nothing better to offer than grudging agreement to do what the emperor wanted him to do: to complete his side of the arrangement and put an end to confessional posturing and irritation.

The sometime Protestants of the Pongau were by this time— by September 1732, fifteen months after the Petition of the 19,000 had surfaced at Regensburg and only ten after the emigration patent—safely out of the way, in Prussian territory. To the south, however, sources of infection or reinfection remained, not only in Salzburg but also in Austrian crown territories. This second, Austrian territorial and confessional aspect of the problem (after the imperial political one) was a serious concern for the emperor and his house. The truth is, it had been right along.

The confessional topography of German Austria after the Thirty Years' War was much like Salzburg's: there were no longer worrisome numbers of Protestants among Austrian no-

---

[43] The point here has less to do with decisions that may have been reached at these meetings than with the manner of their representation: thus the gossipy sources cited above for my accounts. David Fassmann had been an intimate of the king at the Tabakskollegium, along with Morgenstern and Gundling, though he had left the court in 1731; he made a business of publishing accounts of historical and contemporary court doings in a mixed mode of deference and scandal which was exceedingly popular. Corbinus Gärtner, or Maurus Schenkl, who wrote under the name of Corbinus Gärtner, was a Benedictine monk, doctor of both civil and canon law and ecclesiastical councillor, was not a contemporary but a chronicler whose knowledge of the intimate detail of the Salzburg court in Firmian's time is unmatched. Mayr, *Emigration*, describes the Linz meeting with Firmian, pp. 164–66; oddly, he makes no mention of the Prague meeting with Frederick William.

bles or townspeople, but the religious situation in the mountains was unstable, especially in the Salzkammergut of Styria and in Carinthia, both alpine districts that adjoined archepiscopal Salzburg on the east and south. There in the long, high, inaccessible valleys, as along the Salzach, Protestant-like residues or "inclinations" remained among the rural inhabitants, quiescent unless stirred up by counter-reforming zeal on the part of domestic religious authorities, or by Protestant evangelism or outside excitement.[44]

Concern over possible infection of this population had been Vienna's first reaction to the Salzburg religious troubles when they began in 1731. That seems to have been the reason for arresting the Schwarzach delegation in August and extraditing its members to the cellars of the Hohensalzburg, and later for sending troops to seal off Austria's borders with the archbishopric, initially as a quarantine measure.[45] In January 1732 orders were made to prohibit any Salzburg emigrant from stopping over in Austrian crown lands: the columns Prussia was about to organize were to be kept isolated and in motion. Later, in January of 1733, the Prussian colonization patent was banned from Austrian territory, and all circulating copies were ordered confiscated.[46]

The Austrian government's focal concern was for the mines of the Salzkammergut, lying just east of the Salzburg valley of the Salzach (as the Bavarian mines at Berchtesgaden lay just to the west of it). The miners there, like the Dürrnberg miners across the border in Salzburg, had latent Protestant tendencies that were a constant worry, *ob periculum seductionis*, in the official phrase: "on account of the danger of infection," for the memory of the emigration of the Dürrnberger and of the notorious miner-evangelizer Schaitberger in the 1680s was vivid in

[44] Hans v. Zwiedineck-Südenhorst, "Geschichte der religiösen Bewegung in Inner-Österreich im 18. Jahrhundert," *AÖG* 53 (1875), 460–67.

[45] SLA EA 84/108, fols. 75–88 and passim.

[46] Ernst Nowotny, *Die Transmigration ober- und innerösterreichischer Protestanten nach Siebenbürgen im 18. Jahrhundert* (Jena, 1931), pp. 11–12.

official minds. Sporadic Catholic missionary work among the Austrian miners had achieved little, partly because such effort was constrained by fear that working at it too seriously would produce a backlash, in the form of civil violence or of emigration, either of which would bring the mines to a halt and interrupt their revenues.

When the Pongau disorders began, the Salt Office set up its own patrols on the border but got into disagreement with the government at Vienna over how to treat religious dissidence in the workforce. For the Austrian director of mines, *Salzamtmann* Ferdinand Graf Seeau, who was in regular contact with authorities in Salzburg, took the position that the way to get free of the problem was expulsion, Firmian-style; religious troublemakers could be sent to the frontier regions to the east, he pointed out, to the formerly Turkish territory around the middle Danube and Transylvania. The government at Vienna, though, fearing the effects of such deportations on salt revenues, ordered the Salt Office to leave this matter in the hands of religious authorities; and these, at Vienna's direction, pursued a milder and more conciliatory policy designed to keep the mines in operation. After all, ran the instructions, all of us believe in the divinity of Christ and in the Bible and so forth.[47]

The Austrian policy of quarantine and conciliation succeeded in 1732; a smattering of emigrants left the Salzkammergut, but not in serious volume until later in the decade, when religious policy turned more severe as an aspect of a deliberate program of "transmigration" to southeastern Europe. Even then, the Austrian program was aimed at the superfluous peasantry, not the valuable mineworkers. The possibility of infection, however, was a realistic concern in 1731–32, no mere bureaucratic hobgoblin; and infection was in fact one source of the last episode of the Salzburg emigrations of 1731–32: a new outbreak of confessional dissidence in Dürrnberg leading to the emigration

[47] Carl Schraml, *Das ober-österreichische Salinenwesen vom Beginn des 16. bis zur Mitte des 18. Jahrhunderts* (Vienna, 1932), pp. 473–79.

of about eight hundred people in November 1732, almost all of them miners or members of miners' families.

There was no family connection, no regular intercourse, no social analogy between Salzburg's Dürrnberger miners around Hallein and the Pongau mountain farmsteaders, except insofar as both were susceptible to Protestant religious influences. Their conditions of daily life, their occupations, the organization of their work, their very names were quite different.[48] Because the Dürrnberger were fiscally more important and harder to replace, so their official treatment was more circumspect. Religious authorities were ordered to treat the miners with extreme discretion, to avoid any confrontations, and to stay utterly silent about the unrest to the south. When that emigration began, the Pongau emigrants were forbidden to stop over at Hallein, which they were bound to pass on their way northward. But groups of Dürrnberger began to meet, in taverns and out-of-doors in secret, to sing and preach in Protestant idiom, as the emigrant columns passed in the summer of 1732. The Salzburg mine administration began to look about for an alternative labor supply, although the miners on the Austrian side and on the Berchtesgaden side seemed just as vulnerable—even if the Salzburg recruiters had been welcome there, which emphatically they were not.[49]

By midsummer 1732, a substantial number of Dürrnberger—

---

[48] See the list published in Wilfried Keplinger, "Die Emigration der Dürrnberger Bergknappen 1732," *MGSL* 100 (1960), 201–8.

[49] Except where otherwise cited, the narrative of the Dürrnberg emigration relies on ibid., pp. 171–201; with some detail taken from Gärtner, *Chronik*, pp. 380–99 (but here again Gärtner, though richly informed, is careless with chronology). Franz Ortner, *Reformation, Katholische Reform und Gegenreformation in Salzburg* (Salzburg, 1981), pp. 258–61, denies that the Dürrnberger got mild treatment for fiscal reasons and goes so far as to argue (as he implies also respecting the Pongau emigrants) that many of them falsely professed Protestantism so as to be eligible to emigrate for gain. But the Dürrnberger are the one group of emigrants which the Salzburg government made any apparent effort to halt or to recover: the odd instance of the Dutch sea-worms, subjects of the exchange mentioned in note 50 below.

the government thought about two hundred—had set their minds on emigrating. In June, a delegate went north from Dürrnberg, to Regensburg and Nürnberg, to look into possible assistance and opportunities; he was directed by the Saxon ambassador to the ambassador from the Netherlands (of Prussian officials there seems to have been no sign, nor mark of interest in these Dürrnberger), from whom he got letters offering generous settlement conditions in the Netherlands and suggesting a departure date eight weeks thence.[50] The estates of Zealand had sent an emissary to Germany in May, hoping to pick up some peasants to settle their coastal regions; but the mountain farmers, by then under the protection of the king of Prussia, were not available. Now the dissident Dürrnberg miners, in whom Prussia showed no interest, did become available, and a private contract was promptly signed by the ambassador of the States General at Regensburg for the transportation of eight hundred Dürrnberger to the Netherlands.

The Dutch resettlement turned out to be a disaster.[51] The Salzburg immigrants were divided up among Dutch towns who used many of them as lease labor, which they performed unwillingly or not at all. They found themselves lumped together with Quakers, Mennonites, Anabaptists, Calvinists, and other such alien folk of alien nationalities and faiths, about whom they complained bitterly. Meanwhile the disappointed

[50] Keplinger, "Dürrnberger Bergknappen," p. 175, says that the delegate, Tobias Wörndl, went to Nürnberg. It is hard to see how he would have met these ambassadors there, but the Nürnberger (and that was Josef Schaitberger's foster home) certainly played a role in the Dutch connection: the Nürnberg ambassador at the Reichstag wrote a pamphlet defending it when Salzburg authorities tried to discredit it: *Neue Beschreibung der Holländischen See- oder Pfahlwürmer* (Regensburg, 1733), written to refute *Umständlicher Bericht von der Plage der See-Würmer, in den Pfahlen an den Deichen in Holland und Seeland* (Regensburg, 1732), both cited and described in Artur Ehmer, *Das Schrifttum zur Salzburger Emigration 1731/1733* (Hamburg, 1975), pp. 8, 76. I think Wörndl was in both places, to meet with both commercial and diplomatic Dutch agents.

[51] For Dutch-language materials on the Salzburg emigration to Seeland, Ulrich Gäbler, "Österreichs Protestanten und die Niederlande im 17. und 18. Jahrhundert," *JGPÖ* 98 (1982), 211–39.

native Dutch compared them unfavorably with Huguenots, saying that the Huguenots at least had brought money with them, but these Salzburger brought only disease. Most of the immigrants left during the following year, some straggling back to Regensburg in hopes of getting home. The Regensburg town government tried to hurry them along, but the Salzburg government by this time did not want them back, and gradually they dispersed.

The dispersion of the Dürrnberger marked the effective end of the Salzburg emigration, though some repercussions continued outside the archbishopric. In October 1733, a shipment of forty-two scatterlings who had been collected at Augsburg were shipped to the Oglethorpe colony called Georgia, in North America. About a hundred more followed during 1734–36.[52] Meanwhile in Berchtesgaden, the salt-mining district in Bavaria just west of Dürrnberg, some hundreds of families caught the fever, declared their Protestant convictions, and asked permission to emigrate. Hanoverian recruiters had been active there, and early in 1733 close to a thousand Berchtesgadener—peasants and artisans but apparently few if any miners—were allowed to leave, most of them settling in Hanover.[53]

On the eastern or Austrian Salzkammergut side of the

[52] Gerhard G. Göcking, *Vollkommene Emigrations-Geschichte von denen aus dem Ertz-Bisthum Saltzburg vertribenen und in dem Königreich Preussen grössesten Theils aufgenommenen Lutheranern*, vol. 2 (Frankfurt/M., 1737), pp. 528–60; C. Franklin Arnold, "Die Salzburger in Amerika," *JGPÖ* 25 (1904), 238–55. Almost none of the German-speaking settlers in Georgia listed as Salzburger in the earl of Egmont's list published by George Fenwick Jones, "German-Speaking Settlers in Georgia, 1733–1741 (based on the Earl of Egmont's list)," *Report: A Journal of German-American History* 38 (1982), 35–51, can be traced individually to the 1731–32 Salzburg emigration lists. However, a substantial proportion bore surnames that do appear among the Salzburg emigrants or are phonetically similar; probably they were not members of the main 1731–32 movement but splinters from other nearby dates or localities.

[53] For the emigration of the Berchtesgadener, see Fritz Klein, "Die Einwanderung der Berchtolsgadener Exulanten in Kurhannover 1733," *HG* 34 (1980), 159–74; and Göcking, *Emigrations-Geschichte*, 2:413–18.

Salzburg emigration route (where copies of the Prussian colonization patent had been seized and prohibited), Salzamtmann
Seeau at Gmunden ordered some twelve hundred declared
Protestants in 1733 either to abjure or to emigrate; when they
chose to emigrate, though, they were forbidden to do so after
all, having been officially determined instead to be illicit sectarians, thus ineligible for the emigration right protected by the
Peace of Westphalia. Subsequently Austrian policy, quite probably influenced by the success of the migratory transfer of
1731–32 between Salzburg and Prussia, turned to favoring
Protestant emigration from the alpine regions to its own new
eastern territories, especially Transylvania and Hungary. This
transmigration program for Austrian Protestants, carried out
entirely within Habsburg territory, seems to have caused little
stir among north German Protestantism; eventually the practice would even include non-Catholic salt miners, on grounds
that there was plenty of labor available in the mountains anyhow.[54] In Bohemia in 1732, a large group of bondsmen or
serfs—*Leibeigene*—attempted to follow the Salzburg example
with a petition to emigrate to Prussia. Six thousand is the traditional number associated with this enterprise, which came to
nothing; their association was broken up by Austro-Bohemian
authorities who determined it to be a political disturbance with
Hussite connotations.[55]

Thus in an imperial context the main business of the
Salzburg emigration was completed by the end of 1732. Some
odd details worth mentioning remain. The archepiscopal treasury eventually paid Austria 80,000 gulden imperial for the use
of Prince Eugene's regiments, a sum that happens to match

---

[54] Nowotny, *Transmigration*, pp. 1–37 and passim; Schraml, *Salinenwesen*, pp.
476–79; Grete Mecenseffy, *Geschichte des Protestantismus in Österreich* (Gratz,
1956), pp. 198–206.

[55] Eduard Winter, *Die tschechische und slovakische Emigration in Deutschland im
17. und 18. Jahrhundert* (Berlin, 1955), pp. 101–30; Göcking, *Emigrations-Geschichte*, 2:418–25.

quite precisely the amount Salzburg collected as emigration tax.[56] This circumstance is probably an accident, even though it does contains another troutlike anomaly: that in July 1730, Firmian had ordered all income from the emigration tax be earmarked for the expenses of the imperial cameral court at Wetzlar.[57] Some other detail of the transaction is more direct. Chancellor Rall, who did the heavy part of the business, subsequently received a decoration from the Prussian king for being helpful with the financial arrangements: a Prussian "Gnadenkreuz de la génerosité." In February 1740, Rall was raised to the *Reichsfreiherrenstand*, the rank of imperial baron, by Emperor Charles VI shortly before his death. Neither Rall nor his master had much luck at the Vatican, however, which court, like the German archbishop-electorates, kept all possible distance between itself and what it called, in a letter of 1733 to Rall, "these deplorable events," events it blamed on inadequate pastoral attention to the alpine population.[58] So there was to be no papal order for Cristani di Rallo, and no cardinal's hat for Firmian either.

The affair did decidedly little good to the Catholic cause in the Empire, while it gave a distinct stimulus to the morale of German political Protestantism. The garrulous trimmer Baron Pöllnitz in 1734 wrote a postscript to the journal of his 1730 visit to Salzburg, an inserted note about the dispersion of these

[56] Hans Widmann, *Geschichte Salzburgs*, vol. 3, *1579–1805* (Salzburg, 1914), pp. 430–31; Paul Dedic, "Nachwirkungen der grossen Emigration in Salzburg und Steiermark," *JGPÖ* 65–66 (1944–45), 71–134; SLA EA 74: Miszellanea: Verzeichnisse der Emigranten, Undatierte Korrespondenzkonzepte Christanis [emigration tax summary figures], unnumbered.

[57] Gärtner, *Chronik*, p. 417: one of his characteristic free associations.

[58] "Istessi deplorabili avvenimenti . . . che forse ne sia stata la principal causa [sic] la grand' ignoranza nelle cose della nostra Santa Religione di quell' incolta, e rozza Pente. . . . Riflette ancora Sua Beat. che estrema povertà di quegli Abitanti può averli spinti ad abbandonare la vera Fede, per godere nei Paesi eretici quella piu facile sussistènza, che era [lei?] fatta sperare dai Nemici della Religione et della Chiesa." SLA EA 73: Miszellanea: 1731–39 (May 9, 1733); Rall's defensive reply followed on June 18, 1733.

unfortunate subjects of the archbishop of Salzburg, "like the Israelites," to Prussia, "where the King (as I must concede, Catholic though I am), has received them with a magnanimity and a charity truly Christian and royal." That king had spared neither pains nor expense "to let the Universe see that if France is the asylum of unhappy Kings [James Stuart and Stanislav Lesczynski], the States of Prussia are the asylum of oppressed peoples."[59] As for the Pragmatic Sanction, it collapsed utterly in 1740 when Frederick William's successor, Frederick (who came to be called the Great), joined the sanction's other enemies and seized Maria Theresa's richest province for Prussia.

These political considerations and effects of the imperial context lay, of course, quite outside the social and cultural experience of the emigrating peasantry who furnished the material. The migrant farmers' experience was distinct, engaging their own everyday lives, choices, mistakes and opportunities. But even their everyday lives were contained and confined within a political frame of power and necessity.

[59] Pöllnitz, who though Catholic had been raised at the Prussian court, was made master of ceremonies to Frederick II in 1740. His host at Salzburg in 1730 had been the grand equerry at that court, a Graf Truchsess-Ziel, distantly related to the Graf Truchsess von Waldburg who had launched the Retablissement program in East Prussia. Charles-Louis [=Karl Ludwig] Pöllnitz, Mémoires, contenant les observations qu'il a faites dans ses voyages, vol. 2 (Liège, 1734), pp. 98–103.

CHAPTER FOUR

THE MIGRANTS

In the representations contemporaries made and saw of the Salzburger emigration, written and pictorial, two items consistently appear: the book and the child. There are formal and historical reasons why these two signs were used. The book of course signifies the Evangelical emphasis on scripture and on faith, as contrasted with Catholic emphasis on church and works. It was an explicit confessional sign. The child signified the family, following certain highly publicized earlier cases in which the children of emigrated Protestants had not been allowed to follow their parents out of the archbishopric and out of the church. This was not an issue in 1731–32, when no effort was made to retain children, but it had been at the time of the Deferegger expulsion of the 1680s, and possibly in the incidents that had aroused activity by the corpus evanglicorum at Regensburg around 1730. But these two representations are also substantially correct in their joined identification of the elemental social, cultural, and economic unit of the emigrant Salzburg peasantry: the farmstead family.

The reason for this domestic ecology is topographical at the outset. The valley of the Salzach and its tributaries in the Pon-

gau and the Pinzgau is rarely more than a few hundred yards
wide, usually less than that, and the surrounding mountain
slopes are steep and broken by deep wooded ravines and rocky
torrents. In alpine husbandry it was not economically feasible
to trudge about among widely scattered arable strips, as did
the villagers of lower Germany; the cost in time and strength
would be too great; and so Salzburger Bauern families lived not
in compact villages with dispersed family strips, but in dispersed family dwellings on compact farmsteads, each with one
or two outbuildings for livestock and storage, surrounded by
the narrow meadows and steep pastures upon which the family economy was founded. For members of one family to visit
another already meant a slow and difficult trip; for members of
many families to gather at a social location like a church or a
tavern was harder still.

The wide scattering of single-family economic units over the
mountain slopes thus made it difficult for the farmers to attend
and receive regular religious services and difficult for the official church to organize them; it made for reluctant and inadequate pastoral care and missionary attention. But also, and
consequently, these conditions enjoined family devotions as
the main religious exercise of the population; and for family
devotions, the book is a basic implement—indeed, more than
an implement: in the domestic context, it is a holy ritual object,
a totem.[1] In Salzburg these ritual objects were kept in secret
places, at least when priests or policemen were about; later, in
Prussian Lithuania, they were put in prominent display—at
least, when pastors or policemen were about. Book and family
were essentially bound together, as contemporary perceptions
and representations of the emigration recognized.[2]

---

[1] Hartmut Lehmann, *Das Zeitalter des Absolutismus: Gottesgnadentum und
Kriegsnot* (Stuttgart, 1980), pp. 170–71, emphasizes the place of family devotions in the formation of the patriarchal Protestant family.

[2] See for example the illustrations in Angelika Marsch, *Die Salzburger Emigration in Bildern*, 2d ed. (Weissenhorn/Bayern, 1979), passim; or the observations
in Gerhard G. Göcking, *Vollkommene Emigrations-Geschichte von denen aus dem*

Some modern scholars of anthropological bent have noticed unusually high literacy rates among early-modern alpine populations. None of their explanations, strangely, has paid much attention to religious practices. One good recent survey and interpretation of alpine ecology, by Pier Paulo Viazzo, argues (much as I have done early in this book) that the alpine peasantry, despite its geographical situation, was culturally not at all isolated from Germany and Europe, and that a main reason for this was the frequency of seasonal migration or temporary emigration in search of work.[3] Salzburg police too would surely and strongly have agreed with that observation as a start, and with explicit reference to books and to literacy, not vague cultural notions of exposure to a bigger outside world. They examined migrants, and examined their attics and mangers and floor joists specifically for devotional books, and devotional books were almost always Protestant books: books suitable for family devotions which therefore challenged and replaced the organized religious exercises and confessional discipline of the church. The books they found among the Salzburger peasantry were much the same ones that appeared in middle-class Protestant households in lower Germany: Arndt's *Paradiesgärtlein* and *Wahres Christentum*, Lutheran bibles, Habermann's *Gebetbuch* (the ubiquitous "Habermändl"), Schaitberger's *Send-Briefe*. Some of these were new and therefore recently imported, but many were a century old and more.[4]

Ertz-Bisthum Saltzburg vertribenen und in dem Königreich Preussen grössesten Theils aufgenommenen Lutheranern, vol. 1 (Frankfurt/M., 1734), pp. 593–95; or [Christoph Sancke], *Ausführliche Historie derer Emigranten oder vertriebenen Lutheraner aus dem Ertz-Bisthum Saltzburg*, 2d ed. (Leipzig, 1732), pp. 1–5.

[3] Pier Paulo Viazzo, *Upland Communities: Environment, Population and Social Structure in the Alps since the Sixteenth Century* (Cambridge, 1989), pp. 121–52, and earlier studies cited there.

[4] Rolf Engelsing, *Der Bürger als Leser: Lesergeschichte in Deutschland 1500–1800* (Stuttgart, 1974), pp. 56–78; Göcking, *Emigrations-Geschichte*, 1:204–9. Inventories of books found in peasant possession are scattered through all the materials catalogued under "Reformation" in the Konsistorialarchiv, Salzburg (see Bibliography). Notably absent is any sign of the so-called *Hausväterliteratur* of-

The relation among alpine literacy, family devotions, and Protestantism (or heresy), though quite apparent to contemporaries of both major faiths, may have evaded modern scholarly notice on account of squeamish reluctance to assign greater bookishness, and hence greater merit in the learned view, of one confession over another. Another reason is that the prevailing strategic postulate for sociologically or anthropologically inclined study has been the "community," as in the rural village, where it has not been the "class," as in the industrial city (what influence the competing category of gender may have on these strategies is not apparent at this writing).[5] Neither of these categories is really appropriate to the experience of the population of alpine Salzburg. The notion of class has some modified application to the conditions revealed by the emigration, as will appear shortly in the case of the undomiciled farmhands. But there is no real evidence, despite the efforts and the assumptions of historians, of communal institutions or practices among the Salzburger before the *Societäts-Contract*—literally, the social contract—subsequently made between the Salzburger settlers and the Prussian crown in 1736. There are plenty of signs, in demographic materials and in patterns of debt, for example, of family alliances and obligations; and marriage ceremonials were public occasions. But the basic social unit engaged in these was the family, not the community, let alone the state. Unlike townspeople, the Salzburger Bauern knew hardly any social division of labor, or common property rights, or representative institutions. Communal forms of worship, other than official ceremonies held in the towns, were of course prohibited, and evidence of multiple-family

---

ten associated with this society around this time, but these investigators were not looking for this and might not have mentioned it anyhow.

[5] Thus Viazzo relates migration with heresy (*Upland Communities*, pp. 137–38), and literacy with migration (pp. 139–43), but he shies away from relating literacy with heresy (read: Protestantism). The Salzburg example also conflicts with Viazzo's adoption of the village community as a base unit of study and even an "ecosystem" (pp. 26–30).

peasant religious exercise, though assiduously sought after, is really quite scarce and speculative. Even the scriptural clause "where two or three of you are gathered together in My name" does not appear in any of the Salzburg materials I have seen. Neither have I found any invocation of ancient rights or tradition, on the part or on behalf of the Salzburg Protestants. Their claims against the archbishopric were framed on the legal language of the imperial Peace of Westphalia, as provided by the corpus evangelicorum and in Prussian documentation, and on property rights and deeds registered (most of them quite recently) with the Salzburg civil courts.[6] The 1731 rural assemblies at Schwarzach had no apparent precedent and represented no corporate tradition; but they were a step in the direction of one, as meetings called ad hoc to establish collective resistance to the archbishopric's invasion of the sanctified spheres of household devotions: family, book, and child.[7]

The family farmstead or *Gut*, therefore, was the basic unit of the emigrants' experience and so it must be for any social account of the emigration. In the Salzburg uplands this farmstead was called the *Gut*, and in Prussian Lithuania, where the unit of resettlement and administration was also the family farmstead, it was called the *Bauernhof* or *Bauernstelle*. All contemporary sources for the emigrants' history employ this elemental unit of economic, social, and cultural identity, and so shall I. About two thousand such families emigrated from Salzburg in 1732. Table 6 shows the distribution by district of the farmsteads in Salzburg left unoccupied and subsequently offered for sale.

---

[6] GStA PK Rep. 5 Tit. 21 Nr. 15, vols. 1–3: Acta, wegen Liquidation der von den Salzburgern in ihrem Vaterlande zurückgelassenen Forderungen . . . 1735–38.

[7] Thus Gerhard Florey remarks that it was the seizure of the books, and thus the bases of household devotions or *Hausandacht*, which caused the socialization of the Salzburger Bauern in the Schwarzach assemblies: "Die Schwarzacher Versammlungen der Salzburger Protestanten im Jahre 1731," *MGSL* 114 (1974), 245–46.

Table 6. Unoccupied farmsteads, after emigration

District	Abandoned farmsteads	Domiciled emigrants	Average emigrants per household
Golling	3	37	12
Abtenau	32	243	8
Saalfelden	64	667	10
Gastein	50	487	10
Taxenbach	77	550	7
Rauris	45	166	4
Zell/Mittersill	6	539	9
Grossarl	47	512	11
Werfen/Bischofshofen	346	3961	11
Goldegg/St. Veit	268	2838	11
St. Johann	254	2266	9
Wagrain	302	1521	5
Radstatt	382	3096	8
Totals	1,876	16,288	9

Source: Josef Brettenthaler, "Die Wiederbesiedlung," in *REP*, p. 174; KAS 11/69e: Reformation. Emigrationspatent 1731. Verkauf der Emigrantengüter im Beisein des preuss. Gesandten. Verzeichnis der Güter 1734–38, etc. The number of farmsteads is based on a list of properties for sale published by the Salzburg government. The owners had emigrated, and so the list does not include properties already sold or which officials failed to note; thus Table 6 suggests but does not show family size. For an alternative table, see Otto Kerschhofer, "Die Salzburger Emigration nach Preussisch-Litauen," *MGSL* 116 (1976), 177–78.

About 80 percent of the emigrant population were *Angesessene* such as these: domiciled family members or close relatives settled on the farmsteads; the other 20 percent were the undomiciled *Nichtangesessenen*: servants, laborers and the like who might be employed and reside on a Gut but who were not permanent members of the household.[8] These proportions

---

[8] Wolfgang Menger, "Die Salzburger Emigration nach Ostpreussen in den Jahren 1731 und 1732. Eine medizinisch-geschichtliche Studie zum Umsiedlungsproblem," *MGSL* 98 (1958), 93.

among the emigrants mirror those of the resident peasant population as a whole.

No close examination of this great scattering of farmstead families is feasible, not even an anonymous arithmetical mean, let alone a sphere of domestic experience. Moreover I propose to move quickly from a general outline of the emigration movement, to the condition and experience of families that composed it; so I have abandoned or suppressed some customary statistical standards of means, averages, and representativeness. I wish to use the experience of individual families to locate factors that warrant further investigation of a more collective kind on a more general stage.

My preliminary research target will be one administrative district, or *Gericht*, there being no communal or parish groups relevant to the upland peasantry. The St. Johann district is a plausible choice: an area of relatively heavy emigration, in which the proportion of undomiciled to domiciled (about 20%) matches that of the entire emigrant population, as does the ratio of domiciled emigrants to abandoned farmsteads.[9] The market town of St. Johann held the archepiscopal civil administration and church, and a population of something under a hundred artisan and retailing families.[10] Scattered on the slopes around and above the valley lay about three hundred farmsteads; looking over and down from many of these the town is

[9] Computations from Brettenthaler, "Wiederbesiedlung," and Menger, "Salzburger Emigration"; for closer evaluations see also the tallies in SLA EA 79/103: Eingeschickte Beschreibungen der evang. erklärten Unterthanen, die bei den dem Kaiser extradierten Salzburger Bauern verzeichnet gefunden. 1–10 Oktober 1731.

[10] At the end of the eighteenth century, St. Johann town had 87 artisan and commercial establishments representing 30 different trades. In the district but outside the town then were 287 *Bauerngüter*, and in rural trades a handful of sawyers, millers, cobblers, and two weavers. L. Hübner, *Beschreibung des Erzstiftes und Reichsfürstenthums Salzburg*, vol. 2, *Das Salzburgische Gebirgland* (Salzburg, 1796), pp. 431–36. This matches very closely the evidence for conditions in the 1730s.

plainly visible, but it is laborious and slow to reach overland. In all these respects the St. Johann district is not uncharacteristic of the emigration population and topography; what makes it a useful district to examine is the survival of unusually informative administrative records, generated by the expulsion, about the Bauern of St. Johann.

These records name over two thousand individuals who emigrated from the Gericht St. Johann; from among these I have been able to identify and confirm 227 *Bauerngut* households, with the full name of the family head, name of the Gut (all Güter bore names, and many still bear the same names, for Gut names were not family names, nor did families assume the names of Güter they currently owned). This is still too many to examine closely, and besides, I propose to trace the emigrant experience from Bauerngut in Salzburg to Bauernhof in Prussian Lithuania. This is possible for the 89 of the 227 St. Johann Gut owners—about 40 percent—who can also be located as full farmers in Prussian Lithuania: 80 of them as domain peasants or *Amtsbauern* on family-sized shareshold farmsteads held of the crown's leaseholder, and 9 as freeholders, usually *Kölmer*, on farms purchased outright. This is still too many for the detailed work of reconstruction; moreover, I propose also to look closely at a particular area of resettlement, and these 89 families were widely scattered over seventeen districts (*Domänenämter*) of the East Prussian resettlement area. But 51 of these families, more than half, were concentrated in the southeast Lithuanian districts of Budwetschen, Dörschkehmen, and Grumbkowkeiten; and 30 families, about a third of them, were settled the Budwetschen district (*Amt*), of the Insterburg province (*Hauptamt*).

This "core" group thus consists of the thirty families that can be followed quite closely in the administrative, fiscal, and genealogical records, with enough familiarity to be clearly recognizable, despite, for example, wide differences among the various records in the spelling of names and places, and to identify family relationships of marriage, wardship, inheritance, and debt. These families are identified not because they are arithmetically representative of the emigrating population (though they are in no obvious manner eccentric), but because they can be examined and their family histories reconstituted in this manner, whereas a larger group, whose identities and continuities cannot be recognized or many of whose members fade out of the records, could not. Their histories establish and illustrate the *possibilities* that existed among the Salzburg emigrant families, not the statistical *probabilities* of individual fates, a relatively unpredictive and undemocratic procedure as will appear, and in this, incidentally, they more nearly resemble the *Exulanten* of popular tradition and family anecdote than they do any sociological or statistical mean. But they are not hypothetical types or models, either: they have names, they existed, and their existence rests on normal historical documentation and logic. Here are a few; and from these I shall proceed laterally to examine more generally some of the issues and characteristics that the thumbnail family histories suggest.[11]

[11] To cite individual bits of data used to reconstitute these family histories would clutter text and notes intolerably. All may be found by routine research in one or more of the following sources: Hermann Gollub, *Stammbuch der ostpreussischen Salzburger* (Gumbinnen, 1934); Horst Kenkel, *Amtsbauern und Kölmer im nördlichen Ostpreussen um 1736* (Hamburg, 1972); Herbert Nolde, "Alphabetisches Register der Personennamen in den Salzburgischen Emigrationslisten" (typescript, Göttingen, 1972, available at the Geheimes Staats-Archiv, Berlin-Zehlendorf, and elsewhere); Fritz Schütz, ed., "Haupt-Register von denen sämtlichen nach Preussen gekommenen Saltzburgischen-Emigranten, so wie selbige in denen von des Tit. Herrn Geheimten Rath Osten angefertigten Rechnungen sich befinden. Gumbinnen den 20ten August 1756" (Gumbinnen, 1913, available at the Geheimes Staats-Archiv, Berlin-Zehlendorf); GStA PK XX. HA Rep. 100A Nr. 153, I–II: Salzburger Emigrantenlist; GStA PK Rep. 5 Tit. 21 Nr. 15, vols. 1–3: Acta, wegen Liquidation der von den Salzburgern in ihrem Vaterlande zurückgelassenen Forderungen . . . 1735–38; GStA PK XX. HA Pt Budweitschen II–III: Prästationstabellen, 1734, 1739; "Verzeichnuss Derer Zu freyem Kauff feil stehenden Güter Der Emigranten," in KAS 11/69e: Reformation. Emigrationspatent 1731. Verkauf der Emigrantengüter im Beisein des preuss. Gesandten. Verzeichnis der Güter 1734–38, etc.; SLA EA 79/103: Eingeschickte Beschreibungen der evang. erklärten Unterthanen, die bei den vom Kaiser extradierten Salzburger Bauern verzeichnet gefunden. 1–10 Oktober 1731.

Matthes (or Martin) Anlasser is a fairly straightforward case. He was forty-seven years old at the time of the emigration, more than twenty years older than his wife, Regina Merckenschweiger, which was unusual; and he was owner of the Gut Zimmerberg, which included six *Jauch* of plowland (about five U.S. acres), along with substantial pastureage.[12]

Regina and their baby daughter, Maria, emigrated with Matthes, and he was able to carry a moderate amount of cash out of the archbishopric, declaring 175 kfl. (gulden imperial), of which the authorities took 18 kfl. as emigration tax, rounding out the standard 10 percent. Gut Zimmerberg was valued at 1,165 kfl. (the tax valuation was customarily the price at which a property had last changed hands, usually within the past thirty years or so), a sum that seems on the low side for a property of that size, and Anlasser ultimately was able to sell it—or rather, the Prussian commissioner Plotho was—to one Joseph Fend, his being no Pongau farmsteader name, for 450 kfl., of which 50 kfl. was paid in cash. There is no news of the outstanding 400 kfl. Joseph Fend also bought Hans Bacher's Gut Ritterhof, valued at 31,862 kfl., for 1200 kfl. which he paid in cash; possibly he bought others, as investments in land in that buyers' market. Chances are, though, judging by the relatively low assessment, that the six Jauch of plowland on Zimmerberg were not very productive.

By the time his Salzburg property was sold, Matthes Anlasser was settled in Leptuballen (or Plicken; the place appears under both names) in Amt Budwetschen, on a farm of one *Hufe*, a family farm of ordinary size previously operated by a Lithuanian, in the domain leasehold; this was probably around 76,600 sq m or 19 U.S. acres overall.[13] He was liable for a pay-

[12] Reckoning the Salzburg *Jauch* at about 3,600 sq m or .89 U.S. acres, like the Bavarian, Swiss, and Tyrolean *Juchart* and the Bavarian *Morgen*, but unlike the Württemberg *Morgen* or *Joch* or the Prussian *Morgen*. For these measurements, see especially Fritz Verdenhalven, *Alte Masse, Muenzen und Gewichte aus dem deutschen Sprachgebiet* (Neustadt/Aisch, 1968), pp. 15–54 .

[13] For area equivalents see note 12 above. But inasmuch as nearly all Amtsbauern were settled with one Hufe per family, the name presumably did not reflect exact areal measurement but a family unit of labor and production.

ment of 12 Prussian thaler (thlr.) or the equivalent per year for
the farm: 4 thlr. groundrent (*Hufenzins*), 4 thlr. crop share (*Get-
reidepacht*), 4 thlr. service duty (*Scharwerksgeld*). Or more exactly, the leaseholder of the Budwetschen Amt was liable for
these amounts to the Prussian crown on account of Anlasser's
farm. Two other St. Johann farmers were settled nearby: Joseph Reither's son Georg from Gut Oberhöll (the father, Joseph, had died in 1733), and Michael Pilzegger from Gut Gug-
genbichl, along with three Lithuanian families, all named
Lupp, an earlier German settler, and a shepherd.

Like nearly all other immigrant farmsteaders, Anlasser had
both debts and debtors. He told Prussian authorities that Michael Oberstaller, previously from Gut Riedling in St. Johann,
owed him 36 kfl.—perhaps an inherited debt but probably a
loan, since Oberstaller was seventeen years old and living in
Leptuballen near Anlasser. Oswald Griffenberger, Gutsbesitzer
from St. Johann, owed him 100 kfl., and Martin Merckel-
schweiger from Wagrain 50 kfl.; these two, judging by the over-
lapping family names and the even sums, were almost certainly inheritances or marriage portions on Regina's behalf.
There were claims against Anlasser, too. He owed 25 kfl. to
Barbara Kesslerin, "wife of Hans Nisslauer." (She was the
widow Kessler from St. Johann, was owed money by many
emigrants, and was remarried to the fortunate Nisslauer in
1733). Anlasser owed 50 kfl. to Rup Geyer, an enterprising St.
Johanner whose own story comes next; and he owed 100 kfl. to
another prosperous St. Johann farmsteader, Joseph Schleim-
inger. This is an unusual proportion of debt in what appears to
be borrowed cash, though no terms were named nor interest
specified. And one Maria Anlasserin—clearly a relative, probably an unmarried sister—claimed that Matthes owed her 100
kfl., presumably as inheritance and/or marriage portion.

Anlasser's young wife, Regina, had produced another child
along the road, an unusual achievement when many families
were losing theirs; and at the first Prussian head count in 1734,
there were two "servants," unmarried Salzburger without family status, also living on the farm. The Pilzegger and Reither

families were still neighbors then, and one more Lithuanian and one more Salzburg family were settled in the area. By 1739, the four Anlassers and one servant were working the farm. Matthes died, probably in 1745, without male heirs.

Rupp Geyer, 42 years old, emigrated in 1732 with his wife, Mardta Branstätter, 43, and their six daughters: Maria, Magdalena, Barbara, Ursula, Marta, and Brigitta, ages 18 years to 1 year old. Only little Ursula, 5, failed to survive the journey. Rupp left behind him the adjoining Güter called Vorder- and Mitter-Unterberg, just southwest of the town of St. Johann; he also owned mountain pastures in Grossarl, high above his farms, and a small mill in Obkirchen near to his farms. These were substantial holdings. Many farmsteaders had small mills nearby for a variety of domestic uses; but since Rup Geyer named two bakers among his debtors (one of them from some distance away in the town of Wagrain) for 20 kfl. and 30 kfl. respectively, it seems likely that he was in the business of milling in a small way, selling flour for income. With six unmarried daughters, two of them already in their teens, if for no other reason, money was almost certainly often on Rup Geyer's mind. Money was in his pockets, too: Rup carried 300 kfl. with him out of Salzburg, acknowledged for the record, along with his large family, paying the legally stipulated 30 kfl. emigration tenth to the archbishopric. In Prussia he also filed claim to credits in the amount of 160 kfl. "on behalf of his wards" Rupert Aestlechner, Hans Treusteiner, and Martin Creutzsahler, so he was managing the estates of three legal wards as well as his own farms and mill: an honorable and a lucrative condition. And Geyer had no debts at all.

Rup and all his womenfolk, and one manservant, were promptly settled on the usual one Hufe in Auxloepen, in the Budwetschen district. He was still there in 1736; but by 1739, he had become a freeholder, a Kölmer, on no less than four Hufen in nearby Nauwigkaulen (or Kriszullen). That is to say: by this time, Rup had got enough money together to buy a quite large holding, four ordinary farms, for cash from the Prussian crown. His annual obligations were reduced proportionally. Where as a domain share peasant in Auxloepen he had been assessed at 12 thlr. per year for his one Hufe, as freeholder he was paying only 10. thlr. on four Hufen—proportionally only a quarter as much. And he had two servants, few enough, for so large an operation. But all five daughters were still on the farm to help: Maria was now 25 and the rest were coming along, but the prudent Rup so far had paid out no dowries. The Geyers' new neighbors were the Kölmer Johann Christian Loew and Georg Schönhardt, neither of them Salzburger. In fact there were no sharework peasants at all in Nauwigkaulen/Kriszullen, only freeholders. The Geyer family was making its way, in Lithuania as they had in Salzburg.

Thomas Resch—or Reck or Riecke or Röcke or Röck or even Stöck—is unique among these farm family fathers in that he was "naturally" or illegitimately born. I have seen no other illegitimately born among the Gutsbesitzer of St. Johann, which may account for official uncertainty, or indifference, about the spelling of his surname: in any case, Thomas's natural birth is an exception that points to the rule. But he was married to Katherina Lottermoser, honorably born of a family respectable enough, probably a daughter of the well-to-do Simon Lodermoser of Gut Praschlechen. Thomas owned the Gut Hinterstallen, west of the river near where *Georg* Lodermoser, possibly a brother-in-law, owned Gut *Vorder*stallen, and a half-interest in a household mill on the Reinbach, a mountain stream that flows into the Salzach across from St. Johann. All three of Thomas's children—Simon, 5; Thomas, 3; and Margaretha, 1— were legitimately born of his marriage with Katherina.

Still some oddities about the Resch household persist. Three unmarried individuals traveled with Thomas, Katherina, and their children from Salzburg, not full family members, but people who had somehow escaped the expulsion of the undomiciled in autumn 1731: Phillipp Crafft, 30, also "naturally born";

Margaretha Lodermoser, 28, spinster, legitimate; and Lorenz Lodermoser, 13, legitimate. None of these, even Thomas, seems to have carried any money with them, or at least no one declared any; nor did any claim any debts owing to them. There is no sign of who Phillipp Crafft may have been. But Margaretha and Lorenz Lodermoser were presumably relatives of Katherina's who had attached themselves to the Resch family; if, for example, Thomas senior has taken responsibility for Katherina's younger sister and brother, that may explain his favorable Lodermoser marriage and his proprietorship at Hinterstallen despite his low birth. The Resch family situation has other obscure spots; such things seem to exist in clumps. For example, among debts claimed against Thomas Resch, or Röckh or Stöck, is one made by Rosina Hamoser, 34, who claimed he owed her 60 kfl.; and this Rosina Hamoser had a two-year-old daughter named Regina Stöckhl, one of the surnames attributed to Thomas Resch.

Thomas had more trouble getting established in East Prussia, to be sure, than so formidable a figure as Rup Geyer or even the sober Matthias Anlasser. Resch is nowhere to be found in the early 1734 survey, under any of his names. But in 1736 he had a farmstead in Auxloepen, right alongside Rup Geyer; and in 1739 he had two farms, having taken over Rup's first Bauernhof when Rup went to Nauwigkaulen to take over his new big freehold there. One Resch child had meanwhile died, but the three "servants"—perhaps Krafft and the two Lodermoser in-laws—were still with him. Thomas Resch was again making his way.

The Zehendorfer-Burgschweiger case is more complicated but worth tracking for the sake of the strategies it shows to be available to the family economies. It involves three Salzburger Gutsbauern households: those of Leonhard Zehendorfer (or Leonard Zehendhofer), of Rup Schwabe, and of Rup Burgschweiger. Zehendorfer, 52, was owner of the Gut Oberpezelhof in St. Johann, an additional pasture, and a household mill; he emigrated with his wife, Anna Niederlechner, 45, and four children, and was assigned a Bauernhof in Warnalaugen (or Laucken) in the Budwetschen district, where his neighbors were three Lithuanian families, six German colonists, and "schoolmaster Metz." But this Leonhard Zehendorfer was seriously ill by then, officially *gebrechlich*, unable to work, and he died in 1733. His widow Anna was then registered, in the late Leonhard's name, with one-half ownership of a double Hufe, which she held jointly with Rup Schwabe, former owner of Gut Rössellechen in St. Johann. The widow Anna had at that time two nearly grown sons and two servants on the place; so presumably she was working the farm, probably with the help and some supervision from her neighbors the Schwabes. For Rup Schwabe himself was already 74 when he emigrated, and he also died in 1733, leaving behind *his* widow Katharina Pacher, several grown children, and the unmarried maidservant Sabina Rechnerin, 25, who had accompanied them from Gut Rössellechen. After Rup's death his oldest son Jacob stayed on the joint double-holding with his mother and the Zehendorfer widow and orphans, still listed jointly in his late father's name, at least through 1734 (very likely Jacob assumed his father's name at least for the record; that was common practice). By 1739 he was married, with two small children and three "servants," two of these probably being his grown siblings who were still attached to the family. But by this time Jacob had one Bauernstelle on his own. As for the other of the widows' pair: one Rup Burgschweiger had appeared and married the widow Niederlechner-Zehendorfer, finally replacing the late Leonhard Zehendorfer as owner and operator of the farm at Warnalaugen (Laucken). This farm therefore separated from the Schwabe place that Jacob had taken over.

Then who was this Burgschweiger? He was a widower, just the age (forty-five) of his second bride, the widow Anna Niederlechner-Zehendorfer; his previous and younger wife, Eva Stuhlebner, had died on the trip from Salzburg, leaving him with four small motherless children. In St. Johann he had been the owner of the small upland Gut Oberhelmberg, together with a household mill and half-interest in a woodlot, but he had been assigned no farmstead when he arrived in Lithuania. He had no debts (and thus probably no inheritance to share), but he claimed small irregular amounts owing him from each of five former Gut owners in St. Johann and Werfen, almost certainly unpaid back wages from work he had done on farms larger and more prosperous than his own at Oberhelmberg. Rup Burgschweiger had had to struggle for his living in Salzburg, and he got only a slow start, with little help or encouragement from the crown, in Lithuania. But by marriage he took over a farmstead, the one originally assigned to the late Leonhard Zehendorfer. The anomolous joint double-farm arrangement of widows originating with the 1733 deaths of Zehendorfer and of Rup Schwabe ended, through marriage and inheritance, with two separate farms run by two whole families.

These four stories of persistence are taken for purpose of examination from what I have called the core and not meant to be representative or typical of the emigrants. Records of failures and tragedies, except for bare mortality lists and counts, are harder to come by. But such intimate stories offer points of perception from which to see, sift, and interpret such broad summary information as the records allow. I shall focus on three such points: patterns of debt; situation of the undomiciled, the Nichtangesessenen; and the organization of the Salzburg household itself and the process of its reestablishment in Prussian Lithuania.

The core family histories suggest the complex and pervasive structure of debt among the Salzburger Bauern, and its significance for relations among the families. The bare data, assembled mainly by Prussian officials, do not allow the close study this important subject deserves, but taken together with the interpretive hints in the family histories, they clearly show that credit, expressed in money—that is also to say, debt—was a

substantial and ubiquitous component and a binder of this society, expressing economic and moral obligation. Debt was perhaps the most substantial binder among the families except for
marriage itself; and marriage and debt themselves were often
closely connected.

The records identify 559 debts claimed by St. Johann emigrants, almost all claims against other emigrants or against
their properties back in Salzburg.[14] This recorded credit network roughly coincides with the alpine peasant population itself: contained within it and mostly local. The few exceptions,
such as debtors or creditors outside this network, serve mainly,
again, to highlight the rule.[15] Credits are of several kinds:
claims on inheritance, marriage portions, unpaid wages, and
also a small fraction that can be identified as capital lent at interest (always 5%). Some sums simply represent property left
behind with relatives or neighbors by the emigrants (though I
have excluded the Güter themselves or proceeds from their
sale from any of these calculations). It is not always possible to
guess what basis of credit or debt a named sum represents,
though usually there are good grounds for inference from the
size of a debt, from the family relations between creditor and
debtor, or other contexts of the claim. These debts are spread
throughout the mountain society, where other social ligaments
are in truth hard to find. But for all their ubiquity, they do not

[14] For the debts and credits of families, the Prussian lists in GStA PK Rep.
5 Tit. 21 Nr. 15, 3:139–45; for the Nichtangesessenen, claims recorded in Kaufbeuren and Memmingen and published in Johann J. Moser, *Derer Saltzburgischen Emigrationsacta*, vol. 2 (Frankfurt/M., 1733), pp. 553–69; and Moser,
Reichs-Fama, vol. 11 (Frankfurt/M., 1732), pp. 776–86.

[15] There were ecclesiastical endowments and other funds in the archbishopric
in the business of lending money which sometimes lent to peasants at 4.5 to
5% (see KAS 11/69e), but such evidence as I have seen suggests that this practice was not common. My concern is not with the overall economic position
of the Bauern but with the significance of the credit network among them. There
is an excellent analysis of peasant debt patterns in Rudolf Schlögl, *Bauer, Krieg
und Staat: Oberbayerische Bauernwirtschaft und frühmoderner Staat im 17. Jahrhundert* (Göttingen, 1988), pp. 320–42.

point to a society or any stratum hard-pressed by debt: of the thirty core families 23 were debtors, 20 were creditors, and 13 were both; none was neither. Rather, they depict a society or economic landscape where there was little cash, and whose members were accordingly accustomed to long-term credit or debt as a usual element of their economic or familial relations.

Consider first the total numbers of debts, debtors, and creditors. The 559 debts were distributed among 363 creditors: thus most of them are single obligations, almost all within the St. Johann district. Among these, just 100 creditors were owners of Güter; and their individual claims were rather larger than those of 263 non-owners, for the claims of non-owners were commonly for back wages, or for other small sums or obligations left behind them when they emigrated. Of debtors there were 279, averaging therefore two debts apiece: fewer debtors than creditors, then, but not so many more as to suggest a heavy concentration of debt. But among these 279 debtors were 116 Gut owners, a substantially larger proportion than the 100:363 owner-creditors. That is to say, Gut owners are more likely to appear as debtors than as creditors. The amounts owed by owners, however, taken individually are small, often in odd figures, signifying claims for unpaid back wages, unpaid bills, and the like. Another substantial proportion of the total debt owed by Gut owners is quite certainly unsettled inheritance claims, especially made by female relatives or in their names. Debtors, conversely, were almost all male: there are only eleven claims made against women, mostly claims by siblings or in-laws; two or three were made against female Gut owners—there were a few of these—or against widows.

Turning now from the number of debts to the proportions in total volume of debt, and taking creditors first: among a total 45,517 kfl. reliably identified claims for or against St. Johann emigrants, 19,143 kfl. credits were held by the 100 Gut owner-creditors. Reckoning that sum together with the total number of creditors, it appears that when an owner had claims, they were on average almost twice as large (191 kfl.) as those of a non-owner creditor (263 persons claimed 26,374, averaging just 100 kfl. each). Among the claims of Gut owners, 2,052 kfl. (11% of the volume) were made by women or explicitly on their behalf. But among the claims of non-owners, 54 percent of the volume (14,268 kfl.) was claimed by women, claims that judging by their sizes and circumstances included back wages, unliquidated inheritances, or very occasionally dowries.

That is to say: women held about a third of the total obligations, a substantial stake in the structure, and most of the part held by non-owners. I say "substantial," but the credit they held also suggests that unpropertied women were relatively unlikely, for whatever reason, to collect what was owing to them, or, that they preferred to bank their capital or savings that way. Among Gut-owning creditors, women or claims made in women's names amounted to only a tenth. The latter fraction reflects the infrequency of women's ownership of farmsteads but tells little about the place of women in the structure of debt, because it is impossible to say how many of the debts claimed by male Gut owners were actually for amounts owed to their womenfolk (very few of them, however, is my impression; even married women had recognized financial standing and commonly made their own claims).

One final set of calculations helps refine the picture of women's place in the structure of finance and of family: this is to classify debts by size and then relate the sizes of debts to the gender of creditors. Of the total recorded debt (45,517 kfl.) about a thirtieth (1,492 kfl.) was made up of small amounts: 133 claims of 20 kfl. or less (thus up to about the value of two cows, as will appear), and averaging about 11 kfl. Of these 133 small claims, about a quarter (32) were registered by women. At the other end of the scale are claims of 100 kfl. or more—the value of one Morgen plowland, or pasture for two or three cattle—of which there are almost the same number, 135, totaling 25,526 kfl. and averaging 189 kfl. But of these larger claims, 52 (39%) were made by women, a much larger proportion than among the small claims; and moreover, among the large claims, the women's averaged 199 kfl. each (10,355 in all), but the men's a bit less, 183 kfl. each (15,171 in all).

As a result (returning to gender shares in total volumes): women, though seldom listed as owners of Güter, still held a greater proportion of total large-scale debt, a substantial 41 percent, than they did of the small-scale debt, of which they held 22 percent. This undoubtedly reflects the greater share of women in undistributed inheritances and probably some (other) unpaid dowries as well. Where cash did not flow, women could not collect but retained claims against holdings worked by male relatives or their families. Among all 363 St. Johann creditors, however, male and female, I find only one person who is clearly in the business of lending money. This is the widow Margarethe Neukamm, with 650 kfl. capital lent out at interest, some to her brother Simon in Werfen, some to various Gut owners in St. Johann—and 50 kfl. to the weaver Georg Engelmeyer in St. Johann town, all at 5 percent.

The emigration records have less to say about the undomiciled population that was first to leave Salzburg than about the families. These were the folk designated in the official emigration edict as "undomiciled residents, lodgers, wage workers and laborers, servants, and farmhands, of both sexes, who have arrived at their twelfth year." That neither the Salzburg nor the Prussian authorities had much more to say about them is a fact with its own significance; and most of what is to be learned about the undomiciled emigrants comes from lists made by clerks and magistrates in south German Protestant towns as they appeared there and were sent on their ways.[16] From these lists 326 undomiciled emigrants from St. Johann can be identified, probably about 60 to 80 percent of that category of folk initially resident in the district. Almost all of them were unmarried, without property; and 116, just over a third, were female. About one in five claimed that there was money

---

[16] Lists published by J. J. Moser, *Emigrationsacta*, 2:553–69, and *Reichs-Fama*, 11:776–89.

owed him or her, back in Salzburg; this might represent
clothing or other small possessions left behind, or back wages,
although there were also several claims on inheritances or marriage portions, and some indistinct claims of wards against
their guardians for property held in trust.

These were the people whom the archbishopric had been especially hasty to be rid of, and whom the Prussian officials
were less than eager to recruit.[17] Their ages and occupations
show some of the reasons why. Here are the undomiciled and
unemployed St. Johann emigrants quartered in Kaufbeuren at
the end of December 1731:[18]

Age	Number	Status or occupation	Number
1–12	8	farm/household servant,	133
13–20	67	male (*Bauernknecht*)	
21–30	142	farm/household servant,	64
31–40	63	female (*Bauernmagd*)	
41–50	23	peasant's son	7
51–60	16	(*Bauernsohn*)	
61–70	2	artisan	13
	321	wageworker	5
		other	16
			238

The occupational figures offer few surprises, but they raise a
useful question: if the undomiciled *Knechte* and *Mägde* are as-

[17] In justice be it remembered that the undomiciled were exiled late in 1731,
before the Prussian invitation of February 1732; but most of them were still
encamped or drifting about southern Germany at the end of winter and might
have been collected—indeed some were—at the cost of great effort. Of outstanding debts later claimed by Prussia on behalf of Salzburg immigrants, the
undomiciled counted for less than .25%: (Göcking, *Emigrations-Geschichte*, vol. 2
[1737], p. 340).

[18] Moser, *Reichs-Fama*, vol. 10 (1732), pp. 146–66; Moser, *Das Neueste von denen Salzburgischen Emigrationsactis*, vol. 2 (Frankfurt/M., 1733), pp. 80–97. These
do not include emigrants who had found employment in Kaufbeuren or elsewhere by year's end. The totals are unequal because many entries were incom-
plete.

sumed to be a poor and unstable social stratum of this alpine society, how is it that almost half of them were in their twenties: where had they been as children and what became of them when they grew older? Emigration and mortality offer partial answers, but there is another and more instructive one, to wit: the undomiciled were not lifelong inhabitants of an inherited social or economic or moral stratum, but rather they occupied a temporary status determined by their age and location in family development. To be sure, certain caste marks of social and moral taint appear among especially the undomiciled—illegitimate birth and unmarried motherhood, for example, appear somewhat more commonly than among the families—but the category was characteristically one of age, not caste, including young men and women from respectable Gut families and Gut expectations who had not yet entered on their inheritances or married, but who had left home and were in service on other farms. For many and perhaps even for most of them, to be undomiciled was a temporary condition.[19] But the category included most of the "peasant sons, farm-hands, and other young bucks" that the archepiscopal War Council was registering in August 1731, or was meant to include them. There was no shortage of such labor in Salzburg. It was the threat they posed to order and authority, rather than their rôle in the economy or lack of it, that was the most likely reason for the hurried expulsion of the undomiciled.

One curious feature of the official tally of the almost seven hundred undomiciled Salzburg emigrants registered at Kauf-

[19] See similar findings in Michael Mitterauer, "Formen ländlicher Familienwirtschaft. Historische Ökotypen und familiale Arbeitsorganisation im österreichischen Raum," in *Familienstruktur und Arbeitsorganisation in ländlichen Gesellschaften*, ed. Josef Ehmer and Michael Mitterauer (Vienna, 1986), especially pp. 204–6, 280–81, and in Mitterauer's "Servants and Youth," in *CC* 5 (1990), pp. 11–38; see also Peter Schmidtbauer, "The Changing Household: Austrian Households from the Seventeenth to the Early Twentieth Century," *Family Forms in Historic Europe*, ed. Richard Wall et al. (Cambridge, 1983), pp. 360–61, which shows almost identical correlation between age and servitude. Some undomiciled emigrants got married along the trail: see [Sancke], *Ausführliche Historie*, p. 212.

beuren in December 1731 is that about a third of them, despite the haste and violence with which they had been collected into columns by armed soldiers and marched out of the archbishopric, still declared that they had emigrated by their own free choice; two-thirds said they had been forcibly expelled. Conjecture over this has followed, uneasily, confessional lines, although not even partisan Catholic accounts have seriously proposed that the emigration, particularly of the undomiciled, really was a matter of free choice.[20] The most plausible single reason why so many of them declared themselves voluntary religious emigrants is that this status seemed preferable to that of an expelled rebel, reasonably enough. To be a voluntary emigrant, after all, was the status recommended by the corpus evangelicorum and other Protestant authorities; to be a rebellious subject was the status assigned them by the authorities in Salzburg. But bear in mind also that elective migration northward in search of work was nothing new to the alpine undomiciled. And we may be sure that the normal situations of the undomiciled in the alpine domestic economy were thoroughly servile, unpleasant, and precarious, whatever hopes some among them may have had for future entry into family status by marriage or inheritance.[21] Unlike the Gut owners and their resident families, almost none of the undomiciled can be traced through to Prussian Lithuania. The Prussian invitation, to be sure, was issued more than two months after the expulsion of the undomiciled, and the resettlement program, which was explicitly aimed at the families, did not get underway until later still. By that time most of the undomiciled were thoroughly dispersed and they disappear from view.

[20] Among contemporaries of the two confessions see Göcking, *Emigrations-Geschichte*, 1:230–32; Gärtner, *Chronik*, p. 223; among modern historians Peter Putzer, "Das Wesen des Rechtsbruches von 1731/32," *MGSL* 122 (1982), 314, and Franz Ortner, *Reformation, Katholische Reform und Gegenreformation in Salzburg* (Salzburg, 1981), pp. 244–46.

[21] Franz Innerhofer's novel *Schöne Tage*, 4th ed. (Salzburg, 1975), although set in the twentieth century and based on modern experience, offers a caustic remedy for any optimistic inclinations about the place of employee or lateral kin in the "whole house" of the "extended family" of alpine rural life.

The Salzburger family Gut and the East Prussian family Hof were the irreducible and basic elements of the domestic economies of both places, despite their very different topographical features and even rural technologies. The basic agricultural resource of the scattered Salzburg peasant Güter was grass: in pasture and meadow, as feed for cattle. The main product and characteristic diet of the people was based on butterfats: on milk, cheese, and milk gruels, and on meats. Cereals were grown especially on the narrow valley plain of the Salzach, on Güter owned by the wealthier Bauern there; these are easy to identify now but there were not many of them, probably not more than a score or so of some three hundred Güter in the St. Johann district, for example, although many others had small plots planted to cereals where the topography allowed. Multiple holdings were not uncommon—probably about one Bauer in ten owned or operated more than one Gut—but even in such cases the individual Güter kept their names and separate identities, as they did also when they changed hands, a frequent occurrence. Peripheral holdings such as upland summer pastures, woodlots, gardens, and even plowland were usually treated as distinct and could be separately accumulated ("besonders acquiret," in the accounts) or sold off, following family fortunes, without disrupting the integrity of the central domestic farmstead.[22]

The Prussian commissioner, Plotho and his successors, made inventories of properties left behind by Salzburg emigrants; some of these are quite detailed but too irregular to be combined directly and arithmetically into an average Salzburg Gut in all its parts. It is possible, though, to establish an approximate mean total value and then the proportions of this total which consisted in each of the several basic kinds of property;

[22] For multiple holdings and their character, see "Verzeichnuss, derer zu freyem Kauff feil stehenden Güter der Emigranten," in KAS 11/69e: Reformation. Emigrationspatent 1731. Verkauf der Emigrantengüter im Beisein des preuss. Gesandten. Verzeichnis der Güter 1734–38 etc. For turnover and tenure conditions, see the sources cited in the Prologue, above, notes 9 and 10.

from this evidence and these calculations, one can sketch a model inventory based directly on contemporary sources, an inventory that, though contrived, at least would not have surprised anybody if it had turned up on an actual list of properties of emigrated Salzburger.[23]

Following that procedure: the mean value of the St. Johann Güter listed in the emigrants' Prussian inventories was roughly 2,500 kfl.; and this agrees with recent calculations made from Salzburg administrative records.[24] Among those described in detail in the Prussian claims, just over 80 percent of their total value in turn lay in real estate or *Immobilien*, about a fifth of that value being in buildings, the rest in land. Among movable goods (the 20% in *Mobilien*), about a fifth of their total value consisted of seed (usually in the field, plus some stored cereals), two-fifths was livestock, and another two-fifths consisted of tools, implements, and household gear. Here are some of the commonest kinds of rural property in the St. Johann district and their relative values, as reported in the Prussian inventories.

Kind of property	Value in kfl.
Plowland (1 Jauch, c. 3600 sq m)	100–150
meadow (1 Morgen, c. 3600 sq m)	40–70
pasture (per head cattle)	30
woodlot	100
milch cow	10–15
calf	2–8
draft ox	10
horse	20–50

[23] My sources are the inventories in GStA PK Rep. 5 Tit. 21 Nr. 15, 1–3: passim; and Göcking, *Emigrations-Geschichte*, 1:233–34, 597–98. For the perplexed problem of spatial measurements, the most informed and reliable guide is now Verdenhalven, *Alte Masse*, and see also the tables in *Geographisches Taschenbuch*, 2 (1950), 258, and 3 (1953), 528.

[24] Brettenthaler, "Die Wiederbesiedlung," in *REP*, pp. 172–79. For descriptive material and explanation of terms, see Kurt Conrad, "Der Bauer und sein Hof," in *REP*, pp. 151–66.

Kind of property	Value in kfl.
sheep	1
wheat (bushels [*Scheffel*], in the field)	4
oats	1–2
rye	2
pease	1
barley	½
lentils	1

These values can then be distributed proportionally among the kinds of property, following the categories customary at the time, to construct a credible model Salzburger farmstead or Bauerngut.

Kind of property	Value in kfl.
Immobilia:	
House, barn, stables	450
Land: 3-Jauch plowland (1 ha.)	400
8-Morgen meadow (3 ha.)	400
pasture, 20 cattle	600
woodlot	100
Total	1,950
Mobilia:	
Live chattels (*lebende Fahrnis*)	
10 milch cows	120
2 oxen	20
7 calves	35
pigs and poultry	5
Total	180
Dead chattels (*tote Fahrnis*)	
40 Scheffel cereals (in the field or stored)	80
Implements (plow, windlass, rakes, scythes, household)	170
Total	250
Combined total	2,380

This loose reconstruction bypasses the eccentricities of individual inventories, irregularities that make them, moreover, quite impossible to combine into a mean; and it is less liable to spurious claim of precision. The amounts and the proportions within categories would have raised no eyebrows if they had turned up among the inventories of the 1730s, and probably better represents domestic realities than what might be reconstructed, say, out of the tax rolls of the city of Baltimore in 1990. Anyhow the model is quite good enough to provide a rough comparison with domestic economies in Prussian Lithuania. Its one glaring omission is that it does not include horses and wagons, which were surely a normal part of the Salzburger peasant household. In fact Salzburger Bauern with arable land often had excellent horses, noted by contemporary observers. But because the Bauern used them to transport their families and domestic goods on their journey, horses and their gear rarely appear on the claim inventories.

The legendary trek of the Salzburger from their mountain meadows to the Lithuanian plain, being legendary, belongs more properly in the next and concluding chapter. Euphoric reports of their joyful reception and support by co-religionists along the way contained impulses and served purposes of the reporters; and over against these accounts, be it recorded that nearly a quarter of the emigrants died, mostly the very young and the old among them, within two years of leaving their homes, and most of these before resettlement.[25] Most arrivals were quartered on the local inhabitants during the first winter, 1732–33, and then scattered through the southeastern districts of East Prussia, east of Königsberg and south of Memel and Tilsit. Very few went to towns—less than 10 percent, and most of these only temporarily; they were not trained or equipped for town occupations, nor had they been invited to go there. Even fewer went to noble manorial estates: relatively few rural nobles lived in the region, and most were deemed rivals or even enemies of the crown officials and domain economy. The Salzburger had not been invited to serve the East Prussian Junker, either.[26]

---

[25] Menger, "Medizinisch-geschichtliche Studie," p. 115.
[26] For the administrative and legal history of the region in the Prussian tradition, the main authorities are Max Beheim-Schwarzbach, *Friedrich Wilhelms I.*

The rural settled population on and about the East Prussian domains, into which the Salzburg colonists were now introduced among a majority population of Lithuanians, Germans, and Swiss already living there, fall into four main classes or categories. The best-situated class was that of the *Kölmer*, a collective term used to include these peasants who were essentially freeholders, who bought their land from the crown and so were free of most tenure dues and obligations. Second, sharework peasants (*Scharwerkbauern* or simply *Domänenbauern*) were families who received farmstead, land, stock, and tools from the crown and owed substantial regular obligations, through the domain leaseholder, in return. A third category were *Gärtner*, who were settled with cottage and garden plot, with fair security or by contract, most commonly on the domain Vorwerke, for which royal enterprise they provided the nucleus of a permanent labor force, and whom I shall call cottagers. Finally, there were mobile day laborers, variously named but characteristically *Losgänger*, who worked for wages whenever and wherever work was to be found.[27] Kölmer were scarce, never comprising more than about a tenth of the settled families; and at the other end of the scale, there is little more to be learned about the Gärtner or the wage laborers, who quickly disappear from most accounts. What follows pertains mainly to the sharework Bauern on the characteristic family farm of the Salzburger settlements in East Prussia.

The royal invitation of February 1732 had promised each sharework peasant settled on a farm of one Hufe (about 7.6 ha. or 19 U.S. acres) a year's family subsistence plus the following

---

Kolonisationswerk in Litauen, vornehmlich die Salzburger Kolonie (Königsberg, 1879); Rudolph Stadelmann, *Friedrich Wilhelm I. in seiner Tätigkeit für die Landeskultur Preussens* (Leipzig, 1878); and August Skalweit, *Die ostpreussische Domänenverwaltung unter Friedrich Wilhelm I. und das Retablissement Litauens* (Leipzig, 1906).

[27] Under Kölmer I include also *Chataullkölmer, Chataullbauern, Freyen*, and *Erbfreie Bauern*; under *Losgänger* also the category *Instleute*. There are good summary definitions based on the Retablissement documents in Beheim-Schwarzbach, *Friedrich Wilhelm I.*, pp. 65–66.

start-up equipment, to which for the sake of comparison I have attached approximate local cash values in the thaler (thlr.) then current in Prussia and the imperial gulden (kfl.) current in Salzburg.[28]

Equipment	Value in thlr.	Value in kfl.
2 horses	12	18
2 oxen	12	18
2 cows	10	15
Wagon, implements, tools, etc.	17	25
Seed: 30 Scheffel rye	13	20
9 Scheffel barley	3	5
20 Scheffel oats	4	6
1 Scheffel pease	1	1
Total	72	108

Strictly speaking, this land, livestock, seed, and equipment, although heritable in usage, remained royal property, and there was no assurance, or even much regularity, in what the Bauern actually received. But it will serve as an expressed norm, and in fact it matches fairly closely the recent empirical studies that have been made of East Prussian agricultural patterns of the time.[29] The family remained the basic and standard unit of work, production, property, and fiscal responsibility. Each domain peasant was bound to provide, after a three-year

[28] Text of the patent from Moser, *Reichs-Fama* 11 (1732), 698–707; for current prices in East Prussia, see Beheim-Schwarzbach, *Friedrich Wilhelm I.*, pp. 41, 392. Seed-to-crop ratio may be figured on average at about 1:3 (1 Scheffel = 55 liters = about 1.5 U.S. bushels); for seed-to-hectare ratios, see Friedrich-Wilhelm Henning, *Bauernwirtschaft und Bauerneinkommen in Ostpreussen im 18. Jahrhundert* (Würzburg, 1969), p. 87. For Prussian weights and measures, see, in addition to Verdenhaven, *Alte Masse*; H. Roeder, *Zur Geschichte des Vermessungswesens Preussens* (Stuttgart, 1908).

[29] Especially those by Henning, in *Bauernwirtschaft*, pp. 47–82 and passim, and in other excellent studies.

grace period, an equivalent of two days' work per week for the leaseholder on the Vorwerk in summer and one day per week in winter; this was normally rendered as cash or in kind.

This was in important respects a different kind of agriculture for the Salzburger. Here primarily cereals were produced (but almost no wheat—only black bread, then), mainly destined for sale and for export. The family Hof included the usual three buildings: house, barn for storage, and stable, much as in Salzburg. The weather was not dramatically different: somewhat darker and more temperate. But the Salzburg dairying tradition was almost wholly out of place here: the few cattle provided only some milk products and beef for family use, and even those in amounts the Salzburger found painfully scant, along with their loss of wheaten bread.[30]

Accordingly, utilized land consisted almost entirely of arable plots: little woodland by comparison with Salzburg, and very little pasture. Yet the assigned acreage in Prussian Lithuania was much greater than, for example, the acreage of the model Salzburg Bauerngut I sketched earlier, or that of all but very few of the Salzburg inventories preserved by Plotho's commission; moreover, most of it was in plowland, rather than mountain meadow and pasture. This suggests that a former owner of a middle-sized Gut in Salzburg who resettled on a Prussian domain farm was not necessarily worse off for the transaction. As for the freehold Kölmer, who were East Prussian equivalents to the most prosperous of the Salzburg Bauern: it appears (though only through a very fragile chain of monetary and spatial conversions) that an equipped farm the size of which cost the Kölmer family 445 thaler in East Prussia would have cost the equivalent of about 3,000 thaler in Salzburg before 1730.[31] If

---

[30] For data and testimony on these matters, see especially Göcking, *Emigrations-Geschichte*, 2: passim.

[31] In 1744, 237 Salzburger families owned 426 Hufen freehold, for which they had paid the crown 46,915 thlr., or 198 thlr. each for farms thus averaging 1.8

that calculation is anywhere near correct, then this migration theoretically perceived makes considerable economic as well as demographic sense, as a rational re-adjustment of land with labor values. Proportional to their arability, the narrow alpine mountainsides were overcrowded, the Lithuanian plain relatively unoccupied. If a Salzburger family could rescue only a fraction of their home properties and reapply them, they might not be at all badly off for the exchange (those of them to be sure, who survived the transaction). In the actual event, of course, the farmsteader usually did not rescue more than a fraction, or buy a new freehold; and on the far more common share holding, his ultimate obligations to the domain were substantial: usually 12 thaler, about the annual price of a pair of horses or of oxen, or thirty Scheffel (around 1,250 kg.) of rye.

Comparing further the price of a freehold or a Kölmer's Hufe with the fiscal advantage that he had over the sharework peasant through reduced obligations to the domain, it turns out that the Kölmer buyer received a return of almost exactly 5 percent on his investment—just the interest rate on capital loans in Salzburg. And actually, most owners of Kölmer land in East Prussia seem to have been prosperous German-Prussians: often men with military or governmental titles, often women, and often with very large holdings, investments that appear to reflect a feature of the German capital market of the time.[32]

Tallies of 1736–37 show 765 Salzburger families to have been distributed among 241 localities. Thus an average of two or three Salzburger families settled in places where there were any at all, and most Salzburger families were located in places with no more than three or four others:[33]

Hufen. Equipment for a two-Hufen farm was valued at 148 thlr. Calculations are based on Beheim-Schwarzbach, *Friedrich Wilhelm I.*, pp. 41, 380.

[32] Lists in Kenkel, *Amstsbauern und Kölmer*, pp. 161–208; and the tables in GStA PK XX. HA Pt Budweitschen II–III, Prästationstabellen, 1734, 1739.

[33] Beheim-Schwarzbach, *Friedrich Wilhelm I.*, p. 192.

No. of families in locality	No. of such localities	Total no. of families
1	83	83
2	54	108
3	27	81
4	25	100
5	11	55
6 or more	41	338

Ethnically, too, the Salzburger were spatially dispersed, and even in the Budwetschen district, with its relatively heavy settlement of Salzburger (especially from St. Johann) Bauern, they were an ethnic minority. These were the proportions in 1736:[34]

Place of origin	No. of sharework peasants	No. of Hufen distributed
Salzburg	59	59
Germany		
Nassau	61	
Ansbach	5	
Pomerania	11	
Halberstadt/Magdeburg	16	
Total Germany	103	109
Lithuania	115	153
Kölmer (no ethnic identification)	21	72

In other districts there were also Poles and French-speaking Swiss: a gaudy ethnic mix. Yet there are relatively few signs of ethnic friction, apart from a few incidents that point to the rule, such as the case of a Salzburg peasant designated a "schlechter

[34] Calculated from Kenkel, *Amtsbauern und Kölmer*, passim. Figures for Kölmer are from 1740. The Magdeburger Hufe currently used by the East Prussian administration as measure = 30 Morgen = 76,597 sq m = c. 19 U.S. acres. Obviously it did not express that precise figure for the Budwetschen farmsteads but did represent a practical rule of thumb for a family holding.

Bauer" (bad peasant) because he would "never get along with the Lithuanians." Domain officials were obliged to examine each peasant and to report whether he was a good or a bad one, considering such matters as punctuality with his obligations to the domain, industriousness or want of it, susceptibility to alcohol. Among 12,094 families so evaluated in 1736, 90 percent of the Salzburger were identified as good peasants, 86 percent of the Lithuanians, and 84 percent of the Swiss and the other Germans. Thus it appears that the Salzburger were quite readily integrated into their new economy. After 1736 the reporting officials apparently ceased dividing and identifying the population by ethnicity.[35]

These data bespeak both adaptibility among the peasantry and successsful settlement practices on the part of the officials in charge of the program. Also, of the 36 Salzburg families settled in 1734 in the Budwetschen district as full sharework farmers, 33 (92%), had been owners of Güter in Salzburg. Five years later, in 1739, 47 of the 59 farms then settled by Salzburger (80%) were in the hands of former alpine Gut owners or their sons or widows.[36] Comparable figures for the neighboring district of Dörschkehmen (also a main area of settlement for the Salzburger, but these were especially natives of the Radstatt district) show that in 1736, 43 of 69 Salzburger families settled on royal domain farms there had themselves been Gut owners in Salzburg or were their immediate heirs.[37] Such strong continuity, persisting across the migration and the quite dramatic environmental change, may be attributed to calculated royal policy in the allocation of farmsteads, or to the level of expectation and self-esteem of the Bauern themselves; certainly the explicit royal policy throughout the transaction had been to iden-

---

[35] GStA PK XX. HA Pt Budweitschen II–III:Prästationstabellen, 1734, 1736, 1739; Kenkel, Amtsbauern und Kölmer, passim; summary figures for 1736 in Beheim-Schwarzbach, Friedrich Wilhelm I., pp. 272–73, with an ethnic breakdown by district and locality, pp. 276–312.

[36] GStA PK XX. HA Pt Budweitschen, II–III: Prästationstabellen, 1734, 1739.

[37] Computed from the lists in Kenkel, Amtsbauern und Kölmer.

tify and to attract families with these expectations and this sense of themselves.

Some more figures from Dörschkehmen will serve as a rude check, lest the Budwetschen district prove eccentric. In Dörsch-kehmen, 66 of 285 Bauern were Salzburger in 1736; in Budwet-schen 59 out of 277 were Salzburg families—almost identical proportions, 21 and 23 percent, respectively. The percentages of Swiss or Germans were 35 in Dörschkehmen, 37 in Bud-wetschen; of Lithuanians, 44 in Dörschkehmen, 40 in Bud-wetschen. This remarkably even distribution suggests a delib-erate royal policy. The Salzburger, like earlier immigrants, were spread evenly across these main settlement areas, as ear-lier immigrants had been, proportionally to the rural popula-tions already there when they arrived. Each of the districts (Budwetschen and Dörschkehmen) had 49 localities, with Salz-burger families in about half of them, and an average of three such families in each. The most noticeable difference between the districts is in the Kölmer, or freehold, land: this amounted to 72 Hufen (21 owners, including the energetic Rup Geyer) in Budwetschen, but 193 Hufen, almost three times as much, in Dörschkehmen. Among the 52 freeholders in Dörschkehmen was just one Salzburger (from St. Veit), and such others as "Pastor Dressler, 5½ Hufen . . . Constable Lindner, 1½ Hufen . . . Administrator Schleemüller, 6 Hufen . . . bookkeeper Jester, 10.19 Hufen . . . Lt. Col. Buddenbrook, 13 Hufen . . . the town of Schirwind, scattered holdings, 20 Hufen."[38]

The actual work of cultivating investment properties like these was surely the destiny of the many Salzburg families who did not acquire domain or freehold farmsteads of their own. Very few of the undomiciled who might have done such work in Salzburg ever arrived in East Prussia, and few of the Salzburger that did arrive there were placed on the Vorwerke (about 100 families in 1744), or stayed in one of the ten provin-cial towns (about 200 families), or entered service on noble es-

[38] Ibid., for the owners here named, see pp. 178–79.

tates (154 individuals). By the mid-1740s, three times that number, well over a thousand Salzburger families, or about seven thousand individuals, were established independently on domain or freehold farms. These families remain the norm. But over 400 families remained, somewhere on the land but without their own farms (411 such families, including 1,731 individuals, were officially listed). These were families designated as servants (274 families with 1,154 members), or as shepherds and laborers (137 families with 577 members).[39] Some of these farmed for or leased from absentee owners, certainly; but many others were in the service of their more fortunate fellow immigrants and appeared on family assessment lists prepared for the domain, if at all, with that reduced status: an important qualification to my earlier remark on the continuity of family proprietorship.

A summary reckoning of the resettled families themselves affirms this qualification. The average Salzburger domain peasant family, according to the assessment survey of 1739, comprised two parents, three children (half of them old enough to work), and an average of two and a half servants, *Knechte* and *Mägde*, per household. A substantial number of the servants were probably family kin, as the core family biographies and other genealogical evidence suggest. But the rest, and probably the majority, must have come from families who had been Gutsbesitzer, members of independent family farms, in Salzburg before the emigration.

These symptoms of decline in status emphasize further the limitations of the core family biographies such as appeared earlier in this chapter, with their benign bias for showing continuity. Numerically, the proportion of dependent to independent families in Lithuania is not unlike that of undomiciled to

[39] But these 1,731 represent a marked improvement over the 3,232 persons still in service status in 1734. I took summary figures for the province Litauen from Beheim-Schwarzbach, *Friedrich Wilhelm I.*, pp. 165–66, 190–91. Persons located on noble estates, unlike even servants on domain or freehold farms or Vorwerke, were not perceived as family members by royal officials.

domiciled or settled population in Salzburg, so that these proportions taken alone would indicate little social flux. But the proportions, though quantitatively similar, hold different meanings. The category of dependency in East Prussia is not a mainly generational one affecting in principle most families, as in Salzburg, but is rather, one of hierarchy *among* families. The families remained the fundamental social unit, of awareness, of economy, and of administration. But maybe, as they moved from the Salzburg highlands to the East Prussian plain, they were moving away from a condition of individual family autonomy and self-sufficiency, domestic qualities that in the alpine environment and contemporary nomenclature and analysis withstood economic differences of scale, toward one of more varied status within a more differentiated system, one in which each family found its place not alone, but with respect to the others and to the state: into a social and a public differentiation of freehold and domain, of independent and service family, of Bauernhof and Vorwerk, all under the Prussian crown.

This change might even be stylized in the political formulations of the German theorists Pufendorf and Hegel, for example, as a process affecting families as they passed from a "natural condition" of domestic autonomy, to a "civil society," subsumed under the state.[40] For the Salzburger, the process and experience so stylized may have begun with the assem-

[40] Samuel Pufendorf perceived an actual state of nature, "qualis revera existat," as a configuration of scattered patriarchal families (deliberately rejecting the individualist starting point of Hobbes) over which the establishment of state authority is an essential stage of socialization. See Hans Medick, *Naturzustand und Naturgeschichte der bürgerlichen Gesellschaft*, 2d ed. (Göttingen, 1981), pp. 60–62, following Pufendorf's *De jure naturae et gentium* (1672), Bk. 2, Kap. 2, §§4 and 7; and *De officio hominis et civis* (1673), Bk. 2, Kap. 1, §7. Subsequently Hegel, in his *Philosophy of Right* (1821), §157, begins his discussion of "ethical life [*Sittlichkeit*]," with "ethical mind in its natural or immediate phase—the Family. This substantiality loses its unity, passes over into division, and into the place of relation, i.e. into Civil Society," and from this hypothetical condition into the higher immediacy of the state (§256). *Hegel's Philosophy of Right*, trans. T. M. Knox (London: Oxford University Press, 1952), pp. 110, 154–55.

blies that gathered to confront Firmian's missionaries in 1731; but they were to see at the end of the process a great deal more of the king's officials than they had ever seen of the arch-bishop's priests and regulars. And in Prussia, Frederick William's prompt and vigorous program of chapel- and school-building served to replace domestic worship as center of their religious and cultural lives.[41]

Not long after their arrival—continuing in this theoretical vein, for such are this history's odd conceits—the crown endowed them with a social contract—an actual *Sozietäts-Contract*. This was a formal agreement between the Prussian crown and representatives of the Salzburg immigrants, reached in September 1736, to regulate relations between royal officials and the so-called Society of Salzburger on the land. But it also made provision for organized mutual responsibilities within the Salzburger community, under the supervision of 26 elected ward elders (*Schulzen*), each of whom got an extra Hufe in recognition of his public role. The entire society, thus represented, was made responsible for payment of obligations to the crown, "einer vor alle und alle vor einem," in return for which, liability for labor service was definitively abolished, and officials were obliged to accept equivalent payments in kind as well as in cash. The society was authorized to eject slovenly (*liederliche*) farmers from their holdings and put efficient (*tüchtige*) ones in their place, as long as the crown was informed and suffered no disadvantage: thus properties currently in Salzburger hands would remain in Salzburger hands, and the crown promised to add to them wherever feasible. In the event of natural disaster—hail, fire, crop failure, epidemic—mutual aid would be organized under the elders. And, houses would be built out of wood, as in Salzburg, not wattle and daub, as among the Lithuanians.[42]

[41] Göcking, *Emigrations-Geschichte*, 2:256–66.

[42] Text of September 17, 1736, in Beheim-Schwarzbach, *Friedrich Wilhelm I.*, p. 187. See the discussion there, pp. 185–89, and in Skalweit, *Domänenverwaltung*, pp. 262–75.

This curious document has a suitably curious history, one befitting its resonance in political and social theory. It was devised not by the Salzburger, or even for them, but by the earlier Swiss colonists, or more probably on their behalf. King Frederick William, however, sternly refused to allow these internal and external communal powers to the Swiss. "That won't do," he pronounced in 1728. "They must stay under official subordination and discipline [*Subordinatio und Straffe*] because I cannot allow any such state within a state [*stattu in stattu*]."[43] Eight years later he did allow this contract with the Salzburger, though with what real effect it is impossible to say; surely they did not become a state within a state. By the terms of the contract, therefore, their society was an ethnic one. One reason for its ethnic character may have been the Salzburg families' resistance to the rural rhythms of simultaneous planting, harvesting, pasturing, and the like in the Lithuanian settlements among which they had been placed.[44]

But there were other reasons for the particularity of the Salzburger settlers, as the history of the social contract shows. Negotiations began as early as 1733, intended mainly, it appears, to overcome the extreme reluctance, often the refusal, of the Salzburger to swear loyalty to their new royal master. Their obstinacy outraged the king's officials, and the king too—after all he had done for these people. Just why the Salzburger were stubborn about this is not certain; probably there was a combination of reasons. Some said they were against oaths on Lutheran principle and cited Scripture to back them up. "If we wanted to swear loyalty oaths, we could have stayed home in Salzburg," was another common objection. Some Prussian officials thought that the Salzburger still harbored hopes of returning home, hopes that they believed the Prussian oath would extinguish forever. A rumor even swept among the immigrants

---

[43] Skalweit, *Domänenverwaltung*, p. 269.
[44] Thus the *Blut-und-Boden*–tainted explanation of Immo Kretschmar, "Die Salzburger Ansiedlung in Ostpreussen," *Odal* 7 (1938), 582–97.

that a Prussian army had now annexed Salzburg and driven out the archbishop, so that they might go back to their old farms—a revival of the old rumor of impending Protestant rescue which had helped to launch the crisis in Salzburg in the summer of 1731. More realistically it seems certain that many of the immigrants believed that once they had taken the oath to Prussia, all bargaining power would be gone: nobody would listen to their complaints any longer, and the Prussian government would then drop their claims back in Salzburg. Many immigrants stubbornly refused to surrender written documentation of their property claims in Salzburg to Plotho's commission.[45] By stages and under pressure they yielded. (Where else could they run away to? If the king was against them, who would be for them?) The social contract of 1736 ended their resistance and bound them finally to their places in the Prussian state.

Their integration was not always easy, however; and a great many of the officials charged with seeing to it doubted that the crown had made a good bargain over the Salzburger after all. "These clowns are worse than the devil himself [*die Kerle sind ja ärger als der Teufel*]" wrote one frustrated officer; and, wrote another, "the longer one works with the Salzburger, the more one sees, their other vices apart, most of all their laziness, how they reject every chance they are given to work and to earn, and spend their time visiting their friends aroundabout, or if they stay home, leaning on the fence or playing cards."[46] Worst were the undomesticated young people assigned to officials on the Vorwerke and elsewhere as gardeners, farmhands, or servants; these were inclined "even to run away clear out of service!" trying to find their families or former masters.[47] Actually the families were not much better, said the reports, not until

<hr />

[45] On the oath problem see especially Beheim-Schwarzbach, *Friedrich Wilhelm I.*, pp. 156–58; and Göcking, *Emigrations-Geschichte*, 2:289–92.

[46] Beheim-Schwarzbach, *Friedrich Wilhelm I.*, p. 158.

[47] Göcking, *Emigrations-Geschichte*, 2:288–89.

punitive legislation, hunger and cold, and the social contract took the needed effect. Their stubbornness and pigheadedness, *Eigensinn*, especially among the complaining race of Salzburger women who never seemed satisfied with their circumstances— these were a source of endless problems. They had been spoiled by all the attention they had attracted along the way, the officials said to one another, and to their superiors. They had been taught by enthusiasts to think of themselves as a chosen people entering a promised land.[48] Published accounts, official or enthusiastic or both, took pains to minimize or to explain away any disappointments or doubts about the quality of the immigrants; but still they revealed a good many of them in the course of it. "Always remember," wrote the program's semiofficial historian for his second lavishly produced volume of 1737, "that in any field, a single thornbush or thistle makes more of a parade than a hundred stalks of wheat." If the Salzburger were coarse folk, "discourteous and insolent," especially when drunk, he went on, and if they used the familiar Du form of address—even with crown officials and pastors!— that was because in their native Salzburg they had lived scattered and apart, surrounded by their own earth, with little need to learn social graces; but they would learn to be civilized soon enough in their new homes and new circumstances. Their drunkenness, yes, well, they were no worse than the natives and hadn't yet learned to handle the stronger stuff currently in use in Prussia. Immodesty? What could be expected of them, after that long journey, in the way of decent clothing? (Though to be sure the calf-length skirts and the colorful bodices of the Salzburg women were, at very least, questionable.) Unchastity and adultery were notorious among them; but doubtless they had learned these sins from the Salzburg regime of priests, who had forbidden them as heretics to marry and then for a fee

---

[48] See for example the observations in Skalweit, *Domänenverwaltung*, p. 273; and Göcking, *Emigrations-Geschichte*, 2:291–92.

forgave such sins as fornication, and who themselves were in-famous examples of sexual vice and disorder.[49]

But they were skilled and industrious farmers after all, ran the verdict, once they had settled down; the thorn or the thistle was cast aside at the harvest—or at least at the threshing. Such failings of the flesh, once understood, were subject to the usual remedies. And of course their Protestant piety was already leg-endary. Pastor Johann Friedrich Breuer, entrusted with the set-tlement mission, became something of an amateur ethnologist in the course of his many encounters with the Salzburger. Take the matter of the rosary and the scapulary, which the priests in Salzburg had insisted upon, and which a good many of the exiles seem to have brought along with them on the exodus (but now kept out of sight, displaying instead the devotional books that in Salzburg they had kept hidden in their hay-mows). Why do you keep such gewgaws? Breuer wanted to know. I kept my rosary, explained Christian Steiner, formerly of the Radstatt district, to remind me of the popish foolishness that claimed magical powers for it; but of course I never use it now. "Here the man looked at the ground," reports Breuer, who then explained to Steiner how he should thank God for his liberation from such unholy nonsense. The Salzburger looked up at him now and answered, "O yes, yes, I thank God and the most gracious King of Prussia a thousand times for that. Yes my Lord, God! Those Catholics have a really idiotic

---

[49] Göcking, *Emigrations-Geschichte*, 2:283–97, 331–33, 618–47. Regarding mar-riage and adultery: there had in fact been a conflict between Tridentine rules on marriage, which invoked priestly participation early in the formation of a family alliance, and an alpine practice whereby the marriage contract was made, and the bride moved into the household of the groom, often long before the religious ceremony, which took place only when the groom took over the Gut as family head after the retirement or death of the previous generation (Ortner, *Reformation*, pp. 101–2; Göcking, *Emigrations-Geschichte*, pp. 344–45). How much the accusation of adultery, commonly made against the Salzburger Bauern both in Salzburg and in East Prussia, reflects this conflict is not appar-ent.

religion!"[50] Breuer learned also that when, back in Salzburg, the Bauern had been forced to join in singing Catholic songs, they had just opened and moved their mouths without making sounds, so as to escape hostile attention without committing actual blasphemy. Out of love for Breuer, they sang one song before him, though, to show that curious and diligent pastor what thoughts and images the papists were capable of: a song those Catholics sang when they were working in the fields and forests of Salzburg:

> O Tannenbaum, O Tannenbaum,
> Du bist ein edler Zweig.
> Du grünest Winter und Sommer,
> Und auch zur Frühlings-Zeit.

"Evergreen, O Evergreen"—a heathenish, tree-worshiping song of seasons to be sure; which then, after treating of deer and nightingales, concluded with the verse:

> Schön überaus, o werthes Haus,
> Wir grüssen dich von fern.
> Leucht uns, in dieser Pilgerfahrth,
> Allzeit du Morgenstern.

"Loveliest of all, thou goodly house—we greet thee from afar. Lead us, in this our pilgrimage, always, thou morning star." Pastor Breuer rejoiced and praised God that such language and thoughts lay now in his people's past, transcended in the marvelous story of their exile and their redemption.

---

[50] Ibid., 2:297–301.

This "March of the Salzburg Emigrants" is a characteristic contemporary representation. Many of these illustrations incorporated groups or figures copied from other sources and were themselves plundered by others for accounts and commentaries. This version appeared in Johann Heinrich Baum, *Nachlese zu der Salzburgischen Emigranten Wanderschafft, oder fernere March-Route* (Nürnberg, 1734). The male figure with three small children at the left was the promotional theme of the exhibition "Reformation-Emigration: Protestanten in Salzburg," held at Schloss Goldegg in the Pongau during the summer of 1981.

CHAPTER FIVE

THE LEGEND

Marianne Weber opens her 1929 biography of her husband, most famed and influential of German sociologists, with a conventionally prognostic first chapter that invokes family genealogy. In Max Weber's paternal line, she declares, "the family belonged for many generations to the merchant patriciate, and was held together by a proud sense of its heritage [*Sippenbewusstsein*]. Their forebears are said to have been expelled from Salzburg on account of their Protestant [*evangelischen*] faith, and to have introduced the linen trade in their new home," in Bielefeld in Rhenish Westphalia.[1] She places this inherited concurrence of Protestant conviction with entrepreneurial capitalism on the paternal side alongside Huguenot descent on the maternal side in her introduction to Max Weber's life and work.

Arthur Mitzman, among others, picked up Marianne Weber's genealogical metaphor. The first paragraph of his 1970 biography of Max Weber, subtitled *An Historical Interpretation*, states the theme: "On both sides of the family, Weber de-

---

[1] Marianne Weber, *Max Weber: Ein Lebensbild* (Heidelberg, 1950), pp. 29–30.

scended from Protestants who had fled their homeland to escape the wrath of outraged Catholics; but from refugees in the
name of the true religion, they had somehow, by the nineteenth century, become capitalist magnates. For their tor-
mented descendent, sorting out the strange relationships between religious rebellion, asceticism, and productivity was to
become—after his breakdown—a form of autotherapy." On
the paternal side, Mitzman went on, "Weber's ancestors had
been driven from Salzburg because of their 'evangelical' convictions. Karl August Weber, the grandfather . . ." and so on
about the weaver Webers, progeny of the Salzburg Protestant
exiles.[2]

Both biographers, and many other commentators who have
used their accounts, have found this genealogical information
about Weber's descent from the Salzburg Protestant exiles to be
a significant key to his interests and ideas. What seems odd but
especially significant about it, however, is that all but certainly,
it is literally not so. I find no evidence for it prior to Marianne
Weber's introduction, and she herself offered none; meanwhile, the negative evidence to the contrary is overwhelming.
To begin with, there is not a single Weber among all the some
twenty thousand names of Protestant exiles, on either the
Salzburg or the Prussian lists; and that is a great many German
names, to include nobody at all named Weber. Neither, as it
happens, are there any Schusters or Schneiders or Spenglers or
Naglers or Tuchers: none of these proto-industrial occupational
family names. By contrast there are thousands of -bergers and
-bachers, -eggers and -pichls, -bühls and -hofers, all denoting
rural and especially alpine traditions, quite as one might expect. Moreover, standard and authoritative German genealogical sources for *bürgerlich* families show no trace whatsoever of
any Salzburg connection of the Bielefeld Webers, to whom
these researchers pay close attention, or of any of their wives,

[2] Arthur Mitzman, *The Iron Cage: An Historical Interpretation of Max Weber*
(New York, 1970), pp. 15–16.

let alone direct descent, for as far back as the line leads, into the seventeenth century and the beginning of the eighteenth, when the first identifiable Weber-ancestor was peacefully begetting children in Bielefeld, well before the Salzburg expulsion.

By contrast, among the Bielefeld Webers, there are a great many family names and connections in common with places like Hamburg and other north German commercial and industrial towns—again, quite as one might expect.[3] Nevertheless, Marianne Weber's biographical device seems on its way, if it has not already arrived, to becoming part of yet another text of the Salzburg narration, a traditional or legendary text whose origins are the subject of this last chapter. This twentieth-century variant, constructed on the traditional story, proceeds from Max Weber's ostensible Salzburger heritage, on to the Protestant ethic, weaver-capitalists, the "iron cage," and ensuing psychic crises of modern rationality and diligence.

As far as I have been able to discover, Max Weber himself never spoke publicly or wrote anything about a Salzburger ancestry. But the imputed association sticks. It is reiterated because it has made useful sense; and it has made sense because of the traditional history that has been made of the Salzburg expulsion, a history it, in turn, reinforces. It has made useful affirmative sense that Max Weber's Evangelical and entrepreneurial forebears should have been heirs to an earnest and enterprising Protestant folk, recorded in the telling as sturdy emigrants from an anachronistic, stubbornly obscurantist Roman Catholic realm; that Max Weber's own life and thought should be rooted in a crosscurrent of religious fervor with economic calculation; and that Weber's pondering of the distinction between the charismatic and the bureaucratic realms should lead

---

[3] Bernhard Koerner, ed., *Deutsches Geschlechterbuch: Genealogisches Handbuch Bürgerlicher Familien*, vol. 19 (Görlitz, 1911), pp. 442–63. The Kirchen-Vorsteher David Weber (1684–1770) had five children born in Bielefeld between 1712 and 1725. The founder of the linen firm was his grandson, another David (1760–1836), Max Weber's great-grandfather.

back to this pilgrimage from the ultimate German South to the ultimate German North, from the archepiscopal realms of baroque and Italianate Salzburg, to that rationalist, bureaucratic, and ascetic icon of political Protestantism, the Prussia of the great Hohenzollerns of the seventeenth and eighteenth centuries.[4]

I pose these contrasts theatrically because the melodrama of the story is a main reason for the extraordinary attention it attracted and a key to the cultural context of this attraction. The story of the Salzburger was constructed as a homiletic historical text, an eighteenth-century romance of moral propriety and earnest virtue: a middle-class Robinsonade (Daniel Defoe's had appeared in German a dozen years before), put in scene from craggy alpine slopes to the East Prussian plain. An engraving taken from the richly illustrated "Joyous and Most Blessed Journeys of the Salzburg Emigrants to the Royal Prussian Lands," published at Nürnberg in 1732 (the very year of the emigration) offers a contemporary statement of the theme (Illus. 4). It shows what came to be a characteristic family group in the foreground, situated before a column of emigrants leaving Salzburg, and in a panel below, the industrious colonists busily erecting a quite imaginary "St. Johannesburg or New Saltzburg in Prussia."[5] With this rendition, in this final chapter, the story takes on its own life and makes its own future history.

It would be possible, and in some ways instructive, to trace

---

[4] On this theme I am indebted to Hartmut Lehmann, "Ascetic Protestantism and Economic Rationalism: Max Weber Revisited after Two Generations," *HTR* 3 (1987), 307–20.

[5] [Johann Heinrich Baum], *Der Saltzburgischen Emigranten Freuden-müthige und höchst-gesegnete Wanderschafft, in die Königlich-Preussische Lande.* This edition included full-color illustrations, including a foldout map showing routes of passage from the Pongau to "St. Johannesburg od. Neu Saltzburg in Preussen." There was in fact a Johannesburg approximately where the map locates one, but it had nothing to do with the Salzburger so far as I can tell and none settled there; see also Angelika Marsch, *Die Salzburger Emigration in Bildern,* 2d ed. (Weissenhorn/Bayern, 1979), pp. 148, 161, illus. p. 149.

From alpine Salzburg to "New Salzburg in Prussia." From Baum, *Der Saltz-burgischen Emigranten Freuden-müthige und höchst-gesegnete Wanderschafft.*

the entire traditional history backward in time, from present forms to the time of the emigration itself. That is one way to examine the making of such histories. But in this instance it would also be misleading; for this configuration of the story began to form very early, even before the events themselves, was evolved with much publicity as the emigration took place, and was renewed and re-articulated in successive contexts up until the present. The proportion of German Protestants whose family traditions include descent from the Salzburg pilgrims is demographically (and biologically) astonishing, as I have learned since taking an interest in the subject. In many parts of Germany, not just Bielefeld or Berlin, the special economic enterprise associated with a certain place may be explained by the once-upon-a-time settlement of Salzburg Protestant exiles there. My purpose in pursuing this reconstruction is not to debunk any of it, a sterile and probably futile task of showing negatives, or even to question it beyond what seems needed to emphasize the liberation of the created history from its sources but, rather, only to mark the way in which the history was made, less by academic historians than by other cultural mediators; though to be sure, academic as well as less constrained modes of representation participated in the process.

One economical place to see the beginnings of that history is with the production of the Albrecht von Haller's long poem *Die Alpen*, composed or at least conceived in 1728–29 and published in the summer of 1732, just as the Protestant emigration from Salzburg was at its peak. With this classic alexandrine idyll the alpine highlands cease rather abruptly to appear, as by previous convention they had appeared, as a raw habitat of brutes and bandits, and begin their modern career as a romantically severe garden of virtue, productive of moral equality and simplicity, of rejection of ornament, of domestic virtue and sturdy independence.[6] These are qualities common also to the

[6] The Bernese Haller (1708–77) made an alpine tour in 1729, when he was trying to decide between literature and medicine as a career. In 1736 he was

visual representations of the Salzburg exiles which began to flow from the engravings and printing presses during 1731 and 1732.

The calendar offers another neat conjuncture for this starting point: the year 1729 had been the bicentennial anniversary of the Augsburg Confession, doctrinal foundation of German Lutheranism, a commemoration widely celebrated and publicized by German Protestant clergy in the context of the confessional and cultural politics of the Reich. In one elaborate representation of the Salzburg exiles, a *Bilderzyklus*, or series of representations from 1732 with accompanying text, the Salzburger are shown literally acting out, appropriately costumed and with presumed scenic backgrounds and even maps, the successive theological articles of the Augsburg Confession.[7] The corpus evangelicorum began its campaign in imperial politics at the Reichstag with the Lerchner and Bremer petitions in the following year, 1730: this was also the bicentennial year of Melanchthons's submission of the confession to Emperor Charles V at the Imperial Diet at Augsburg.

Literary historians may consider *Die Alpen* a link between Old Testament and classical pastoral literary traditions; but as with the theological representations of the Salzburger, it actualizes these traditions into contemporary reality. It asserts the element of stern scenic romance which proceeds to frame and to explain the remarkable appeal of the Salzburg story to its contemporary and succeeding recipients. Haller's alpine topography, moreover, is no mere backdrop, but an explicit context for *Eintracht, Treue und Mut*: a place where, as he wrote, "Harmony, Fidelity, and Fortitude, with their unbroken power," are

---

made professor of botany and medicine at the new university at Göttingen, where he founded the Reformed congregation, before returning to Bern in 1753. I follow the Reclam text of Haller's *Die Alpen und andere Gedichte* (Stuttgart, 1965), pp. 3–37. Line numbers are noted in text. On changing representations of the Alps, see generally Jacob Frey, *Die Alpen im Lichte verschiedener Zeitalter* (Berlin, 1877).

[7] Reproduced in Marsch, *Salzburger Emigration*, illus. nos. 110–14.

able to defy "the yoke that half Europe still must bear," a culture of Roman Catholicism, "where all around us there is suffering, and starving in chains; and the Paradise of the Romans—*Welschlands Paradies*—harbors crippled beggars" (*lines 296–300*). The moral integrity of Haller's mountain peasantry does not require even a society. There are no towns, no merchants, guilds, or even villages: the family is the elemental social unit, standing, without mediation, in direct moral and political relation with the whole.

Haller's authorship of *Die Alpen* is a reminder of another contextual dimension to the Salzburg expulsion: alpine poem and alpine exile were located culturally within the theodicy debate that exercised the learned and confessional world of the 1730s. As a demonstration that virtue and piety could emerge from so rude and, seemingly, so godforsaken a region, and from the deeds of so brutal a prince of the church, the expulsion and redemption were a reassuring and a telling note in debates about the goodness of God, and the riddles of his hidden ways of fulfilling his benevolent intentions. Haller's own literary contribution to the debate followed immediately upon *Die Alpen* in his 1733 poem "On the Origin of Evil" (begun in 1732, during the emigration). His brilliant career at Göttingen as physician and natural scientist may be understood in the light of these troubled questions of what, or whether, divine purpose might live in what seemed cruel and base.[8]

Such a note was particularly welcome to the German Prot-

---

[8] Virgil Nemoianu, *Micro-Harmony: The Growth and Uses of the Idyllic Model in Literature* (Bern, 1977), p. 35; Franz R. Kempf, *Albrecht von Hallers Ruhm als Dichter: Eine Rezeptionsgeschichte* (New York, 1986), esp. pp. 131–48; Thomas P. Saine, *Von der Kopernikanischen bis zur Französischen Revolution* (Berlin, 1987), pp. 89–90. For the literary construction of the pious countryman in the eighteenth century, see Wolfgang Brückner, "Zum Wandel der religiösen Kultur im 18. Jahrhundert," in *Sozialer und kultureller Wandel in der ländlichen Welt des 18. Jahrhunderts*, ed. Ernst Hinrichs and Günter Wiegelman (Wolfenbüttel, 1982), pp. 65–83. On Haller's theodicy, see Eduard Stäuble, *Albrecht von Haller 'Über den Ursprung des Übels'* (Zürich, 1953). Text of the latter poem is in *Die Alpen und andere Gedichte*, pp. 53–79.

estant pastorate, then confronting the divisions and the challenges to their doctrinal foundations raised by what cultural historians have called the "early enlightenment," by which term I include here the ecumenical tendencies of enlightenment, together with the doctrinal indifference or inconformity of evangelical pietism.[9] The theodicy debate was one symptom of that challenge to the established clergy and their moral arsenal. Other symptoms were the commemorative celebrations of the Confession of Augsburg, which led to sharp religious clashes in that confessionally divided city, a place where the passage of the Salzburger was especially dramatized and advertised. The extraordinary publicity accorded to the emigration of the Salzburger was surely another sign of that challenge. The lawyers of the corpus evangelicorum in Regensburg, certainly, had played an essential part in launching the emigration, by adopting the cause of Salzburg Protestants in 1729 and 1730. But it was the German Protestant pastorate, more than any other group or agency, that seized upon the exile of the Salzburger and made it legendary. A revitalized and concretized confessional rhetoric, expressing an essential unity of German Evangelical Christendom, was the Protestant clergy's share in the Salzburg exchange.

The publicity was massive, by the standards of any time. During the early 1730s, Protestant Germany was saturated with news of the expulsion, of the qualities of the expellees, and their rescue and adoption into Prussia. I find listed over three hundred independent titles, not counting serials or administrative materials, printed in 1732 and 1733 alone, published in sixty-seven different places, led by Augsburg (with 28 titles), Frankfurt am Main (27), Leipzig (24), Nürnberg (23), Berlin (16), Dresden (14), and Regensburg (10). These ranged from

[9] On this point I am indebted to comments by Hartmut Lehmann and Heide Wunder, at seminars in Washington and Göttingen in 1989 and 1990 respectively, and also to language found by Hans Medick for a translation of my observations into German.

Detail from a foldout map showing the migration routes of the Salzburg Protestants. From Göcking, *Emigrations-Geschichte*.

learned legal and theological treatises about the religious history, condition, and constitutional rights of the Salzburger, through multivolume and multidisciplinary treatments in quarto, fashionable fictional dialogues over particular points of doctrine and law, and richly illustrated and multicolored treatises that became sources for fliers and occasional verse, and for an elaborate iconography of exile and of pilgrimage.[10]

Some of this is work of quite remarkable quality, done with great care and at great expense. For example, a corner vignette from a colored foldout map in quarto shows the Salzburgers' routes of passage (Illus. 5).[11] There is even an oratorio, titled "The Great Sign of Our Time, to be Seen through the Salzburg Emigrants," composed by Reinhard Keiser: it has vocal parts for Jesus Christ, for the Prophet, for Faith, Hope, and Love, for the True Christian Believing Church, for a Chorus of the Salzburg Emigrants, and for another Chorus of Inhabitants of Christian-Evangelical Places.[12] There were public campaigns and collections for the relief of the Salzburg exiles; an "emigration chest" was set up in Regensburg and by October 1732 had accumulated some 34,000 thaler from donors led by the kings of Sweden and Great Britain and the cities of Hamburg, Regensburg, and Frankfurt am Main.[13]

[10] The tally of publications is compiled from Ernst Dannappel, "Die Literatur der Salzburger Emigration, 1731–1735" followed by "Ein Beitrag zu E. Dannappels Literatur," NABB 47 (1886), 33–41, 65–71, 97–103; and 267–75; and Arthur Ehmer, Das Schrifttum zur Salzburger Emigration 1731/1733 (Hamburg, 1975). Over seventy major items give no place of publication. I have also excluded from the count controversial literature that invokes the Salzburg emigration but is not devoted mainly to it.

[11] Taken from Gerhard G. Göcking, Vollkommene Emigrations-Geschichte von denen aus dem Ertz-Bisthum Saltzburg vertribenen und in dem Königreich Preussen grössesten Theils aufgenommenen Lutheranern, vol. 1 (Frankfurt/M., 1734).

[12] It is instructive to note that Keiser's oratorio (listed in Ehmer, Schrifttum, p. 33) is the single publication identified with the Enlightened free city of Hamburg, while at the same time Hamburg was a leading contributor to the emigrants' relief.

[13] Göcking, Emigrations-Geschichte, 1:292–93; Fritz Klein, "Die Einwanderung der Berchtolsgadener Exulanten in Kurhannover 1733," HG 34 (1980), 166–67;

But above all it was sermons, endless extended sermons by eminent and would-be–eminent Protestant divines, that took and made of the Salzburg emigration a legendary text. Many of these were printed and distributed through ecclesiastical channels and religious associations. A closely related mode of publicity was the "Report" or "News," "Description" or "History" of the passage of the Salzburger through the places along their route. These were usually composed by pastors in these places (but with growing convergence of language among them), and account for most of the sixty-seven identified localities where printed literature was produced. Like the sermons, the reports and histories also expressed formulary amazement at the exemplary virtues of the Salzburger, their piety and honesty, and, despite lack of religious training, their strict Lutheran orthodoxy, upon which they were repeatedly and triumphantly examined. Though they had been forbidden schools or teachers in their native mountains, still they knew and held precisely to Evangelical doctrine, marveled Pastor Christoph Sancke of the Thomaskirche in Leipzig, among many others. Their piety matched their diligence. When certain others went to the taverns, these folk stayed home and read their bibles. While others slept at night, they pursued Christian devotions. They had been mocked and cursed, as befit a godsend: for God has sent these people to us, the pastors agreed, to test and to redeem our own faith.[14]

Usually a celebratory sermon, one that had been planned or preached before the itinerant Salzburger by the pastor-author, was included in such a history or report; and almost invariably, there was also an account of the wave of charitable emotion and pious expression their example inspired among the local

---

Theodor Krüger, *Die Salzburger Einwanderung in Preussen, mit einem Anhange denkwürdiger Aktenstücke und die Geschichte des Salzburger-Hospitals zu Gumbinnen nebst dem Statute desselben* (Gumbinnen, 1857).

[14] [Christoph Sancke], *Ausführliche Historie derer Emigranten oder vertriebenen Lutheraner aus dem Ertz-Bisthum Saltzburg*, 2d ed. (Leipzig, 1732), Vorrede.

congregation. During the earlier stages, this literature emphasized the Salzburgers' innate habits of loyalty and submission:
that they had obediently attended and observed Roman Catholic religious exercises at home in Salzburg: communion in one
kind, masses, processions, and the rest. They had never be-
haved violently or mutinously, which would have been out of
keeping with their "old Germanic simplicity and loyalty [*alten
teutschen Einfalt und Treue*]," as Pastor Sancke put it.[15] Soon,
however, as the story evolved, the possible imputation of
hypocrisy in this deferential posture was transformed into
Evangelical steadfastness and disappeared. So did some earlier
imputations of illiteracy, which initially had made the Salzburgers' doctrinal purity appear the more marvelous; but these
very soon were erased and gave way, by the end of 1732, to
their intimate identity and familiarity with the Bible.

Such pastoral enthusiasm followed, where it did not antici-
pate, the Salzburger columns in their march from one end of
Germany to another. It seems clear too that pastors put special
emphasis on the peaceability and honesty of the emigrants so
as to counteract the traditional suspicion of their congregations
and the civil magistrates against wandering strangers approaching their gates: *fahrende Leute*, alien wanderers likely to
be armed and certainly not to be trusted. Actually there are
many signs, half-hidden in contemporary accounts, that civic
authorities were decidedly less enthusiastic than the pastors at
the transit of the Salzburger, viewing them as a police problem
and a burdensome expense. Thus the migration had to be legitimized as a pilgrimage, putting firm emphasis on the qualities
of sobriety, civility, and diligence; and usually, though not always, on their sponsorship and protection by the otherwise
rather unseemly king of Prussia.

Biblical support texts were not hard to find, especially in Old

---

[15] Ibid., or similarly the anonymous *Umständliche und Wahrhafftige Nachrichten
von der Saltzburgischen Emigration. . . . Martio. 1732, nach dem Berliner Exemplar*
(n.p., 1732) pp. 3–8.

Testament histories and prophecies and in the Revelation, but also on New Testament interpretations of the Old. Pastor Hofmann of the Lorenzkirche in Nürnberg preached on "Abraham's Emigration Staff; or, the Pious Example of Abraham for Christian Emigrants," on a text from the Book of Hebrews: "By faith Abraham, when he was called to go out to a place which he should later receive for an inheritance, obeyed, and he went out, not knowing whither he went."[16] The parallel between the Jewish Exodus and the Salzburger expulsion was an obvious representation, and by no means a makeshift or a transient one. A history published at Magdeburg in 1733 depicted a column of the Israelites of the Exodus, the men in high-crowned hats and the women with long skirts, being led to the Promised Land by the pillar of cloud; and parallel to them marches a procession of Salzburger, the women identified by short skirts and both sexes by their wide-brimmed hats, and this procession is led by an oversized Prussian eagle (Illus. 6). The verse caption attests to the equivalence of these agencies:

> Thou, oppressed Israel, wert led by fire and cloud
> When thou quittest Egypt's ban, estranged to start anew,
> And so to thee, poor folk of Salzburg, was God's Grace allowed,
> When thus before thy footsteps, Frederick William's eagle flew.[17]

For the Protestant pastorate, especially in those central places whose clerical establishments were already engaged in dubious battle to recapture and retain the attention of increasingly secularized burgher congregations, this Exile was indeed a Godsend. It was an affirmation of their faith and a proof of its power, and an occasion to assert and elevate their own roles, values, and purposes in community and state. The regular

---

[16] Georg Jeremias Hofmann, *Abrahams Emigrantenstab oder das erbauliche Exempel Abrahams für Christliche Emigranten, in einer Predigt über Ebr. 11, v. 8* (Nürnberg, 1732).

[17] Taken from *Die Getröstete Saltzburger Oder Gespräch Im Reiche der Lebendigen, Zwischen einem . . . Saltzburger . . . Und einem Waldenser* (Magdeburg, 1733).

Dich, bedrängtes Israel, führte Feuer- und Wolcken Seule,
Als dein Fuß in fremde Lande aus Egypten's Gräntzen zog,
Dir, O Saltzburgs armes Volck, ward auch Gottes Huld zu theile,
Weil vor dir auf deiner Reise Friedrich Wilhelm's Adler flog.

The emigration of the Salzburg Protestants compared with the Exodus of the Israelites from Egypt. From *Die Getröstete Saltzburger.*

qualities of obedience, candor, and loyalty which came publicly to be attributed to the essentially contrary, suspicious, and defiant Salzburg peasantry are a consequence of the pastoral transmission of the story, as embodied in these published sermons and pastoral accounts, in which these positive qualities attributed to the Salzburger were linked in turn to their piety.

Furthermore, pastoral economy being what it was and is, the printed sermons and reports from the sixty-seven places undoubtedly provided material for exponentially more sermons, delivered by lesser pastoral lights in lesser places throughout Protestant Germany, who found in them their weekly texts. When we take into account this multiplier effect, the power of publicity which came to bear on the Salzburg emigration, through the pastoral medium, is quite staggering. It is hard to imagine any informational system of the time which was at all comparable. It combined print with oral communication, integrating and multiplying their respective transmissions and their receptions. The process of diffusion was internally energized, self-generated by the wills and interests of the bearers of the message. By comparison with this engine, the famed but sulky Prussian administrative apparatus was primitive and inert, for all King Frederick William's murderous disciplinary goads. The pastoral network might challenge modern structures of persuasion for saturation and authority, making up in persistence what it lacked in velocity.

The pastors' message overlapped and reinforced the king's in important respects. The economic interests and passions of the Prussian crown matched the confessional interests and passions of German Protestantism, proceeding from a mix toward a match as the story evolved. The plot (or text) ultimately included the erratic and cruel archbishop, the calm and steadfast exiles, the identification of Prussia as leader and savior; then the flourishing of Prussia's domains as refuge for these Protestant spirits. In the production of this history, the Salzburger were transformed in several ways. The sham Catholicism they had affected in Salzburg was dissolved, as already noted, in a language of steadfast and sturdy Evangelical belief, and then it disappeared altogether. The endless trouble they made for the officials and pastors in East Prussia, their frequent refusal to work, or stay where they were put, the commonplace drunkenness and adultery: these too were replaced or submerged in a story marked by the qualities of piety, order, diligence, and frugality. The episode became a romance of moral propriety, a melding of Prussian and Protestant destinies into a bürgerlich, or middle-class epic, articulated into anecdote and image. I say bürgerlich because, countryfolk though the Salzburger were and remained, they came to be endowed with qualities such as thrift and industry which eighteenth-century culture, quite decidedly, had not perceived in peasants or mountain people before. So construed, the story was picked up and adapted at appropriate times by appropriate means in succeeding years and decades. Salzburg stories and Salzburg pictures became regular grist for the illustrated moral weeklies and monthlies that provided ideology for the German middle classes especially of the nineteenth century—*Gartenlaube, Illustrierte Welt, Daheim*—and for the countless journals and proceedings of local historical societies.[18]

During the late eighteenth century relatively little seems to have been made of the story, probably because its implicit religious contentiousness was condemned by the dominant public culture and out of style.[19] This Enlightened temper is suggested, at least, by one passage that has come to my attention: in Johann M. Schröckh's popular "General World History for Children," which first appeared in 1781. There the story was taught as a reproof to religious hatreds that, although repressed in the interest of peace and civility, still had cropped up even in that present century. The text shifts into boldface to

---

[18] For examples of the former see Marsch, *Salzburger Emigration*, pp. 225–40; and the bibliographies in Ehmer, *Schrifttum*.

[19] The fullest bibliography lists almost no references during this period, and those that do appear are mainly interested in the American settlements in Georgia: see Ehmer, *Schrifttum*, pp. 79–113.

emphasize that "the Archbishop of Salzburg lost in that way around thirty thousand staunch [*getreue*] and industrious subjects"; and the prose narration is accompanied by an engraving that shows a loose column of very depressed and disheveled migrants, quite unlike the triumphant processions depicted in the 1730s. But, Schröckh assured his tender readers, this time of intolerance was safely past.[20] The Protestant imperial patriot (but no friend of Prussia) Friedrich Karl von Moser sounded a confessional note in 1787 (echoing Haller) in his essay on the governments of the German ecclesiastical states: "How many thousands of good industrious subjects have emigrated out of the paradisiacal regions of upper Germany, to the sandy wastes of Brandenburg and Prussia, and to the American forests, just because a few Jesuits, . . . " whereupon the rest of the sentence was blanked out, ostensibly by censors.[21]

At the end of the century, however, the poet Goethe used the Salzburg story as the basis for what was to be his most popular long poem, *Hermann und Dorothea*, transposing a romantic pastor's tale of religious expulsion in the 1730s into a story of political exile from the French revolution in the 1790s and transforming the sturdy peasant qualities of Salzburg mountaineers, deliberately and significantly, into the small-town virtues of Rhineland refugees (Haller's *Die Alpen* had been among the young Goethe's early readings).[22] In 1809 the

[20] Johann M. Schröckh, *Allgemeine Weltgeschichte für Kinder*; I have used the second edition (Leipzig, 1792), pp. 434–35. The illustration is reproduced in Marsch, *Salzburger Emigration*, illus. 227.

[21] Friedrich Karl von Moser, *Über die Regierungen der geistlichen Staaten* (Frankfurt/M., 1787), pp. 173–74. See also the 1797 representation by Johann Penzel of the expulsion of the Salzburger as the "ecce homo" scene of the passion of Christ, in Marsch, *Salzburger Emigration*, illus. 228 (source not further identified).

[22] Richard Friedenthal, *Goethe: Sein Leben und seine Zeit* (Munich, 1963), pp. 37, 450–52; Hermann Schreyer, "Einleitung" to *Goethes Sämtliche Werke, Jubiläums-Ausgabe*, vol. 6 (Stuttgart, 1902), pp. xvi–xvii. Goethe's particular source is said to have been [Johann Avenarius], *Das liebthätige Gera gegen die Saltz-*

East Prussian liberal reformer Theodor von Schön pronounced to King Frederick William III that "the Lithuanian province owes its present cultural condition mainly to the immigrant Salzburger. It was they who first showed the natives what Providence provides, and how to make use of it in ways worthy of a rational being. They are the founders," Schön told the king, " of the present spiritual and industrial culture [Geistes- und Gewerbekultur]."[23]

These turn-of-the-century examples resume a process whereby, in the nineteenth and into the twentieth century the Salzburg emigration came to articulate and to represent a Protestant alliance among middle-class virtues and loyalties, economic enterprise, and the dynamics and discipline of the Prussian state. The popular revival of the story as history, however, may be located with Karl Panse's "History of the Emigration of the Protestant Salzburger in the Year 1732: A Contribution to Church History, Written from the Sources," which appeared at Leipzig in 1827. Panse had previously published the "Library of Good Old German Comedies" in 1826 and went on to a "History of the Prussian State, from the Beginnings up to the Present Time" in six volumes in 1830–32. The Salzburger history that came between these efforts was the first lengthy treatment of the subject since the 1730s, and it really did rest on a thoroughgoing perusal of the extensive public documentary

---

burgischen Emigranten; Das ist: Kirtze und wahrhaftige Erzehlung, wie dieselben in der Gräflich-Reuss-Plauischen Residentz-Stadt Gera angekommen, aufgenommen und versorget, auch was an und von vielen derselben gutes gesehen und gehöret worden; Mit eilfertiger Feder entworfen (Leipzig, 1732), pp. 27–29.

[23] Quoted by Otto Kerschhofer, "Die Salzburger Emigration nach Preussisch-Litauen," MGSL 116 (1976), 201. Schön had been born in 1773 as son of a Domänenpächter in Schreitlaucken, Prussian Lithuania—a district in which, oddly enough, no Salzburger at all had been settled in the 1730s: Horst Kenkel, Amtsbauern und Kölmer im nördlichen Ostpreussen um 1736 (Hamburg, 1972), pp. 107, 183–84. He was appointed director of the Lithuanian provincial government at Gumbinnen in April 1809: Aus den Papieren des Ministers und Burggrafen von Marienburg Theodor von Schön, vol. 1 (Halle, 1875), p. 103.

sources.[24] A popular version went through five editions between 1830 and 1841, and three more by 1871.

Panse's telling of the story was unremittingly anti-Catholic,
railing in the name of tolerance against Romanist intolerance;
but especially interesting here is the ecological scheme of men-
talities which Panse employed, similar in some respects to a
scheme I employed in the Prologue. Panse began with an
idyllic description of alpine scenery, in the manner of Haller
but updated by the expostulative sentimentality of the 1820s,
and then he went on to explain how these surroundings had
produced in those who dwelt among them a Protestant culture
of independence, piety, and thrift. The Salzburger farmer was
environmentally conditioned to seek his God, alone; for "his
dwellings lie far apart from one another; and villages of the
kind that cover the plains of Germany are unknown here; and
each builds his cottage in the center of his fields and cuts himself off from his neighbors, or he perches it on on a steep cliff-
side that allows no living sociability." From this condition it
follows that "the long winter leads the awakened spirit to God,
in need of whose grace it stands; and solitude makes of it an
inquirer [Forscher]." Thence (after anthropologically conventional nods to Hunter and Shepherd) Panse turned to the ty-
pology of Merchant as analogue to the Salzburg exile: "The
Handelsmann has seen the world outside his mountains, and
when he comes back home, he has become a doubter of
Rome's infallibility [Untrügbarkeit]; he has not had the time to
seek his God by way of endless ceremonials, and discovers to
his surprise that his soul's refreshment has no need of them.
He must take the nearest path to Heaven, and he is a Protestant, unawares [ohne es zu heissen]."[25]

---

[24] Karl Panse, Geschichte der Auswanderung der evangelischen Salzburger im Jahr
1732. Ein Beitrag zur Kirchengeschichte. Nach den Quellen bearbeitet (Leipzig, 1827);
idem., Bibliothek guter alter deutscher Lustspiele (Leipzig, 1826); idem., Geschichte
des preussischen Staates seit der Entstehung bis auf die gegenwärtige Zeit, 6 vols.
(Berlin, 1830–32).

[25] Panse, Geschichte der Auswanderung, pp. 3–7.

Probably the most widely and frequently distributed rendition of the Salzburg history, however, was Wolfgang Menzel's in his "History of the Germans, Up to the Most Recent Times." This radically anti-Catholic and nationalist version first appeared at Zurich in 1824–25, where, as political activist and cofounder of the Jena *Burschenschaft*, Menzel was living in exile along with Karl Follen and others who had been implicated in such affairs as the Wartburg Festival of young German nationalism and the assassination of the playwright August Kotzebue. But the real history of Menzel's "History" begins with its serial reissue in 1734–35 by the powerful Cotta press at Stuttgart, where Menzel meanwhile had resettled in the course of his political transubstantiation to the conservative camp. After that it went through four more large editions by 1872.[26]

Menzel's account was enlivened docudramatically with a number of fabricated quotations, as: "'No matter!' said the archbishop, 'I'll have those heretics out of the land, though henceforward nothing but thorn and thistle will grow upon it.'" Menzel also quoted a Salzburg official thus: "'I sh——something in the Evangelium!'" and he opined that the Salzburg peasants had most likely got the idea of the salt-licking ceremonial at Schwarzach from the secret lore of Paracelsus, who had seen a powerful elemental force in salt.[27] Most of the invented quotations, and the role of Paracelsus, eventually disappeared from later editions, although the part about the thorns and thistles, and to a lesser extent the defilement of the Evangelium, became favorite themes of other popular ac-

---

[26] I have found no copy of Menzel's 1824–25 Zurich edition (3 vols. published by the radical Gessner firm), which bore the subtitle *Für die reifere Jugend und zum Selbstunterricht fassl. beschrieben*. I have used the second edition, *Geschichte der Deutschen bis auf die neuesten Tage*, one volume in seven installments (Stuttgart, 1834–35), of which many copies have survived and are easy to find. For the Young German radical scene at Zurich in the 1820s and the role of the Gessner firm, see Edmund Spevack, "Charles Follen (1796–1840)" (Ph.D. diss., Johns Hopkins University 1992), chap. 3.

[27] Menzel, *Geschichte der Deutschen*, pp. 620–21.

counts. In 1870 Menzel—still in Stuttgart—published a timely "What Has Prussia Achieved for Germany?" and in it listed many positive accomplishments, including King Frederick William I's recognition of the military merits of "a stalwart and heroic race," and his *kerndeutsch* hatred of the French; and along with these the Prussian king's invitation of "many thousand honest and industrious Salzburger, who had been driven out of their homes by the intolerant regime of the Catholic South."[28]

The Salzburger history had become a regular medium for political expression of Protestant passion and Prusso-German redemption. In this construction it rode the wave of patriotic enthusiasm of 1840, when King Frederick William IV's coronation arrived on the centennial anniversary of the succession of Frederick II, the Great. Franz Kugler told the story in his famous "History of Frederick the Great" published in that portentous year, lavishly illustrated by Adolph Menzel and republished many times, but especially during the 1840s: probably the most popular and longest-lived of all biographies of that king.[29] Eduard Duller told it too in his 1840 "History of the German People," paraphrasing Wolfgang Menzel (no relation to Adolph) but with some added detail: the archbishop "wanted to exterminate them [*ausrotten*] altogether, willingly turning his land into a desert. . . . [He] tore the farmers away from wife and child, hunted them from their plows, seized all their goods, and mocked them with the rudest possible insults to their faith; but the children they held back, and turned them over to Jesuit schools for training. . . . The miserable Reichstag at Regensburg raised not a hand in defense of the oppressed."[30] This popular history too, illustrated by the essential Bieder-

---

[28] Wolfgang Menzel, *Was hat Preussen für Deutschland geleistet?* (Stuttgart, 1870), pp. 18–19.

[29] Franz Kugler, *Geschichte Friedrichs des Grossen*, 2 vols. (Leipzig, 1840–42).

[30] Eduard Duller, *Geschichte des deutschen Volkes, mit hundert Holzschnitten und Originalzeichnungen von Ludwig Richter und J. Kirchhof* (Leipzig, 1840), pp. 528–30.

meier artist Ludwig Richter, was promptly expanded and reis-
sued in 1841 and had reached its fifth edition by 1874. Adolph
Menzel used the story again to illustrate the first volume of the
new critical edition launched by Frederick William IV of the
collected works of his great forebear, which began to appear in
1846 (See illus. 7).[31]

During the 1850s and 1860s the story of the exiles took on
still more explicit political connotations, mediated, especially in
the popular accounts, by religious pathos. In the 1850s Friedrich Christoph Schlosser found space for the story in the sixteenth volume of his massive "History of the World, for the
German People," telling of the Salzburgers' persecution by the
"fanatical archbishop" and their rescue by the Prussian king.[32]
Now popular journalism took a lead from popular history. *Gartenlaube*, most popular of the family journals, published in 1861
a long and provocative article by Robert Keil, historian of
the *Burschenschaft* movement (and presumably a relative of
Gartenlaube's enterprising publisher Ernst Keil), entitled "The
Salzburger Afflictions," emitting outrage as he contemplated
the "spectacles of wretchedness" exemplified by the German
South, owing to the "priest-ridden benumbing of the people,
in concert with the narrow egoistic practices of the courts,
which through the centuries has prevented the most decent,
the sturdiest, the most gifted of the German tribes from achiev-
ing the high place it deserves in social, religious, and political
life: stultified by the hand of an egoistic, power-hungry clergy,
by religious intolerance and fanaticism, allied with an antina-
tional politics of treachery on the part of so ambitious and yet
so feeble princes, with the disastrous meddling of non-German

---

[31] *Oeuvres de Frédéric la Grand*, vol. 1 (Berlin, 1846), p. 202; this reproduction is
from Adolph Menzel, *Illustrationen zu den Werken Friedrichs des Grossen: Jubi-
leums-Ausgabe*, vol. 1 (Berlin, 1886), no. 6.

[32] Friedrich Christoph Schlosser, *Weltgeschichte für das deutsche Volk*, ed. G. L.
Kriegk, vol. 16 (Frankfurt/M., 1854), p. 111. In that same year, Cotta's *Augsburger Allgemeine Zeitung* reported that "the most distinguished families of Sa-
vannah" in Georgia were descendants of the Salzburger.

The Salzburg emigrants cross the border into Prussia. Illustration by Adolph Menzel for a special edition of *Oeuvres de Frédéric le Grand*.

cabinets in German affairs; these it was that brought about the unholy desolation and destruction of our fatherland in the seventeenth century, these it was, who even in the first half of the last, of the *eighteenth* century committed an act of brutality in one of the most beautiful lands of the German South, which raised among all the other German homelands [*Gauen*], and even abroad, a cry of outrage and of deepest sympathy—" all this in one long breathless sentence, interrupted only by a full-page depiction of supposed Salzburg peasants in a forest clearing, praying, vowing, gazing skyward, dipping salt. *Gartenlaube* told how Protestants had been tortured and buried alive by the "raging fanaticism and the bestial brutality" of the—note—imperial soldiery, whose conduct matched the "abominations of the Bourbon regime at Naples." King Frederick William of Prussia had spent "ten tons of gold" as the price of their rescue.[33]

Thus spoke *Gartenlaube*, symptomatically of the growing accommodation between Biedermeier and Borussian modes which would characterize the culture of the Second Empire. In mid-1865, as Prussia's contest with Austria for Germany moved visibly toward its climax, *Die Illustrierte Welt* invoked the Salzburger under the title "The Year 1731: German Staunchness in Belief [*Überzeugungstreue*]," with its sequel "Frederick William I of Prussia, the Wise Economist." This rang the old alarm anew: "As the news spread through the world that the Tyrolean Diet had passed a resolution on February 25, 1863, in the deep hours of the night, a resolution that the land and people of Tyrol henceforth must lie under the ban of religious uniformity, and no person who is not of the old patristic faith shall be allowed to remain or to come to the land with equal rights, except under conditions which make those of independent mind all but helpless: then a shudder went through

---

[33] *Gartenlaube: Illustriertes Familienblatt* (1861), no. 27, pp. 420–24; no. 28, pp. 440–43. Keil returned to the theme in *Gartenlaube* (1863), no. 44. The illustration mentioned is reproduced in Marsch, *Salzburger Emigration*, illus. 235.

all Europe." It was the Jesuits again, of whom the notorious "von Röll" in his time had himself been one, even as the "dim-witted" archbishop Firmian had been the Jesuits' tool as they strove to add Württemberg, Salzburg, and Poland to the conquests they had already made of Bavaria, Saxony, and Belgium. They had promised Firmian much gold and silver, but all he had got was the thorns and thistles that had desolated his land ever since.[34]

This immediate threat to Germany and Europe was overcome when Austria was isolated and defeated by Prussia in the course of the 1860s, and the Prusso-German Empire was proclaimed in 1871. The perspicacious Thomas Carlyle wrote a six-volume *History of Friedrich II of Prussia, Called Frederick the Great*, which appeared in German and in step with that political process, between 1858 and 1869. Carlyle devoted some twenty pages to the "movingly idyllic nature" of the Salzburger story, this "remarkable business" set in the "legendary Tyrolean valleys" of Salzburg, a tale "which all Germany still thinks upon, and even sings about." Carlyle too invented speeches: for a cynical but hysterical Reverend Father Sir Firmian, for a shrewd but magnanimous Prussian King Frederick William, and for other players in his melodramatic rendition of the tale. Carlyle concludes his telling with a reference to Goethe's hexameter version called *Hermann und Dorothea*, projected by the poet "into airy regions" and "still worth reading."[35] It is no longer possible, of course, to locate, let alone describe, the many places where the Salzburg history was invoked in print during these years. But as to the singing, as Carlyle called it: a specialized bibliography of fictional literature of the nineteenth and early twentieth centuries mentions ten novels, fifteen

[34] *Die Illustrierte Welt: Blätter aus Natur und Leben, Wissenschaft und Kunst, zur Unterhaltung und Belehrung für die Familie, für Alle und Jeden* (1865), 218–22, 250–55.

[35] Thomas Carlyle, *Geschichte Friedrichs II. von Preussen gen. Friedrich der Grosse*, trans. J. Neuberg, 6 vols. (Berlin, 1858–69), appeared in many editions after the first; I quote from the first edition, vol. 2 (1863), pp. 331–47.

"tales [*Erzählungen*]," four epic poems, and twelve dramatic representations of the Salzburg expulsion, the last group being mainly pageants and popular dramas designed for amateur and church-related exercises.[36] These, too, are now hard to find, though many were frequently reprinted. To represent them all I take Kurt Delbrück's "The Salzburger: A People's Stageplay in Six Scenes."

Delbrück was a gymnasium professor at Weimar who also published a novel called "Beethoven's Last Love," and patriotic dramas including a "Festival Play in Memory of Emperor William, the Great" and "William of Orange, the German."[37] His Salzburger melodrama was printed in some seventy pages of blank verse, with a dozen spoken parts and constantly shifting scenes: no easy undertaking for amateurs, but intended for presentation, according to its title pages, by Protestant lay associations and youth groups; it had already played, announced the preface to a third edition (1910), before audiences of many thousands, including the Evangelical Union of Essen West, at the Bierhalle Cronenberg, in Neuruppin at the Stadtgartensaal, and a great many other places large and small.[38]

Leading the action was a Salzburger family to which Delbrück gave the name of Schaitberger, as a reminder of the famous *Send-Briefe*, reissues of which were still in print. No clergy appear onstage, perhaps out of deference to the estate of the cloth; villainy is embodied rather in a "Count Werfen," who, amid an opening Schaitberger family scene, appears with a band of Austrian soldiers. These with his connivance have been brutalizing the native population, upon whom they are quartered, twenty of them on the farm of the rich widow

[36] Ehmer, *Schrifttum*, pp. 109–13.

[37] Kurt Delbrück, *Beethovens letzte Liebe* (Halle, 1925), *Festspiel zum Gedächtniss Kaiser Wilhelms des Grossen* (Hannover, 1897), and *Wilhelm der Oranier, der Deutsche* (n.p., 1916).

[38] I have used the third edition (Hannover, 1910), which identifies Delbrück as a pastor in Berlin-Schöneberg, and have seen a second (Hannover, 1902) but not a first edition.

Schwarzenegger (who has one of the two female speaking roles; Schaitberger's daughter Maria is the other; meanwhile, offstage a woman is burned alive in a stove whither she has crept to escape the attention of the soldiery). Werfen and the soldiers are hunting Schaitberger's son Joseph, who had resisted their persecutions of the helpless; when they do not find him, the Schaitbergers are driven out into the storm.

Schaitberger then calls Protestant family heads together at a secret place, contemplating no violence, he insists, but "to take holy counsel." He reveals to the others that he has sent his son, Joseph, to Regensburg seeking support, and he recalls the salvation of the Huguenots by Prussia. "'Away, away; the land of freedom!'" cry the assembled fathers and they dip salt (here there are stage directions: *see II Chronicles 13, 5*). At this, however, Count Werfen reappears, escorted, and arrests them all; a resister is cut down by a soldier, and the rest are hustled off to imprisonment on bread and water in the dungeons of the Count's castle.

In a room of the castle, Count Werfen confronts the group and demands their conversion to Catholicism. He mocks their protest that the Protestant estates of the Empire will defend their rights: Who cares for the estates? sneers Werfen; no *prince* will draw the sword in their behalf; and he orders in the young Joseph Schaitberger, who has been intercepted and arrested on his way back from Regensburg. For his treasonous behavior Joseph must die, says Werfen, and he points out the window to where the bloody scaffold already stands. But wait; mercy before justice! If only father Schaitberger will turn to the bosom of the true church, Joseph will be spared and everybody may go home free.

Schaitberger ponders the distressful choice before him. What shall he do? Just a couple of words will save everybody, insinuates Werfen. It is all up to you, he says. Schaitberger: But at what a price! Finally he decides: Son Joseph, it is all up to *you*: "'Will you / Be freed from death, but at betrayal's cost?'" Joseph sees that this would break his father's heart, and urges

Schaitberger not to yield: "'Better . . . to end upon the bloody scaffold / Than be judged false at God's eternal throne / . . . Count, be quick.'" He is led off and executed offstage, and the headless corpse is brought to a place from which the actors can see it (stage direction: *but out of sight of the audience*).

When the fathers, despite the bloody spectacle offstage, still refuse to say the few words that would save them, Werfen orders them all to the scaffold; but he grants them a brief moment to pray, and as they do, *Outside, a trumpet sounds*. It is Herr Dankelmann, newly arrived envoy from Regensburg. Again Werfen sneers: who cares about the Reichstag? nobody who matters does. But Dankelmann then reveals himself to be no mere agent of the Old Empire but additionally, a true servant of the king of Prussia, who will give succor to the persecuted Protestants; and the archbishop has agreed to let them go. Dankelmann displays the emigration order; Werfen reads it with, if he follows stage directions, trembling hands: "'All my trouble in vain!'" he cries. He goes out.

Finally the peasant columns are formed, herded together by the soldiers, under whose treatment the aged father of the rich widow Schwarzenegger expires onstage. ("'Do you hear? the angels sing! Such a light!'") The other female player, Schaitberger's daughter Maria, is seized and hustled off as a final vengeful act, to be brought up Catholic, and the rest of the cast marches out singing in chorus "A Mighty Fortress Is Our God," in which, again according to stage directions, the audience joins.

The family journal *Daheim* contemplated the meaning of the Salzburger history at New Year's 1884, its reflections including a large foldout illustration of the migrant columns' arrival at Berlin-Zehlendorf, replete with festively dressed Salzburger, children, books, and a beaming Frederick William I. "The sorrows which an unbridled religious fanaticism inflicted on the Salzburger brought with them rich blessings. The steadfastness of the martyrs brought countless Protestants to realize what they possessed in the pure Evangelium; to their migration, finally, we owe one of the most beloved poems of Goethe. An event, which occurred then at Gera, inspired the great poet to write "Hermann and Dorothea."[39] This is the point at which to note that Marianne Weber, in exactly the place where in her biography she attests Max Weber's Salzburg heritage, also invokes *Hermann und Dorothea* to describe the small-town, "early-capitalist" Bielefeld where her husband's poetically perceived Salzburg ancestor had settled and opened his trade: that was the Bielefeld, "as Goethe sang," she writes, of Max Weber's revered grandfather, the actual personage "whose type he [Max] captured in his essay on the capitalist spirit".[40]

It was always, of course, possible to write a soberer and quite factual account of the expulsion—for example, the rendition in Gustav Adolph Harald Stenzel's "History of the Prussian State," which followed the richly documented early treatments by the Prussian official Göcking and the Catholic chronicler Gärtner.[41] Academic historians too—*wissenschaftliche*, in the German sense of scholarly—recalled the story, though with less dramatic color and perhaps less imagination; and they were more inclined to see the political and economic monuments it revealed, though they never lost sight of the religious component that dominated the popular accounts. Among historians of the established order, Leopold von Ranke, who knew very well the political circumstances of the Salzburg migration and its relatively small place in the Prussian Retablissement program of economic development, declared nevertheless that it was the Salzburg Protestants who "first gave the whole program genuine character." Otto Hintze in his popular but serious and authoritative 1915 history, "The Hohenzollerns and Their Work," assimilated the entire Retab-

---

[39] *Daheim* (Leipzig, 1884), pp. 4–8. The original painting from which the illustration was made is reproduced in Marsch, *Salzburger Emigration*, illus. 244.

[40] See note 1 above. Marianne Weber attributes the comparison to her late husband's mother, of Huguenot descent.

[41] Adolph Harold Stenzel, *Geschichte des preussischen Staates*, vol. 3, *1688–1739* (Hamburg, 1841); Gärtner, *Chronik*; Göcking, *Emigrations-Geschichte*.

lissement history into the story of the Salzburg migration.[42] In still more recent times, Carl Hinrichs, historian of the pietist and Prussian spirits, called the Prussia of Frederick William I, "the first complete embodiment of the Protestant-bourgeois world of work [der protestantischen-bürgerlichen Arbeitswelt]."[43]

Social, cultural, and administrative theorists followed a pattern parallel to that of the historians. Gustav Schmoller wrote that the East Prussian rural domain administration had "generated [erzogen] a prosperous, bourgeois [bürgerlichen], entrepreneurial middle class, far above the level of the backward and petty [spiessbürgerlichen] artisanry of the time: industrious, thrifty, energetic."[44] This was the Schmoller who, as guiding spirit of the "Society for Social Policy" (Verein für Sozialpolitik), started the young Berliner immigrant Max Weber (following Weber's work on the rural constitution of classical Rome) on his early study of the East-Elbian rural work system. Weber's great rival Werner Sombart published a study called Der Bourgeois in 1920, the same year as Weber's essay, "The Protestant

[42] Leopold von Ranke, Zwölf Bücher Preussischer Geschichte, 2d ed., vols. 3–4 (Sämtliche Werke 27–28 [Leipzig, 1879]), p. 174; Otto Hintze, Die Hohenzollern und ihr Werk (Leipzig, 1915), pp. 299–300; and see Gerd Wunder, "Die Schweizer Kolonisten in Ostpreussen 1710–1730 als Beispiel für Koloniebauern," in Bauernschaft und Bauernstand 1500–1970, ed. Günther Franz, (Limburg/Lahn, 1975), p. 183.

[43] Carl Hinrichs, Preussen als historisches Problem: Gesammte Abhandlungen (Berlin, 1964), p. 32. Neither Frederick William I nor the Salzburger can be called pietist in a theological sense, but Pietism in the vaguer sense that associates the Prussian state with the "improvement" Pietism at Halle is loosely but commonly attributed to both.

[44] Gustav Schmoller, "Das brandenburgisch-preussische Innungswesen von 1640 bis 1800," in his Umrisse und Untersuchungen zur Verfassungs-, Verwaltungs- und Wirtschaftsgeschichte besonders des preussischen Staates im 17. und 18. Jahrhundert (Leipzig, 1898), p. 169. The East German economic historian H. H. Müller argued in 1965 in the Jahrbuch für Wirtschaftsgeschichte that the domain leasing system succeeded because of transformation of leases into essentially secure private property, in which leasers reinvested their profits as capital. See his "Domänen und Domänenpächter in Brandenburg-Preussen im 18. Jahrhundert," JWG (1965), 152–92.

Ethic and the Spirit of Capitalism." In counterpoint to Weber, Sombart traced the entrepreneurial spirit to the historical experience of a culture, rather than to a transcendent predisposition of its values; and he supported his logic with a historical argument about migrations, with special attention to Scots, Huguenots, Yankees, and Jews. "Migration or the change of native place *as such*," he emphasized, "is the basis for the strongest development of capitalistic spirit." Migration was, moreover, "a selective process" that identified "the most energetic, the strongest-willed, boldest, coolest, most calculating and least sentimental natures, no matter whether they turned to emigration on account of religious or political oppression, or for economic gain." Such oppression at home was in fact "the best preparatory school [*Vorschule*] for capitalistic development [*die kapitalistische Ausbildung*]."[45]

These remarks by Hinrichs, Schmoller, and Sombart were not addressed directly to the episode of the Salzburger, though they seem to encircle it within their constellation of Protestantism, migration, and economic enterprise. One might, conceivably, develop a theoretical argument that the Salzburg Gutsbesitzer who became East Prussian Hofbauern, country folk though they were, did in effect own capital, which they exploited for profit and reinvested, and even that there was something entrepreneurial in their departure from a static and constrained economic universe into one of wider invitation and opportunity; or even, though still more remotely, that the respective ecclesiastical conditions in Salzburg and East Prussia had something to do with this mutation. Clearly the emigrant Salzburger Bauern had more in common with the king of Prussia than they had with the archbishop of Salzburg. But it was not entrepreneurial daring or economic calculation that the Salzburger legend celebrated. It was diligence, constancy, and sacrifice, and their transcendent rewards. (Illus. 8)

[45] Werner Sombart, *Der Bourgeois* (Munich, 1920), pp. 380–98; the quotations are from pp. 391–92.

This frontispiece to the first volume of Gerhard Göcking's *Vollkommene Emigrations-Geschichte* (1734) shows the king and queen of Prussia elevated above a plethora of allegorical royal bureaucrats at work. A putto surveys the Pongau in Salzburg, scribes keep a tally of the arriving colonists, who are depicted in conventional arrangements (compare the Nürnberg engraving of 1734 at the beginning of this chapter), and a Prussian eagle has Lithuania firmly in its grasp. The frontispiece to Göcking's second volume (1737; not shown) shows Crown Prince Frederick and his bride, subject to the stern scrutiny and recording hand of Kronos.

For this last episode of the Salzburg transaction is about the making of a history as a moral idea, not about learned adaptations of social theory. This history was made in a particular context of German confessional politics, one that tied the expulsion of the Salzburg Protestants, both at the end of the story and at its outset, to the organizing energies and dynastic vigor and tradition of the Hohenzollern monarchy and its administrative state of the eighteenth century and beyond, and so to its central role in the formation of German political culture. Located there, the parable of the Salzburg exiles is no more trivial or accidental than Marianne Weber's biographical strategem. It is a religious parable in the ethical formation of political and moral culture, then—one that finds its place, though, in the story not so much of Protestantism and a spirit of secular capitalism but more nearly of German Protestantism and the spirit of Prussia; or yet again, another reminder of the problematic relation among them.

BIBLIOGRAPHY

ARCHIVALIA

Konsistorialarchiv Salzburg (KAS): *Konsistorialakten*

11/53a: Reformation, 1686–1695. Hallein, Zell, Grossarl, Hüttau, Dienten, Bischofshofen, Freisach, etc.

11/53b: Reformation. Religions Kommissions-Akten 1672–1728. Verschiedene Orte. Verhöre.

11/53c: Reformation. Religions-Commissions Berichte. Verschiedene Orte 1732–1781.

11/54a: Reformation. Ketzer Bekehrung 1627–1808.

11/54b: Reformation. Verschiedene Orte: Werfen, Radstadt, Goldegg, Hüttau, Gastein, Altenmarkt 1706–1726. Verhöre.

11/54c: Reformation. Werfen, Wagrain, Radstadt, Bischofshofen, St.-Johann, Goldegg. Relig. Kommission 1695–1706. Verhöre etc.

11/65a: Reformation. Altenmarkt. Relig. Commission. Verhöre 1686–1706.

11/66g: Reformation. St. Johann i. Pg. Verhöre 1704–1706.

11/66h: Reformation. St. Johann i. Pg. Verhöre 1727–1730.

11/69b: Reformation. Verhöre, Personenverzeichnisse u. Anderes 1601–1698.

11/69c: Reformation. Reform der Kleidertracht, Abstellung des Lasters der Unkeuschheit aus den Gebirgen. Pars I, 1729–1731; Pars II, 1732–1738.

11/69e: Reformation. Emigrationspatent 1731. Verkauf der Emigrantengüter im Beisein des preuss. Gesandten. Verzeichnis der Güter 1734–38, etc.

11/71a: Reformation. Gastein. Relig. Verhöre 1731.

Salzburger Landesarchiv (SLA): *Emigration 1731/44* (EA)

69: Kommissionsakten der von F. Baron Rehlingen mit dem preuss. Gesandten Frh. v. Plotho vorgenommenen Bereisung des Gebirges 1736.

73: Miszellanea: 1731–1739.

74: Miszellanea: Verzeichnisse der Emigranten, Undatierte Korrespondenzkonzepte Christanis.

74–75/98–99: Kommission im Gebirge, Jul. 1731.

76–77/100–101: Schwarzacher Zusammenkunft, Gesandschaft der Bauern nach Regensburg, etc.

78/102: Oktober 1731. Verpflegung der eingerückten kaiserlichen Völker; Einberufung und Beschreibung aller Schutzen; Entwaffnung.

79/103: Eingeschickte Beschreibungen der evang. erklärten Unterthanen, die bei den vom Kaiser extradierten Salzburger Bauern verzeichnet gefunden. 1–10 Oktober 1731.

80/104: Emigrationspatent; Entwaffnung, Verzeichnisse. 2 Nov.–3 Dez. 1731.

81/105: Spezifikationen der Schutzen, Wehrhaften Bauern, deren Söhnen und Knechten und anderen Burschen. 1731.

83/107: Aufgefangene verdächtige Briefe . . . etc. 25 Februar–13 Oktober 1732.

84/108: Korrespondenz mit dem Kaiser . . . Ankunft des kaiserlichen oö. Geh. Rates von Gentilotti . . . Beschwerde des Corpus Evangelicorum . . . 25 Juli [1731]–2 Oktober 1732.

92/116: Marschrouten der Emigranten durch das Reich in das kgl. Preussische . . . von den Pfleggerichten eingeschickte Spezifikazionen der emigrirten Personen.

93/117: Von den Pfleggerichten eingeschickte Spezifikationen der Emigranten und deren Kinder.

95/119: Dürrnberger Emigranten, Jesuitenmission dortselbst, Vertrags-
punkte mit den Generalstaaten Holland.
97/120: Von der hf. Gesandschaft in Regensburg eingelaufene relationen . . . etc.

Geheimes Staats-Archiv, Preussischer Kulturbesitz (GStA PK)

162A: Findbuch, für die Prästations-Tabellen.
Rep. 5 Tit. 21 Nr. 1: Register der nach Preussen gekommenen
Salzburger mit Angabe der salzburgischen Gerichtsbezirke, 1732.
Rep. 5 Tit. 21 Nr. 14: Acta wegen Anfertigung von Tabellen über die
Salzburger . . . in Königsberg, in den Landstädten in der Königs-
berger Departements und auf den adeligen Gütern. 1734.
Rep. 5 Tit. 21 Nr. 15, vols. 1–3: Acta, wegen Liquidation der von den
Salzburgern in ihrem Vaterlande zurückgelassenen Forderungen . .
. 1735–38.
XX. HA Pt Budweitschen II–III: Prästationstabellen, 1734, 1736, 1739.
XX. HA Rep. 100A Nr. 153, I–II: Salzburger Emigrantenlist (originals
in SLA EA 92/116, 93/117).

PUBLISHED TITLES.

This selective list does not include every work consulted or mentioned in the notes, but only titles that are cited more than once in
any chapter of the text (therefore at least once by short title) and
others of special relevance and importance. Lengthy bibliographies
of the emigration itself appear in the Dannappel and Ehmer works
listed below.

"Alte deutsche Längen- und Flächenmasse." *GT* 2 (1950), 258.
Ammerer, Gerhard. "Funktionen, Finanzen und Fortschritt: Zur Regionalverwaltung im Spätabsolutismus am Beispiel des geistlichen
Fürstentums Salzburg." *MGSL* 126 (1986), 341–518, and 127 (1987),
151–418.
Arnold, Carl F. *Die Ausrottung des Protestantismus in Salzburg unter Erzbischof Firmian und seinen Nachfolgern.* 2 vols. Halle, 1900–1901.
Arnold, C. Franklin. "Die Salzburger in Amerika." *JGPÖ* 25 (1904),
222–61.

Barton, Peter. "Die jüngste Literatur über die evangelischen Salzburger- oder—Das Ende des ökumenischen Zeitalters?" *JGPÖ* 107 (1981), 175–212.

[Baum, Johan Heinrich]. *Der Saltzburgischen Emigranten Freuden-müthige und höchst-gesegnete Wanderschafft, in die Königlich-Preussische Lande.* Nürnberg, 1732.

Beheim-Schwarzbach, Max. *Friedrich Wilhelms I. Kolonisationswerk in Litauen, vornehmlich die Salzburger Kolonie.* Königsberg, 1879.

——. *Hohenzollernsche Colonisationen.* Leipzig, 1874.

Belster, Ulrich. *Die Stellung des Corpus Evangelicorum im Reichstag.* Tübingen, 1968.

Biederbick, Andreas. *Der deutsche Reichstag zu Regensburg im Jahrzehnt nach dem Spanischen Erbfolgekrieg 1714–1724.* Düsseldorf, 1937.

Blickle, Peter. *Landschaften im Alten Reich; Die staatliche Funktion des gemeinen Mannes in Oberdeutschland.* Munich, 1973.

Borgmann, Karl. *Der deutsche Religionsstreit der Jahre 1719/20.* Berlin, 1937.

Breiter, Herbert, ed. *Johann Christoph Dreyhaupt: Anecdotes de Saltzbourg oder Geheime Nachrichten von dem Erzstift Salzburg.* Salzburg/Braunschweig, 1977.

Brettenthaler, Josef. "Die Wiederbesiedlung." In *REP*, pp. 172–79.

Bruckmüller, Ernst. *Sozialgeschichte Österreichs.* Vienna, 1985.

Brückner, Wolfgang. "Zum Wandel der religiösen Kultur im 18. Jahrhundert." In *Sozialer und Kultureller Wandel in der ländlichen Welt des 18. Jahrhunderts*, edited by Ernst Hinrichs and Günter Wiegelmann, pp. 65–83. Wolfenbüttel, 1982.

Bülow, Heinrich W. v. *Über Geschichte und Verfassung des Corporis Evangelicorum.* [Regensburg], 1795.

Caspari, Johannes Baptist [=Giovanni Battista Caspari di Nuovomonte]. *Aktenmässige Geschichte der berühmten salzburgischen Emigration.* translated by Franz X. Huber. Salzburg, 1790.

Clarus, Ludwig [= Ludwig Völkel]. *Die Auswanderung der protestantisch gesinnten Salzburger.* Innsbruck, 1864.

Clauss, Hermann. "Josef Schaitberger und sein Sendbrief." *BBK* 15 (1909), 105–23, 153–66.

Conrad, Kurt. "Der Bauer und sein Hof." In *REP*, pp. 151–66.

Currie, Pamela. "Moral Weeklies and the Reading Public in Germany 1711–1750." *OGS* 3 (1968), 69–86.

Czybulka, Gerhard. *Die Lage der ländlichen Klassen Ostdeutschlands im 18. Jahrhundert*. Braunschweig, 1949.

Dannappel, Ernst. "Die Literatur der Salzburger Emigration, 1731–1735," followed by "Ein Beitrag zu E. Dannappels Literatur," *NABB* 47 (1886), 33–41, 65–71, 97–103, 267–275.

Dedic, Paul. "Nachwirkungen der grossen Emigration in Salzburg und Steiermark." *JGPÖ* 65–66 (1944–45), 71–134.

———. "Verbreitung und Vernichtung evangelischen Schrifttums in Innerösterreich." *ZKG* 57 (1938), 433–58.

"Die deutsche Siedlungs- und Feldmasse." *GT* 4 (1953), 524–28.

Dissertori, Alois. *Die Auswanderung der Deferegger Protestanten 1666–1725*. Innsbruck, 1964.

Dollinger, Robert. "Regensburg und der österreichische Protestantismus nach der Pax Augustana." *ZBK* 28 (1959), 71–96.

Dreyhaupt, Johann C. *See* Breiter, Herbert.

Droysen, Johann G. *Geschichte der preussischen Politik*, Vol. 4, Part 3. Leipzig, 1869.

Dürlinger, Josef. *Historisch-statistisches Handbuch vom Pongau*. Salzburg, 1867.

Ehmer, Artur. *Das Schrifttum zur Salzburger Emigration 1731/1733*. Hamburg, 1975.

Engels, Rolf. *Die preussische Verwaltung von Kammer und Regierung Gumbinnen*. Cologne, 1974.

Engelsing, Rolf. *Der Bürger als Leser: Lesergeschichte in Deutschland 1500–1800*. Stuttgart, 1974.

Erdmannsdörffer, Bernhard. *Deutsche Geschichte vom Westfälischen Frieden bis zum Regierungsantritt Friedrichs des Grossen 1648–1740*. 2 vols. Berlin, 1892–93.

Faber, Anton [=Christian Leonhard Leucht], ed. *Europäische Staats-Cantzley*. Vols. 55–67. Nürnberg, 1730–36.

Fassmann, David. *Leben und Thaten Friderici Wilhelmi, Königs von Preussen*. Vol. 1: Hamburg, 1736; Vol. 2: Breslau, 1741.

Florey, Gerhard. *Geschichte der Salzburger Protestanten und ihrer Emigration 1731/32*. Vienna, 1977.

———. "Die Schwarzacher Versammlungen der Salzburger Protestanten im Jahre 1731." *MGSL* 114 (1974), 243–70.

Förster, Friedrich. *Friedrich Wilhelm I. König v. Preussen*. 3 vols. and 2 documentary vols. Potsdam, 1834–36.

Forstreuter, Adelbert. "Salzburgerstamm auf ostpreussischem Boden." *Odal* 3 (1934–35), 847–57.

Franz, Günther, ed. *Bauernschaft und Bauernstand 1500–1970*. Limburg/Lahn, 1975.

Gäbler, Ulrich. "Österreichs Protestanten und die Niederlande im 17. und 18. Jahrhundert." *JGPÖ* 98 (1982), 211–39.

Gärtner, Corbinus [=Maurus Schenkl]. *Geschichte der Bauernauswanderung aus Salzburg, unter dem Erzbischoff Firmian*. Salzburg 1821. Part 10 of J. D. Zauner, *Chronik von Salzburg*, q.v.

Gaspari, Johannes B. *See* Caspari.

Gesellschaft für Salzburger Landeskunde. *Festschrift für Herbert Klein*. Salzburg, 1965.

Göcking, Gerhard G. *Vollkommene Emigrations-Geschichte von denen aus dem Ertz-Bisthum Saltzburg vertribenen und in dem Königreich Preussen grössesten Theils aufgenommenen Lutheranern*. 2 vols. Frankfurt/M., 1734–37.

Goldbeck, J. F. *Vollständige Topographie des Königreichs Preussen. Erster Theil welcher die Topographie von Ost-Preussen enthält*. Königsberg, 1787. Reprint Hamburg, 1966.

Gollub, Hermann. *Stammbuch der ostpreussischen Salzburger*. Gumbinnen, 1934.

Günther, Adolf. *Die alpenländische Gesellschaft*. Jena, 1930.

Hansiz [=Hansitz], Marcus. *Germania Sacra*. Vol. 2, *Archiepiscopatus Salisburgensis*. Augsburg, 1729.

Harnoch, Agathon. *Chronik und Statistik der evangelischen Kirchen in den Provinzen Ost- und Westpreussen*. Neidenburg, 1890.

Heckel, Martin. "Itio in partes: Zur Religionsverfassung des Heiligen Römischen Reichs Deutscher Nation." *ZRG Kan* 95 (1978), 130–308.

——. "Parität." *ZRG Kan* 80 (1963), 261–420.

Heinisch, Reinhard R. *Die bischöflichen Wahlkapitulationen im Erzstift Salzburg 1514–1688*. Vienna, 1977.

——. *Salzburg im dreissigjährigen Krieg*. Vienna, 1968.

Henning, Friedrich-Wilhelm. *Bauernwirtschaft und Bauerneinkommen in Ostpreussen im 18. Jahrhundert*. Würzburg, 1969.

——. "Die Betriebsgrössenstruktur der mitteleuropäischen Landwirtschaft im 18. Jahrhundert und ihr Einfluss auf die ländlichen Einkommenverhältnisse." *ZAA* 17 (1969), 171–93.

——. "Die Differenzierung der landwirtschaftlichen Produktion in Ostpreussen im 18. Jahrhundert." *ZAA* 18 (1970), 197–220.

——. *Studien zur Wirtschafts- und Sozialgeschichte Mittel- und Ostdeutschlands*. Dortmund, 1985.

Henökl, Aurelia. "Evangelische Richtungen im Pongau." In *REP*, pp. 72–76.

——. *Studien zur Reformation und Gegenreformation im Pongau unter besonderer Berücksichtigung der Vorfälle im Pfleggericht Werfen*. Vienna, 1979.

Hinrichs, Carl. *Preussen als historisches Problem: Gesammte Abhandlungen*. Berlin, 1964.

——. *Preussentum und Pietismus: Der Pietismus in Brandenburg-Preussen als religiös-soziale Bewegung*. Göttingen, 1971.

Horn, A. *Die Verwaltung Ostpreussens seit der Säkularisation*. Königsberg, 1890.

Hsia, R. Po-Chia. *Social Discipline in the Reformation: Central Europe, 1550–1750*. London, 1989.

Hübner, L. *Beschreibung des Erzstiftes und Reichsfürstenthums Salzburg*. Vol. 2, *Das Salzburgische Gebirgland*. Salzburg, 1796.

Jones, George Fenwick, "German-Speaking Settlers in Georgia, 1733–1741 (based on the Earl of Egmont's list)." *The Report: A Journal of German-American History* 38 (1982), 35–51.

——. *The Salzburger Saga*. Athens, Ga., 1984.

Kenkel, Horst. *Amtsbauern und Kölmer im nördlichen Ostpreussen um 1736*. Hamburg, 1972.

——. *Französische Schweizer und Réfugiés als Siedler im nördlichen Ostpreussen (Litauen) 1710–1750*. Hamburg, 1970.

Keplinger, Wilfried. "Die Emigration der Dürrnberger Bergknappen 1732." *MGSL* 100 (1960), 171–208.

Kerschhofer, Otto. "Die Salzburger Emigration nach Preussisch-Litauen." *MGSL* 116 (1976), 175–254.

Klein, Fritz. "Die Einwanderung der Berchtolsgadener Exulanten in Kurhannover 1733." *HG* 34 (1980), 159–74.

Klein, Herbert. "Die bäuerlichen Lehen im Erzstift Salzburg." *MGSL* 69 (1929), 148–68.

——. "Die Bauernschaft auf den Salzburger Landtagen." *MGSL* 88–89 (1948–49), 51–78.

——. "Salzburg und seine Landstände von den Anfängen bis 1861." In *FHK*, pp. 115–36.

——. "Das Türkenjahr in Salzburg." *MGSL* 112–113 (1972–73), 86–91.

Kurtze Historie Der Evangelischen Emigranten, wie die Göttliche Providentz dieselben nach vielen ausgestandenen Drancksalen aus dem Ertz-Stifft

Saltzburg in ein Land geführet, worinnen Milch und Honig der Evangelischen Wahrheit fliesset. Mit schönen (28) Kupffern gezieret. Memmingen, [1733].

Lehmann, Hartmut. "Ascetic Protestantism and Economic Rationalism: Max Weber Revisited after Two Generations." *HTR* 3 (1987), 307–20.

——. *Das Zeitalter des Absolutismus: Gottesgnadentum und Kriegsnot.* Stuttgart, 1980.

Lehmann, Max. *Preussen und die katholische Kirche, 1640–1740.* Leipzig, 1878.

Lepner, Theodorus. *De Preusche Littauer.* Danzig, 1744.

Leucht, Christian. *See* Faber, Anton.

Loesche, Georg. *Geschichte des Protestantismus im vormaligen und neuen Österreich.* 3d ed. Vienna, 1930.

——. *Neues über die Ausrottung des Protestantismus in Salzburg 1731–32.* Vienna, 1929.

Lucanus, August H. *Preussens uralter und heutiger Zustand.* 3 vols. Lötzen, 1901–12.

Marsch, Angelika. *Die Salzburger Emigration in Bildern.* 2d ed. Weissenhorn/Bayern, 1979.

Martin, Franz. *Salzburger Fürsten in der Barockzeit 1587 bis 1812.* 4th ed. Salzburg, 1982.

Martin Lodingers von Gastein Trost-Schrifft und Briefe, Welche er fast vor Zweyhundert Jahren an seine Lands-Leute im Salzburgischen abgehen lassen. Edited by Gustav Georg Leitner. Nürnberg, 1732.

Mayhew, Alan. *Rural Settlement and Farming in Germany.* New York, 1973.

Mayr, Josef. *Die Emigration der Salzburger Protestanten von 1731/32: Das Spiel der politischen Kräfte.* Salzburg, 1931.

Mecenseffy, Grete. *Geschichte des Protestantismus in Österreich.* Gratz, 1956.

Medick, Hans. *Naturzustand und Naturgeschichte der bürgerlichen Gesellschaft.* 2d ed. Göttingen, 1981.

Menger, Wolfgang. "Die Salzburger Emigration nach Ostpreussen in den Jahren 1731 und 1732. Eine medizinisch-geschichtliche Studie zum Umsiedlungsproblem." *MGSL* 98 (1958), 89–128.

Meyer, Moritz. *Geschichte der Preussischen Handwerkerpolitik.* Vol. 2, *Die Handwerkerpolitik Königs Friedrich Wilhelm I.* Minden, 1888.

Mitterauer, Michael. "Formen ländlicher Familienwirtschaft. Historische Ökotypen und familiale Arbeitsorganisation im österreichischen Raum." In *Familienstruktur und Arbeitsorganisation in ländlichen Gesellschaften*, edited by Josef Ehmer and Michael Mitterauer, pp. 185–323. Vienna, 1986.

——. "Servants and Youth." *CC* 5 (1990), 11–38.

——, ed. *Grundtypen alteuropäischer Sozialformen*. Stuttgart, 1979.

Mitzman, Arthur. *The Iron Cage: An Historical Interpretation of Max Weber*. New York, 1970.

Morgenstern, Salomo. *Über Friedrich Wilhelm I.* N.p., 1793.

Moser, Friedrich Karl. *Über die Regierungen der geistlichen Staaten*. Frankfurt/M., 1787.

Moser, Johann J. *Akten-Mässiger Bericht von der jetztmaligen schweren Verfolgung derer Evangelischen in dem Erz-Bisthum Salzburg*. Leipzig, 1732.

——. *Das Neueste von denen Salzburgischen Emigrationsactis. 11 Stücke*. Frankfurt/M., 1732–33.

——. *Reichs-Fama*. Vols. 9–19. Frankfurt/M., 1732–36.

——. *Derer Saltzburgischen Emigrationsacta*. 2 vols. Frankfurt/M., 1733.

——. *Von der Landes-Hoheit im Geistlichen*. Frankfurt/M., 1773.

——. *Von der Teutschen Religions-Verfassung*. Frankfurt/M., 1774.

Müller, H. H. "Domänen und Domänenpächter in Brandenburg-Preussen im 18. Jahrhundert." *JWG* (1965), 152–92.

Mylius, Christian O. *Corpus Constitutionum Marchicarum*. 6 vols. Berlin, 1737–55.

Nagl, Heinz. " Der Zauberer-Jackl-Prozess: Hexenprozesse im Erzstift Salzburg 1675–1690." *MGSL* 112–113 (1972–73), 385–539, and 114 (1974), 79–241.

Nemoianu, Virgil. *Micro-Harmony: The Growth and Uses of the Idyllic Model in Literature*. Bern, 1977.

Nolde, Herbert. "Alphabetisches Register der Personennamen in den Salzburgischen Emigrationslisten." Typescript, Göttingen, 1972, available at the Geheimes Staats-Archiv, Berlin-Zehlendorf.

Nowotny, Ernst. *Die Transmigration ober- und innerösterreichischer Protestanten nach Siebenbürgen im 18. Jahrhundert*. Jena, 1931.

Oertel, Christian G. *Repertorium derer gesamten Religionsbeschwerden . . . 1720–1770*. Regensburg, 1770.

Ortner, Franz. *Reformation, Katholische Reform und Gegenreformation in Salzburg*. Salzburg, 1981.

Panse, Karl. *Geschichte der Auswanderung der evangelischen Salzburger im Jahr 1732. Ein Beitrag zur Kirchengeschichte. Nach den Quellen bearbeitet.* Leipzig, 1827.

Pariset, Georges. *L'État et les églises en Prusse sous Frédéric-Guillaume Ier, 1713–1740.* Paris, 1896.

Passler, Paul. "Die lutherische Bewegung im Defereggental." *JGPÖ* 49 (1928), 1–107.

Pichler, Johannes W. *Die ältere ländliche Salzburger Eigentumsordnung.* Salzburg, 1979.

Pöllnitz, Charles-Louis [=Karl Ludwig]. *Mémoires, contenant les observations qu'il a faites dans ses voyages.* Vol. 2. Liège, 1734.

Pütter, Johann S. *Historische Entwickelung der heutigen Staatsverfassung des Teutschen Reichs.* 2d ed. Vol. 2. Göttingen, 1788.

Putzer, Peter. "Das Wesen des Rechtsbruches von 1731/32." *MGSL* 122 (1982), 295–320.

———. "Der konfessionelle Hintergrund der Salzburger Protestantenemigration 1731/32." *ÖAK* 33 (1982), 13–34.

Randt, Erich. *Die Mennoniten in Ostpreussen und Litauen bis zum Jahre 1772.* Königsberg, 1912.

Raupach, Bernhard. *Evangelisches Oesterreich; das ist, Historische Nachricht von den vornehmsten Schicksahlen der Evangelischen-Lutherischen Kirchen in dem Ertz-Herzogthum Oesterreich.* Hamburg, 1732–41.

Roth, James L. "The East Prussian Domänenpächter in the Eighteenth Century: A Study in Collective Mentality." Ph.D. diss., University of California at Berkeley, 1979.

Sahm, Wilhelm. *Geschichte der Pest in Ostpreussen.* Leipzig, 1905.

Saine, Thomas P. *Von der Kopernikanischen bis zur Französischen Revolution.* Berlin, 1987.

Sallaberger, Johann. "Das Eindringen der Reformation in Salzburg und die Abwehrmassnahmen der Erzbischöfe bis zum Augsburger Religionsfrieden 1555." In *REP,* pp. 26–33.

———. "Die Trientiner Familien Firmian und Cristani di Rallo." *SMB* 42 (1981), 1–3, 10–12.

[Sancke, Christoph]. *Ausführliche Historie derer Emigranten oder vertriebenen Lutheraner aus dem Ertz-Bisthum Saltzburg.* 2d ed. Leipzig, 1732.

———. *Ausführliche Historie derer Emigranten oder vertriebenen Lutheraner aus dem Ertz-Bisthum Saltzburg Zweyter Theil.* Leipzig, 1732.

Schaitberger, Joseph. *Evangelischer Send-Brief, Samt noch etlichen andern Unterrichts- Vermahnungs- und Trost-Schriften, An seine liebe Lands-Leute in Saltzburg und Tefferecken-Thal*. Graitz im Voigtlande, 1732.

Schauroth, Eberhard C. *Vollständige Sammlung aller Conclusorum, Schreiben und anderer übrigen Verhandlungen des Hochpreisslichen Corporis Evangelicorum*. 3 vols. Regensburg, 1751–52.

Schelhorn, Johann Georg. *Historische Nachricht vom Ursprunge, Fortgang und Schicksale der Evangelischen Religion in den Salzburgischen Landen, darinnen die Kirchen-Geschichte seit der Reformation erläutert wird*. Leipzig, 1732.

Schilling, Heinrich. *Der Zwist Preussens und Hannovers 1729–1730*. Halle, 1912.

Schindling, Anton. "Der Westfälische Frieden und der Reichstag." In *Politische Ordnung und soziale Kräfte im alten Reich*, edited by Hermann Weber, pp. 112–53. Wiesbaden, 1980.

Schlaich, Klaus. "Corpus Evangelicorum und Corpus Catholicorum. Aspekte eines Parteiwesens im Heiligen Römischen Reich Deutscher Nation." *Der Staat* 11 (1972), 218–30.

———. "Maioritas-protestatio-itio in partes-corpus Evangelicorum. Das Verfahren im Reichstag des Hl. Röm. Reichs Deutscher Nation nach der Reformation." *ZRG Kan* 63 (1977), 264–99, and 64 (1978), 139–79.

Schmidtbauer, Peter. "The Changing Household: Austrian Households from the Seventeenth to the Early Twentieth Century." In *Family Forms in Historic Europe*, edited by Richard Wall et al., pp. 347–78. Cambridge, 1983.

Schmoller, Gustav. "Das brandenburgisch-preussische Innungswesen von 1640 bis 1800." In his *Umrisse und Untersuchungen zur Verfassungs-, Verwaltungs- und Wirtschaftsgeschichte besonders des preussischen Staates im 17. und 18. Jahrhundert*, pp. 314–456. Leipzig, 1898.

———. "Die Epochen der preussischen Finanzpolitik, bis zur Gründung des deutschen Reichs." In his *Umrisse und Untersuchungen*, pp. 104–246.

———. "Ländliche Kolonisation des 17. und 18. Jahrhunderts." Reprinted in *Moderne Preussische Geschichte*, edited by Otto Busch and Wolfgang Neugebauer. Vol. 2 pp. 911–950. Berlin, 1981.

———. "Die Verwaltung Ostpreussens unter Friedrich Wilhelm I." *HZ* 30 (1873), 40–71.

Schönberger, Matthias. "Bevölkerungsstatistik eines Salzburger Gebirgstales, 1621–1920." *MAGW* 66 (1926), 271–78.

Schraml, Carl. *Das ober-österreichische Salinenwesen vom Beginn des 16. bis zur Mitte des 18. Jahrhunderts.* Vienna, 1932.

Schütz, Fritz, ed. "Haupt-Register von denen sämtlichen nach Preussen gekommenen Saltzburgischen-Emigranten, so wie selbige in denen von des Tit. Herrn Geheimten Rath Osten angefertigten Rechnungen sich befinden. Gumbinnen dem 20ten August 1756." Gumbinnen, 1913, available at the Geheimes Staats-Archiv, Berlin-Zehlendorf.

Schwarz-Oberhummer, Gertraud. "Die Auswanderung der Gasteiner Protestanten unter Erzbischof Leop. Anton von Firmian." *MGSL* 94 (1954), 1–85.

Skalweit, August. *Die ostpreussische Domänenverwaltung unter Friedrich Wilhelm I. und das Retablissement Litauens.* Leipzig, 1906.

Sombart, Werner. *Der Bourgeois.* Munich, 1920.

Stadelmann, Rudolph. *Friedrich Wilhelm I. in seiner Tätigkeit für die Landeskultur Preussens.* Leipzig, 1878.

Terveen, Fritz. *Gesamtstaat und Retablissement: Der Wiederaufbau des nördlichen Ostpreussen unter Friedrich Wilhelm I.* Berlin, 1954.

Urlsperger, Samuel. *Ausführliche Nachricht Von den Salzburgischen Emigranten, die sich in America niedergelassen haben.* Halle, 1735.

Vehse, Eduard. "Der Hof zu Salzburg." In *Geschichte der deutschen Höfe.* Vol. 4, Part 12, pp. 131–76. Hamburg, 1859.

Verdenhalven, Fritz. *Alte Masse, Muenzen und Gewichte aus dem deutschen Sprachgebiet.* Neustadt/Aisch, 1968.

Viazzo, Pier Paulo. *Upland Communities: Environment, Population and Social Structure in the Alps since the Sixteenth Century.* Cambridge, 1989.

Völkel, Ludwig. *See* Clarus, Ludwig.

Wächter, Hans-Helmut. *Ostpreussische Domänenvorwerke im 16. und 17. Jahrhundert.* Würzburg, 1958.

Wagner, Hans. "Politische Aspekte der Protestantenaustreibung." In *REP*, pp. 92–100.

Weber, Lothar. *Die Parität der Konfessionen in der Reichsverfassung von den Anfängen der Reformation bis zum Untergang des alten Reichs im Jahre 1806.* Bonn, 1961.

Weber, Marianne. *Max Weber: Ein Lebensbild.* Heidelberg, 1950.

Weiss, Richard. *Das Alpenerlebnis in der deutschen Literatur des 18. Jahrhunderts*. Leipzig, 1933.

Widmann, Hans. *Geschichte Salzburgs*. 3 vols. Gotha, 1907–14.

Witzleben, A. v., ed. "Briefe des Königs Friedrich Wilhelm I. an den Fürsten Leopold von Anhalt-Dessau." *ZPG* 8–9 (1871–72).

Wolff, Fritz. *Corpus Evangelicorum und Corpus Catholicorum auf dem Westfälischen Friedenskongress. Die Einführung der konfessionellen Ständeverbindung in die Reichsverfassung*. Münster, 1966.

Wopfner, Hermann. "Güterteilung und Übervölkerung Tirolischer Landteile im 16., 17. und 18. Jahrhundert." *SDF* 3 (1938), 202–32.

Wunder, Gerd. "Die Schweizer Kolonisten in Ostpreussen 1710–1730 als Beispiel für Koloniebauern." In *Bauernschaft und Bauernstand 1500–1970*, edited by Günther Franz, pp. 183–95. Limburg/Lahn, 1975.

Wunder, Heide. *Die bäuerliche Gemeinde in Deutschland*. Göttingen, 1986.

Zaisberger, Friederike, ed. *Reformation/Emigration: Protestanten in Salzburg*. Salzburg, 1981.

——. "Der Salzburger Bauer und die Reformation." *MGSL* 124 (1984), 375–401.

Zauner, Judas T. *Chronik von Salzburg*. 11 parts in 10 vols. Salzburg, 1796–1826.

Zwiedineck-Südenhorst, Hans v. "Die Anerkennung der pragmatischen Sanction Karls VI." *MIÖG* 16 (1895), 276–341.

——. *Deutsche Geschichte im Zeitraum der Gründung des preussischen Königtums*. Vol. 2. Stuttgart, 1894.

——. *Dorfleben im achtzehnten Jahrhundert*. Vienna, 1877.

——. "Geschichte der religiösen Bewegung in Inner-Österreich im 18. Jahrhundert." *AÖG* 53 (1875), 457–546.

INDEX

Library of Congress Cataloging-in-Publication Data

Walker, Mack.
  The Salzburg transaction : expulsion and redemption in eighteenth-century
Germany / Mack Walker.
    p. cm.
  Includes bibliographical references and index.
  ISBN 0-8014-2777-0
    1. Salzburgers—Emigration, 1731–1735. 2. Salzburg (Austria : Land)—
Church history. 3. Prussia (Germany)—History—Frederick William I, 1713–
1740. 4, Prussia (Germany)—Church history. I. Title.
BR817.S3W34 1992
274.36'307—dc20   92-52774

Hamburg

UNITED
NETHERLANDS

Magdeburg

Halle

Cologne
(Köln)

Gotha
Gera

L

Meiningen

Frankfurt/
Main
Schweinfurt

Bamber

Nürnl

Nördlinge

FRANCE

Ulm

Augsbu

Memmingen
Munic

Kempten

Innsbruck

SWITZERLAND

Bolzano

Veni